Socialism, *Perestroika,* and the Dilemmas of Soviet Economic Reform

Published in cooperation
with Radio Free Europe/Radio Liberty

Socialism, *Perestroika,* and the Dilemmas of Soviet Economic Reform

EDITED BY

John E. Tedstrom

Westview Press

BOULDER, SAN FRANCISCO, & OXFORD

This Westview softcover edition is printed on acid-free paper and bound in library-quality, coated covers that carry the highest rating of the National Association of State Textbook Administrators, in consultation with the Association of American Publishers and the Book Manufacturers' Institute.

Published in 1990 in the United States of America by Westview Press, Inc., 5500 Central Avenue, Boulder, Colorado 80301, and in the United Kingdom by Westview Press, Inc., 36 Lonsdale Road, Summertown, Oxford OX2 7EW

Library of Congress Cataloging-in-Publication Data
Socialism, *perestroika,* and the dilemmas of Soviet economic reform /
    edited by John E. Tedstrom.
        p.   cm.
    ISBN 0-8133-8017-0
    1. Perestroika. 2. Soviet Union—Economic policy—1986–
I. Tedstrom, John E.
HC336.26.S62 1990
338.947′009′048—dc20   90-12137
                                                                             CIP

Printed and bound in the United States of America

          The paper used in this publication meets the requirements
     ∞   of the American National Standard for Permanence of Paper
          for Printed Library Materials Z39.48-1984.

10   9   8   7   6   5   4   3   2   1

Contents

Foreword

This book is the result of a conference held in the summer of 1989 at Radio Free Europe/Radio Liberty in Munich, West Germany. The subject of the conference was the process of economic modernization in the Soviet Union under *perestroika*. The authors offer a variety of institutional, disciplinary, and cultural perspectives on this subject.

A major theme that emerges in the chapters of this volume is that Soviet economic planners and politicians must come to recognize the need to make fundamental changes, not simply incremental refinements, in the failing Soviet system. For political leaders, this means addressing the issue of a multiparty system or at least of a more responsive and democratic legislature that can serve to check and balance executive power. For economic leaders, it means grappling with new institutional arrangements such as forms of private ownership which are fundamentally at odds with traditional Soviet policies and practices. Thus, the contributors to this volume devote less attention to the administrative and bureaucratic changes that have emerged under Gorbachev's leadership than to the fundamental steps that are required to make the Soviet economy work. They make clear that some of these necessary radical steps have been attempted, some have been only discussed and debated, and others have yet to be broached seriously at all.

A second major theme that emerges in this volume is that *perestroika* is a process, not an event and that it is too early to construct a balance sheet on its achievements, at least not one that has a bottom line. The contributors to this book examine the dynamics of the process of *perestroika* as much as they do the complexity of individual economic issues, and in so doing they elucidate the social pressures that to an increasing degree impel and inform Soviet economic policy.

The book is intended for a general audience, for all those interested in the transformations being ventured in the Soviet Union, as well as for specialists in Soviet-type economics.

S. Enders Wimbush
Director, Radio Liberty

Acknowledgments

This book is the product of many people's efforts, and I am indebted to them for their help. The management of RFE/RL , Inc., in particular Mr. S. Enders Wimbush, Director of Radio Liberty, and Mr. Gene Pell, President of RFE/RL, Inc., deserve much credit. They approved the conceptual, organizational, and budgetary questions that were involved not only in producing this volume but also in organizing and holding a conference in July, 1989, that generated early draft chapters. In a real sense, they made this project possible. A large note of thanks goes to Karen Whitehouse of the Radio Liberty Editorial Department. Without the assistance of Karen, the publishing process would have been a much more difficult experience. The assistance of Patricia Early and Burga Pattinson, both of Radio Liberty, was indispensable, from the early days of planning the conference through the final days of preparing the book.

A number of people either read draft chapters or participated in the conference. Wolfram Schrettl, Vladimir G. Treml, Mario Nuti, Christoph Royen, Theodor Schweisfurth, George Urban, Keith Bush, Erik Whitlock, Viktor Yasmann, O. Ralph Raymond, Charles Trumbull, Iain Elliot, D. J. Peterson, Michael Thompson, and Pierre Audiger deserve special mention. The usual caveats concerning responsibility for errors and omissions of course apply here. The contents of the book do not necessarily represent the views or policies of Radio Free Europe/Radio Liberty, Inc., or the Board for International Broadcasting.

John E. Tedstrom

Introduction

John E. Tedstrom

The transformations undertaken in the Soviet Union and Eastern Europe in the late 1980s and early 1990s are likely to be looked upon by future analysts as among the most important political and economic developments in the twentieth century. Fundamental changes in both the domestic and foreign policies of the USSR have captured the attention of people throughout the world. Even if *perestroika* were to suffer a major setback, the process of social maturation in Soviet society has already gone too far to permit a full and permanent reversal. East-West tensions are at an all time low, in large part a result of initiatives taken by the Soviet Union within the rubric of "new thinking," reflecting the Soviet Union's desire to play a more positive role in global politics and economics. Internally, the USSR took what many have regarded as a decisive step towards democratization when it held and then honored the results of limited multicandidate elections to the new Soviet legislature, the Congress of People's Deputies. Soviet citizens took advantage of the opportunity presented to them by the elections to elect a number of reformist legislators and reject many Communist Party (CPSU) officials running on the ballot in constituency districts, even when the latter were running unopposed. After the first session of the Congress of People's Deputies, a radical pressure group consisting of nearly four hundred deputies and known as the Interregional Group was formed and has since taken a number of radical legislative initiatives.[1] The formation of the People's Fronts in the Baltic republics a year or so earlier somewhat foreshadowed the development of autonomous political movements both at the grass-roots and at the legislative level. Such independent political formations have come to enjoy what amounts in many instances to veto power if not virtual control over political life in their respective republics. They are, for all practical purposes, independent political institutions often standing in opposition to the CPSU. The key difference between these popular movements and other new political institutions such as the Congress of People's Deputies and the restructured Supreme Soviet is that the latter have all been reforms *à la russe*, or from the top down, initiated by the leadership in an effort to perpetuate whatever legitimacy it had in the face of the current systemic crisis. The popular movements (as well as numerous "informal" groups that have sprung up in Soviet society during the *perestroika* period) have, however, been grass-roots phenomena—popular will in action.

---

[1] There are approximately 90 members of the Interregional Group in the Supreme Soviet as well, but a seat in the Congress is the basic criterion for membership.

An important function served by the emerging populist organizations such as the Lithuanian Popular Front "Sajudis" and the semi-oppositionist legislative faction, the Interregional Group, is that they take the initiative away from the traditional Soviet power elite. Moreover, the ideas embodied in their programs, and still more the implicit dynamic of the organizations themselves, tend to be much more radical than even Soviet leader Mikhail Gorbachev's concepts of "radical" societal transformation. Taken together, the current political reforms in the Soviet Union are quantitatively and qualitatively different from earlier reform efforts, and their effects cannot help but be more profound and may—short of some abrupt and increasingly unlikely termination of the reform process—fundamentally alter the political norms of Soviet society.

The nature of the current economic reforms is different from those of the past as well. Gertrude Schroeder, one of the West's keenest observers of the Soviet economy, has said that the Soviet economy was on a "treadmill of reforms."[2] Her point was that the Soviet leadership was constantly tinkering with its command-administered economy—shifting personnel, reorganizing ministries, revising prices, etc., without attacking the fundamental problems of the Soviet economic system. To be sure, there have been steps on the treadmill under Gorbachev. He has overseen the amalgamation of various ministries and departments; has shifted scarce resources among the competing end users of defense, investment, and consumption; and has focused on "the human factor" in hopes of generating more productivity from the shrinking Soviet work force—all changes within the traditional economic system.

There has, however, at least since 1987, been a qualitative difference between the "treadmill" reforms of the past and the reforms of *perestroika*. Instead of being constrained by conventional Soviet economic dogma, Gorbachev has initiated a set of reforms based on economic concepts hitherto believed to be inimical to socialism.[3] Instead of trying to perfect the existing system, he seeks to change that system fundamentally by reassessing features long and dogmatically held to be guarantors of its socialistic essence. Crucial to this reassessment is the concept of a legal "private" economy in which the state does not own or control the means of production and in which individuals have owner-

---

[2] Gertrude Schroeder, "The Soviet Economy on a Treadmill of 'Reforms'," in *Soviet Economy in a Time of Change*, Joint Economic Committee, US Congress, Vol. 1, October 10, 1979, pp. 312-40.

[3] It is probably more political necessity than anything else that Gorbachev still speaks of returning to Leninist principles—that is, he advertises his reforms in terms of ideological continuity. Many other, perhaps less official, reformers have already dumped that baggage and denounced the Marxist-Leninist set of ideals. See Elizabeth Teague's contribution to this volume.

ship incentives and can earn income not commensurate with their labor. Probably more than any other component of the current economic reforms, it is the introduction of a "private" sector that sets them apart from past, failed attempts to "perfect" the Soviet economic system.

While current Soviet political and economic reforms fail to sum to a Western understanding of liberal democracy, the common conceptual framework that holds them together seems to comprehend, on the one hand, a rejection of Marxism-Leninism as a political and economic system and, on the other hand, an espousal of certain basic liberal principles even if this theoretical framework largely remains inchoate in practice. As Robert Campbell stresses in his contribution to this volume, however, "*Perestroika* [is] a long-term, multidimensional process—one that will take longer and affect the societal structure more widely and deeply than its proponents originally intended, or probably realize even now." Another analyst, Francis Fukuyama, has gone so far as to see in the reforms the eventual "death" of Marxism-Leninism as a viable political philosophy and an "end of history."[4]

Implicit in both Campbell's and Fukuyama's assessments is the notion that the changes occurring in the Soviet Union are not merely a reaction to immediate material circumstances alone but are of a deep, conceptual nature that goes well beyond who sits in the general secretary's chair or the size of the Soviet budget deficit. Campbell and Fukuyama are referring to an acceptance by the Soviet people of an ideology of human government that is essentially different from the one they were taught to believe in for the past three-quarters of a century. Granted this transition may experience setbacks, but the dynamic of the process that has begun shows signs of the potential to endure.

This book focuses attention on economic modernization in the Soviet Union. The volume builds on earlier studies which have focused on the question of why the Soviet economy functions so poorly to address what has been ventured by the Soviet reformers so far and what is still left to be done. The following chapters attempt to provide more than diverse snapshots of the still-evolving program for Soviet economic restructuring. Rather, they aim to present an in-depth view of the dynamics of the whole process. The opening chapters serve mainly to establish a conceptual and historical framework within which the subsequent chapters explore their respective themes. The first chapter, by Campbell, develops a schematic of Soviet economic reform in general, raising the issues that must be addressed by Soviet reformers if *perestroika* is to be successful. In this regard, Campbell argues that "*perestroika* involves an extensive resort to privatization, and not only

---

[4] Francis Fukuyama, "The End of History?" *The National Interest*, No. 16, 1989, p. 18.

with respect to economic decisions and rights, but also with respect to many other kinds of rights." That is a long-term notion, and Campbell distinguishes that from the problems of the medium term, around which a good deal of the current debate over *perestroika* revolves. Such medium-term issues include some, such as administered prices and soft-budget constraints, that have been problems for the Soviet economy for many years. Others, such as the emergence of a budget deficit, however, are new to the USSR and present special difficulties. Campbell both examines the various problems and suggests appropriate directions for corrective policy. In his shorter-range view of *perestroika*, Campbell addresses the issue of the ability of the leadership to generate improvements in living standards quickly enough to buy time for some of the more difficult reforms to be implemented and produce results.

One of the key problems, not widely expected at the outset of *perestroika*, is the great range of opinions on how the reforms should be designed and implemented. At first, attention—both in the USSR and abroad—tended more commonly to focus on the alleged obstacles of bureaucratic inertia and other vested interests. But, as Elizabeth Teague points out in Chapter 2, there is even disagreement among the reformers on key questions concerning the relationship of the individual to the workplace, government, and society. The inability of the reformers to unite around a common concept of society is itself proving to be a stumbling block for *perestroika*. Teague's examination of the current debate over the nature of socialism in the Soviet Union foresees a radicalization of Soviet economic policy and the eventual dismantling of the one-party system justified as it is by an obsolescent ideology.

Not surprisingly, considering that many in the Soviet intelligentsia had been acculturated to assume the superiority of their own system, whatever its gathering difficulties, Soviet reformers initially sought to find answers to current and projected problems by examining their own past experience. As Mark von Hagen argues in Chapter 3, this understandable tendency led, among other things, to a reinterpretation of the New Economic Policy no longer as a tactical "retreat" or "breathing space" (*peredyshka*) but as Lenin's final legacy.[5] This tendency also contributed to the rehabilitation of Nikolai Bukharin and others of the "right opposition." Indeed, it helped extend *glasnost'* into the treatment of the history of the pre-1932 period and even the formative years of the Soviet state when Lenin was still alive. But for all the freshness involved in reexamining the Soviet economic experience and searching for new solutions to be found there, Soviet reformers, especially in the early days of *perestroika*, simply lacked the sophistication to place their own economic past into a comparative political-economic context.

---

[5]   See, for one of the more famous examples, Nikolai Shmelev, "Avansy i dolgi," *Novyi mir*, No. 6, 1987, pp. 142-58, especially pp. 142-43.

Western analysts have also found themselves turning towards the NEP for historical analogies, but von Hagen shows that there is little in the Soviet past, including the NEP, to draw on, as far as positive lessons for *perestroika* are concerned. The NEP, von Hagen asserts, was a time of terrible hardship for the proletariat, which did not regard it as "the golden age" until they had experienced the Stalinist terror.[6] Also, the problems of the 1920s are dramatically different from those of the late 1980s, and any successes of the NEP are likely to be peculiar to the problems of the past, not of today.

The next chapters examine the nature of a "private" economy and how it may be applied in the socialist system. Chapter 4, by Philip Hanson, outlines the historical economic debate over the issues of ownership and property, discusses the debate among reformers about the role of property and ownership, and examines the various types of "private" economic activity in the Soviet Union. Several important themes emerge in this treatment of ownership Soviet-style. First is the fact that neither the economic theory of Marx nor of Lange, von Mises, von Hayek, or Schumpeter has been able to resolve fully the conceptual puzzle of ownership. Most of the Western literature on comparative economic systems, Hanson points out, has focused on the importance of the market as a resource allocation mechanism, balancing supply and demand. Ownership has been treated as a secondary issue, not vitally involved in either system equilibrium or system development. Many East European economists, however, are now claiming that the focus on the market as an efficient resource allocator has been misguided and that the various examples of market socialist economies (devolved decision-making within the state sector) have failed to create an efficiently operating market and have not solved the problems besetting the East European economies. Private property, seen in this light, takes on renewed practical importance.

Hanson also notes that the cooperative movement has been the only form of "private" ownership to develop rapidly during the Gorbachev era. The scope of individual labor activities is small compared with the cooperative movement, and much of the "privatization" on the farm has been in name only. Leasing, Hanson points out, is an ambiguous term with multiple and imprecise meanings and is usually combined with cooperative activities. Hanson's conclusion is that there is a strong logic leading from market-socialist reforms to reforms that embrace private ownership. But while the logic may be there, Hanson is skeptical about the ability of the socialist world to (at least in the

---

[6] It is worth noting here that the NEP was pro-peasant and effectively dethroned the urban proletariat from the position of chief beneficiaries, economically and "spiritually," of the new system. The peasants generally benefited under the NEP and quite legitimately recall it as "a golden age."

foreseeable future) absorb the concept of private property and all that it entails. He notes that to many people who are not accustomed to a private, market economy, the instability, risk, and hard, responsible work that it requires may be overwhelming arguments for maintaining the status quo.

Observing that in many cases the economic reforms in Eastern Europe antedate *perestroika*, Vladimir Sobell in Chapter 5 extends the discussion in Hanson's chapter in an attempt to draw lessons from those countries, especially Hungary and Poland. The thrust of the chapter, however, is that any lessons to be learned are of the negative sort—what not to do. Even in Hungary and Poland, Sobell argues, economic reforms have by and large been half-hearted. They have thus far failed to cross the boundary between economic decentralization of the market-socialist type to a system that incorporates a significant private sector. Only now, when the systems face near total collapse, have the ideologues loosened their grip on the societies and economies in question in an effort to generate economic welfare. Sobell describes a cycle of reform and regression-to-orthodoxy which, for the countries of Eastern Europe at least, has been a net economic drain. Not all of this experience has been in vain, however, and "the reformers have realized that it is necessary to move from markets in limited areas such as agricultural produce to markets in capital and labor." Sobell's conclusion is that the Soviet Union needs to look to the East European reform cycle and do its utmost to avoid the same trap.

Subsequent chapters narrow the focus a bit more and examine in detail specific aspects of the Soviet private sector. Chapter 6, by John Tedstrom, charts the development of the Soviet cooperative movement, looking at the political process of establishing the cooperative movement, the social attitudes that affect the way the movement has progressed, and the economics behind some of the successes and failures of the system.

While the cooperative movement tends to stand out as the "flagship" of the Soviet private sector, Tedstrom notes that it has experienced numerous problems along the way. Most problematic for the cooperatives is the schizophrenic attitude towards issues of ownership, income, and labor on the part of the Soviet public. On the one hand, cooperatives clearly help to ease the shortage of consumer goods in areas where they have been allowed to flourish. On the other, high prices, high incomes, and the employment of one man by another offend the widespread Soviet understanding of social justice. The Soviet leadership also seems incapable of transcending such ideological obstacles and has on occasion regressed from its own expressed reform commitments by taking a series of steps to curb the growth of the cooperative sector. Such actions not only create legal obstacles to Soviet entrepreneurs, but also engender an increasing measure of uncertainty and risk that dampens the entrepreneurial spirit and makes private enterprise a less attractive alternative.

Chapter 7, by Karl-Eugen Wädekin, analyzes the extent to which the reforms of the Soviet agricultural sector have resulted in a "privatization." Wädekin presents a comprehensive picture of the various types of decentralized economic arrangements such as renting and leasing, family farms, the brigades, etc., and he assesses the impact of these arrangements on agricultural production. His conclusion about the nature and impact of the privatization in the Soviet agricultural sector parallels those of other authors in this volume. Specifically, he sees less "privatization" of Soviet agriculture in practice than Soviet propaganda would have one believe and he sees the impact of "half-hearted" measures as minimal.

Chapter 8, by Hans Heymann, Jr., takes up the question of the effect of the reforms under Gorbachev on innovation in the Soviet socialist economy. Applying some of Joseph Berliner's pioneering work to the contemporary Soviet situation, Heymann turns attention away from questions of resource allocation and efficiency to discuss the prospects for an acceleration of Soviet technological development.[7] Heymann first develops an analytical framework built on the necessary and sufficient conditions for technological innovation. Employing the axiom that individual creativity and innovation require a breadth of individual freedom and incentive, Heymann then evaluates the prospects of Soviet technological advance in the context of contemporary Soviet social, political, and economic conditions and the nature of draft reforms on the book. Heymann notes that, perhaps because the "commanding heights" of the Soviet economy occupy such an important place in Soviet economic thought, very little more than reorganization and administrative reforms have been applied in Soviet industry. He concludes that because Soviet planners have yet to introduce a sufficient environment for entrepreneurial activities, the qualitative leap forward in innovation that Gorbachev is searching for is still out of sight.

Chapter 9, by Perry Patterson, examines the possibility for the development of capital markets in the Soviet Union. Patterson notes the Soviet attempts to find answers to their wholesale-trade and capital-allocation problems in the systems of other socialist and Western countries and also describes how current Soviet reformers are looking to the institutions of the commodity exchange (*tovarnaia birzha*) and financial exchange (*fondovyi otdel'*) of the NEP period for guidance. Patterson documents the activities of these exchanges during the 1920s, showing that in many respects they were relatively large and similar to

---

[7]   For example, Joseph Berliner, *The Innovation Decision in Soviet Industry*, Cambridge, Massachusetts, MIT Press, 1976.

those of the West. Patterson concludes that for some heavily traded, homogeneous commodities and contracts, *birzhi* may be reasonably efficient resource allocators. In the Soviet case, this might include such commodities as oil, cotton, grains, and foreign currency, among others. The establishment of financial and commodity exchanges in the Soviet Union would require the breakup of existing monopolies and granting small firms full right of access to the markets. In short, Soviet economic relationships would have to shift from the traditional hierarchical arrangement to a decentralized one based on ownership of factor inputs and competition among buyers and sellers if the *birzhi* were to be effective.

The question of what effect the establishment of modern economic institutions—including private ownership—has on the lives of Soviet citizens is addressed in the last two chapters. Chapter 10, by Michael Alexeev, studies how the Soviet consumer might be affected by, and change his spending patterns in, the state and private sectors of the economy as the result of a retail price reform, one of the most important reforms the Soviet leadership is now contemplating. As Alexeev notes, the existence of appropriate market institutions is crucial for the work of the price mechanism. Among these institutions, private ownership of the means of production and well-functioning capital markets are particularly important. Alexeev argues that even in the Soviet economy, consumers have choices of how to spend their time and money because of the existence of a substantial "parallel second economy." While this parallel economy is now a mixture of nonstate and nonlegal economic institutions, a main point of Alexeev's argument is that it tends to operate on more-or-less market-based principles and as if private property were the basic ownership arrangement. Moreover, as other chapters in this volume argue, the long-term trend is towards the organization and legalization of this second economy into a system much more similar to traditional private, market-oriented economies. Retail price reform is most likely to result in an increased price level in the state sector because of the pervasive subsidies there. But the effects on the second economy are ambiguous. Alexeev maintains that prices there might even go down, depending on if and what kind of an income reimbursement scheme is incorporated into the reform. If the price differential between the state and nonstate sectors decreases, that could well result in a significant invigorating shift of consumer activity from the state sector to the nonstate sector.

The final chapter, by Aaron Trehub, examines the impact of *perestroika* on personal rights in Soviet society. Implicit in Trehub's analysis is that *perestroika* generates a "Catch-22" situation that may doom it to self-destruction. First, the inability of *perestroika* to arrest the deterioration of Soviet living standards threatens the existence of the reforms themselves: "In order to succeed, Gorbachev's reforms require nothing less than the enthusiastic participation of millions of Soviet citizens. Mere acquiescence will not do." On the other hand, a successful *perestroika*—which incorporates a policy of decentralization, marketization, and privatization—"cannot but undermine social protection in the Soviet Union—and, with it, the post-Stalin 'social contract,' which . . . rests on egalitarianism, stability, and security." Trehub catalogs the Soviet Union's record as the premier welfare state and finds its ability to feed, clothe, care for, and employ the majority of the Soviet population wanting. The hesitancy of the state to delegate some of these responsibilities to the nonstate sector and the hesitancy of the Soviet populace to accept the idea of economic winners and losers make it very difficult to predict a successful solution in the foreseeable future.

A common theme of the chapters is that the Soviets have begun a journey down a long and difficult path of social modernization. Most of the chapters conclude that, while substantial progress has been made in reconceptualizing the nature of the future Soviet society, much more is left to be done in the way of changing people's attitudes towards various economic and social relationships. The difficulties arise because the Soviet reformers find themselves in a complicated and unique situation, with few positive lessons to be found either in other countries' experiences or in the Soviet past. The emergence of a significant private sector and market, while critical to a vital, growth-oriented economy, will be particularly problematic because of the way in which personal property and entrepreneurship contradict traditional socialist teachings. Nonetheless, the already impressive development of the cooperative sector and the increasing number of positive discussions of private ownership in the Soviet press signal the beginnings of things to come.

Socialism, *Perestroika,* and the Dilemmas of Soviet Economic Reform

1

How to Think about
Perestroika

Robert W. Campbell

THERE are many ways to think about *perestroika*, and in following what is happening in the USSR and considering the possible outcome multiple perspectives may be useful.

THE LONG-RANGE PERSPECTIVE

First, *perestroika* can be viewed as a long-term, multidimensional process—one that will take more time and affect the societal structure of the USSR more widely and deeply than its proponents originally intended or probably realize even now. Fundamentally, it is an effort to *modernize* socialist society, to bring it into the twentieth century, and to do so—it is hoped—by the time the twenty-first century arrives. A process that goes beyond mere decentralization and marketization of the *economy* to take on something like the task of "societal institution-building," *perestroika* will ultimately require a whole new understanding and philosophy of how a society works. One of Soviet leader Mikhail Gorbachev's themes has been *novoe myshlenie*, or new thinking, which conceivably has greater potential for stimulating change than does *perestroika* itself.

From another angle, *perestroika* can be thought of as a new round in the age-old effort by Russian rulers to catch up with, and create the basis for competing with, the West. The history of that effort is an ambiguous one, alternating between high-pressured, superficial, and eventually self-defeating attempts to catch up, such as those of Peter the Great, and attempts to create the prerequisites for modernization through more fundamental emulation of Western institutions. *Perestroika* may be interpreted as a return to the latter approach after the momentous interruption of the Great October Revolution and Stalin's forced industrialization under central control.

Seen in this way, *perestroika* involves modernizing the political and social spheres of the nation's life as well as the economic sphere. It means some move towards constitutionalism, legitimation of the Party's leadership role on the basis of shifting from a zero-sum concept of political power (we/they, *kto-kogo*) to a variable-sum concept, and creation of the conditions for "a civil society." Important Soviet reform thinkers who have spelled out this vision are Leonid Abalkin,[1] Tat'yana Zaslavskaya, and Boris Kurashvili.[2] Interpreted thus, *perestroika* involves an extensive resort to privatization, not only with respect to economic decisions and rights but also with respect to many other kinds of decisions and rights.

In the economy, reform means "creeping marketization." The word "creeping" is meant to convey the notion that the reform architects will be driven to widen progressively the sectors and functions of the economy within which market processes determine the production and allocation of goods and resources. Marketization must go beyond control over just current decisions about production and allocation and extend to control over decisions about investment, foreign trade, and utilization of the society's capital. The last two extensions imply an open economy and separation of ownership and control by "unbundling" the collection of ownership rights that come under the heading "socialist property." This separation or unbundling will require the creation of various kinds of financial instruments and contracts to permit shifting some of these rights to private individuals and institutions and will have to entail the marketization of these rights as well. This last step is an important component of privatization.

Finally, as progress is made on marketization two additional problems will inevitably arise—i.e., equity in income distribution and macrostabilization. Solving these problems will require the modernization—and, in many cases, the creation from the ground up—of institutions for conducting fiscal and monetary policy.

This is the agenda for the long-term program whether Gorbachev and his reforming allies have read to the end of it or not and whether they acknowledge it or not. As for acknowledging it, the impression is that the political actors who are pushing reform see further ahead than they are always willing to state for public consumption. Moreover, what they have been willing to reveal of their vision often implies a deeper and more pervasive set of changes than they seem to realize. In any case, all these elements of the long-term program for economic and

---

[1] See his "Novaya kontseptsiya tsentralizma," *Ekonomicheskaya gazeta*, No. 50, 1987, p. 2.

[2] A convenient collection of Zaslavskaya's essays showing the evolution of her views is *Essays by Tatiana I. Zaslavskaia*, edited, and with an introduction, by Murray Yanowitch, Armonk, New York, M. E. Sharpe, 1989.

societal modernization have surfaced in the discussion and debate surrounding *perestroika*, even if many of them are still controversial at this stage and even if the most far-reaching suggestions have not yet affected policy or institutions.

This interpretation of *perestroika* is based in part on the experience to date of the East European countries and China. Some of these countries have been working at reform and modernization longer than the USSR (twenty years already for the Hungarians), have thought reform through more nearly to the end, and have learned more about the necessary scope of an effective reform. The East European reformers certainly did not envisage the whole program at the outset. They were pioneers, who had to learn by doing. In addition, they always had the USSR looking over their shoulder to curb adventurism. There is little reason to believe *perestroika* in the USSR will necessarily recapitulate this process in the same sequence or on the same time scale. It is evident that some phases have already been telescoped in the USSR—*glasnost'* came earlier than it did in Eastern Europe, and political reform is starting earlier in relation to economic reform than it did in Eastern Europe and in China. The Soviet reformers are free to chart whatever path they can persuade the elites and the population to accept. Though the Soviet case has numerous distinctive features, the USSR can learn from the experience of the pioneers, and it is possible that reform there may proceed faster and more directly than it did in Eastern Europe.

The implications of what has been said so far are that *perestroika* will take a long time, that it is somewhat groping in its development, and that it may end up at a destination somewhat different from that now intended. With experience, the Soviet leaders will realize that the agenda stretches beyond current notions of what needs doing. All this means that it will be impossible to evaluate *perestroika* on the basis of an annual balance sheet of its progress or even on the basis of a balance sheet of Gorbachev's administration as a whole, should he be dismissed somewhere along the way. As an evolving process, *perestroika* ought not to be impatiently judged by taking current programmatic statements as a yardstick or by seeing it as a transition to be completed by, say, 1995 that can then be rated a success or a failure.

The objection to this long-range view of *perestroika* will doubtless be something like the following: "If Gorbachev and his successors let reform proceed as you suggest, what then would be socialist about the kind of society to emerge? Gorbachev does not intend to preside over the liquidation of the socialist system, and it will be impossible for the process to go as far as you say." The answer to "what then would be socialist about the kind of society to emerge," is—though it is unlikely the leaders of socialist societies are ready to accept it openly yet—that socialism as it has been understood in the Soviet Union is mostly an illusion. The fundamental socialist goals come down to some fairly general shibboleths—social justice, abolition of exploitation of man by man, arrangements that ensure "production for the sake of people, rather than for the sake of profit" (socialist ideologists have always mistaken the latter as the end rather than the instrument of the market economy) or "production for the sake of people rather than for the sake of production" (the practical outcome of the Soviet system was to reverse this order), and "socialist abundance." The shibboleth that is probably most explicit in the definition of socialism is "public owner-ship of the means of production." The irony is that in the USSR and elsewhere people are coming to see that socialism's ultimate goals are best served not by "public ownership of the means of production" but by arrangements that guarantee everyone access to the decision-making processes in the two great spheres of social life—the economy and the polity. In other words, the best way to guarantee efficiency and equity is to institutionalize some variant of the market process and some variant of political democracy. Winston Churchill did not propose to preside over the liquidation of the British empire, but under the press of objective circumstances that empire is gone.

THE SHORTER-RANGE PERSPECTIVE

The above is the long view of "how to think about *perestroika*." But there ought to be a shorter-range view as well, a sense of what to focus on in the more immediate future. What is actually being done? How fast can the process go? What about sequences? What about alternative routes from here to that distant point on the horizon? Which obstacles should be outflanked, and which directly assailed? The treatment of this shorter-range perspective that follows is organized around issues that must be resolved and tasks that must be undertaken. What are some of the most important strategic and tactical issues in *perestroika*, and how should they be thought about?

MARKETIZATION

It is taken as axiomatic here that real reform must involve marketiza-tion. If the reformers want a significant improvement in performance, the reform must cross the threshold between administrative decentrali-zation and marketization. Underlying this view is the conviction that "perfect administration" of the economy is not attainable, mainly because of the game-like character of the relationship between the managers and the managed, between the central authorities and the enterprise-level executors of commands. An asymmetric distribution of power between the top and bottom of the administrative hierarchy (with formal authority concentrated at the top and with information, which confers a less explicit but effective form of power, in the hands of the managers) results in a defective bargaining structure in which both sides lose. This interaction is a non-zero-sum game structured to lead to a less than optimal outcome.

The three pillars of the administered economy are output targets and allocations, administered pricing, and a cyclically repetitive control process. As long as these pillars remain, the attention of managers will be focused on pleasing (perhaps by deceiving) their superiors, not on catering to customers or bargaining with suppliers. The only way to get rid of these three pillars is to destroy the apparatus whose job it is to perform the functions they represent. This conclusion can be reached in a kind of deductive way, or it can simply be inferred from the experience and insights of the East European reformers.

The Soviet reformers have so far adopted a schizophrenic stance towards undermining the three pillars. They have talked about "combining plan and market," and they have tried to institute a hybrid system where some production activity was market-directed while the remaining production was to be guided by the old principles under the guise of *goszakazy* (state orders). They have legislated freedom for enterprises in the new Law on State Enterprises but have left in place the old bureaucratic apparatus to interfere with the exercise of that freedom. They have so far done virtually nothing to move away from administered prices. As time has passed and they have gained experience, however, the reformers have come to realize they must go further towards real marketization, and in their general policy and actions they have moved in the direction of radicalizing the reform. In short, the reformers have learned they cannot really change the behavior of the bureaucratic apparatus but must simply abolish it.[3] They are held back in this task more by the political problem than by any lingering expectation that they can reform the bureaucrats. The tactics are to chip away at the administrative apparatus, to free individual sectors, to marketize certain categories of prices, and so on. Under such a piecemeal approach, there will be inconsistencies, but the experience of Eastern Europe suggests that it is probably impossible to proceed directly to a full-blown market system. What is important is to keep moving in the right direction.[4]

---

[3] This line of thought is systematically and interestingly developed in *Ekonomicheskie korni byurokratizma* by R. G. Khudokormov, Moscow, Ekonomika, 1988.

[4] I am reminded of Albert Hirschman's view on economic development (see Albert O. Hirschman, *The Strategy of Economic Development*, New Haven, Connecticut, Yale University Press, 1958). Critics of development programs always decry their inconsistencies and disproportions. Hirschman's idea is that this is an unhelpful point of view. The important thing is to do *something*. It is *not* possible to deal with all aspects of a program in a fully coordinated way, so

PRICE REFORM

It is not possible to marketize without reforming the price mechanism. Marketization, properly understood, is a process in which markets not only allocate resources but also generate the information needed for the economic decision-making underlying allocation. In shifting from vertical communication between bosses and executors to lateral negotiation between producers and users the goal is not to settle only decisions about quantities but also to get a reading from all interested parties on how much inputs and outputs are worth. What has to be reformed is not prices per se but the price *mechanism*. If economic reform is to improve economic performance, price reform must go beyond having Goskomtsen (State Committee on Prices) introduce "reformed prices" to removing the process from the hands of Goskomtsen altogether. This is one of the cases where it may be necessary to take one step first and then a second, but in this case such a transition is like the policy of protecting "infant" industry. As long as Goskomtsen is there to reform prices, it is itself the biggest obstacle to reforming the price mechanism.

Some of the reformers understand that administered prices must be eliminated. In a round-table discussion between Soviet reformers and Czech economists that was organized by the Soviet journal *Kommunist* and the Czech journal *Nova mysl* and that generated a clear-headed explication of reform, one of the Soviet participants, Nikolai Petrakov, made it plain on the question of market-based prices that despite what any price fixer may choose to do there is such a thing as the real value of any commodity and that only markets in equilibrium can reveal this value. "A price that equates supply and demand takes into account all factors on both the production side and the consumption side."[5] In one of the sharpest criticisms of the official line on *perestroika* that has yet been made, Abalkin said something similar at the Party conference in the summer of 1987.

The big argument here is one of sequence. The official line is that before prices can be reformed markets must first be brought into equilibrium. There are too many shortages, and freeing prices would lead to disaster in the form of inflation and redistribution of income. Even the reformers are now accepting this line. The argument is less reasonable than it sounds, of course. The threat of inflation does not

that imbalances and bottlenecks will inevitably emerge. But that is no excuse for not starting—imbalances and bottlenecks will define very clearly what direction the next steps must take.

5   "Za novoe ekonomicheskoe myshlenie: 'Kruglyi stol' zhurnalov *Nova mysl* i *Kommunist*," *Kommunist*, No. 15, 1988, pp. 91-104. The Soviet participants were Leonid Abalkin, Nikolai Petrakov, Gelii Shmelev, Viktor Starodubrovsky, and two of the editors of *Kommunist*, Otto Latsis and Egor Gaidar.

flow, as many current Soviet discussions would have it, from inadequate production but from too much money, which creates too much demand. An expansion of consumer-goods output would, *ceteris paribus*, expand the money in the hands of the population by the same amount as the supply of goods increased. V. V. Novozhilov explained this to Soviet policymakers long ago in the context of the shortage of goods in the 1920s, and it is interesting to see that someone has now mustered the good sense to reprint one of his articles on the subject.[6] The prices that will create market equilibrium can only be found by letting them emerge via the market. Unfortunately, given the supply of money now in the hands of the population, a price level for consumer goods that would make the population willing to go on holding it would be far above the current level of prices. As Petrakov puts it in the discussion with the Czechs, "the problem of curing the monetary system is a life-or-death problem for economic methods of control. . . . The problem of reforming the price system must be solved simultaneously with the reforming of the monetary system."

THE SOFT OR HARD BUDGET CONSTRAINT IN ITS MICRO- AND MACROFORMS

One of the standard problems of the Soviet-type economy is the absence of "a hard budget constraint." This term, first introduced by Janos Kornai, has acquired a wide variety of meanings, but basically it refers to the fact that Soviet-type economies, even in a semireformed version, lack institutional arrangements to force financial responsibility on the state and on its creatures—ministries of finance, banks, enterprises, and such. The crucial sanction that is missing is bankruptcy, which adherents of the socialist system have always been very reluctant to accept.

The softness of the budget constraint has micro- and macroeffects. On the microlevel, it reduces the pressure to correct past errors in investment, economic structure, and allocation. Incentives for cost control are weak in the Soviet-type economy. This fact is neatly captured in the Russian description of the Soviet system as a *zatratnyi mekhanizm* (expense mechanism). One Soviet term for input-output is *zatrat-vypusk* (expense-output), a probably unconscious pun suggesting that the Soviet system eats up inputs without producing outputs. Enterprises often produce the wrong things, are not strongly cost conscious, systematically overexpend resources, and fail to cover costs out of revenues. But an inefficient enterprise can continue to operate because the bank extends credit to cover its overexpenditure period after period and not infrequently forgives the loan. The rules of the

---

6 V. V. Novozhilov, "Nedostatok tovarov," first published in *Vestnik finansov* in 1926, reprinted in *EKO*, No. 12, 1988, pp. 10-31, and early in 1989 in *Ekonomicheskaya gazeta*.

system have generally been that when faced with the alternative of extending credit beyond the plan or holding an enterprise to planned credit and thus forcing a shutdown, the bank is to provide liquidity for the continued operation of the enterprise. In the semireformed systems, central authorities also often accord special treatment to weak enterprises in other forms—special exchange-rate coefficients that give them an advantage compared with the general rate of exchange, relief from taxes, special dispensation with respect to wage payments, and direct subsidies. The result is that uneconomic production continues, and resources are not shifted to more desirable activities.

On the macrolevel, either of these processes (direct extension of unrepayable credit by the bank or extension of budget-based or budget-wrecking favors) creates excess demand. The first leads directly to an expansion of the money supply. The second entails extension of credit by the monobank to the state rather than to enterprises to cover budget deficits. Whatever the mechanism, this excess liquidity generally ends up as cash held by the population.

Under the old system, the enterprise sector was simply a channel for transforming new credits into cash held by the population. It had no motive to hold money itself or little way to use it to influence resource allocation. The best way for an enterprise to use extra money is to try to elicit more effort by increasing wage expenditures. As the economy becomes marketized, however, enterprises will begin to have reasons to hold money. They will begin to exhibit portfolio behavior—i.e., make choices about the best way to hold their assets, one way being to turn money into producer goods, which will affect the price of these goods.

The excess cash generated by the soft budget constraint leads to loss of incentives, corruption, price increases for those consumer goods and services that are not price-controlled, or price creep for those that are price-controlled, via familiar mechanisms that need not be spelled out here. The bank does not worry about the growth of outstanding liabilities in the form of notes backed on the asset side of its balance sheet only with worthless IOUs. The monobank itself, having no hard budget constraint, will never have to redeem those notes.

This mechanism of inflationary monetary expansion has been operating for a long time in the USSR but became especially active during the Eleventh and Twelfth Five-Year Plans. With economic reform the inflationary process accelerates. Fewer prices are controlled. Under the new Law on State Enterprises, Soviet managers have won more freedom to expand wage expenditures. Plans that envisage structural change and reallocation of resources end up generating excess demand, because without a hard budget constraint to remove the old claimants they continue as an undiminished drain on resources. Soviet reformers from Gorbachev on down are filling the pages of the press with admonitions that "we must live within our means." As

Gorbachev put it in his speech to the plenum of the Central Committee, in April, 1989, "not a single ruble must be spent without tying it to the quantity and quality of output."[7] As yet, though, neither the Soviet reformers nor the architects of the already semireformed economies have created an institutional mechanism to enforce that desideratum.

A hard budget constraint could conceivably be imposed at the microlevel by "commercial banks," operating under a "solvency or bankruptcy" constraint and a liquidity constraint imposed by a central bank. In such a situation the banks would be forced to conduct their dealings with the enterprise sector on the basis of truly commercial principles, extending credit only to creditworthy borrowers for economically justified purposes. But controlling the macroeffects would require Gosbank to take on the responsibility for regulating system liquidity as its commercial banking functions were shifted to local banks. Some entity would also need to take on the bank regulatory function as a way of forcing a hard budget constraint on the commercial banks—remember the fiasco of the US savings and loan associations. No reforming society in Eastern Europe has yet succeeded in creating such a banking system, and the consequences—in the form of inflationary pressure—are obvious. The Hungarians have gone furthest in this area and now have something close to the kind of system described above. This is one area in which the USSR ought to be able to telescope the reform process a bit, but its bank reorganization effort so far does not touch the essential features.[8] Setting up specialized banks, as the USSR has done, does not necessarily make them commercial banks. The five banks split off from Gosbank are more like subcontractors for carrying out the loan and settlement operations that Gosbank used to perform directly. It is true that some new kinds of banks are beginning to emerge—cooperative banks and inter-firm banks. The cooperative banks must almost inherently feel a hard budget constraint, but the system of government-sponsored banks as a whole will not do so until Gosbank takes on the traditional central banking role of regulating the reserves of the system.

Because the reformers have generally postponed the effort to deal with the soft budget constraint, the monetary horse is already out of the barn, certainly in the Soviet Union. As mentioned above this creates an

[7]   *Ekonomicheskaya gazeta*, No. 18, 1989, p. 3.

[8]   What has been done is to create five specialized banks (Prombank, Agroprombank, Vneshekonombank, Zhilsotsbank and Sberegatel'nyi Bank). All enterprises now deal with these rather than with Gosbank for settlement and credit services, leaving Gosbank "to implement a unified policy in the field of monetary circulation, lending, financing, settlements, cash and foreign exchange operations" (see the interview with N. V. Garetovsky, chairman of the Board of Gosbank, in *Ekonomicheskaya gazeta*, No. 50, 1987, pp. 4 and 9).

almost insuperable obstacle to retail price reform. Even if a hard budget constraint were instituted now, there is already a huge monetary overhang in existence. One estimate is that the excess supply of cash is about 70 billion rubles. In addition, about 300 billion rubles are held in savings accounts, and these holdings are growing rapidly. Two researchers from the Savings Bank Research Institute (NIIBank) estimate the level of "unsatisfied demand" at 120 billion rubles with estimates by others ranging from 60 to 200 billion rubles.[9]

It does not appear that anyone in the USSR has really thought analytically about this problem yet. The Soviet discussions seem quite unsophisticated, generally failing to distinguish between stocks and flows in talking about the size of excess demand. It is interesting that in all the new statistical information now being published little is to be found on the household income and expenditure account. To think about how the problem might be handled requires going back to the fundamentals of the demand for money—the transactions motive, money held as a store of wealth, and precautionary demand. How much inflation there will be if prices are freed depends on where the money is held and the accompanying motivations. To get some perspective on how excessive the stock may be, consider the major element—i.e., transactions demand. Savings accounts averaged 258 billion rubles in 1987, and to this should be added possibly as much as 100 billion to 200 billion rubles of cash. Household expenditures in 1987 for the major categories—retail goods, household and communal services, and personal taxes—were about 400 billion rubles. Soviet workers are generally paid biweekly, and the transactions demand for cash to cover that much turnover would be a very small fraction of the flow, say 1/40th.[10] If all incomes were biweekly and spending equaled income, holdings on payday would amount to 1/26th of spending, and by the end of the two-week period would fall to zero for an *average* holding of 1/52nd of annual spending. Collective farmers' receipts have a much longer cycle, except for receipts from collective-farm sales, which are much more frequent. The full statement of household incomes and expenditures would be much more complex, though the big elements of expenditure are taken into account here. A more systematic analysis would require disaggregation by rural and urban components.

---

  [9] *Ekonomicheskaya gazeta*, No. 18, 1989, p. 12. Like most of the Soviet commentators, they are a little confused in how to think about this. The Western concept would be excess stock of money—i.e., the portion of the stock that exceeds what households are comfortable with holding at the existing level of prices, purchases, interest rates, and so on.

  [10] The dynamics are also very interesting. The ratio of the big expenditure items to savings deposits has fallen from 2.0 in 1980 to 1.5 in 1987.

But however crude the analysis above may be, it is hard not to believe that much of the stock of cash and savings is unwanted, held only because it is very difficult to spend.

The transactions demand is, of course, only one of the demands for money. There is probably considerable variation in the motives for holding this money among different groups of the population, and it may be that the extent of balances held unwillingly is not as overwhelming as often thought. With the growth of a free market sector, there begins to be a rationale for holding money for speculative purposes—for example, to finance investment in cooperatives and to buy assets from the state. This motive may begin to arise for enterprises as well. Given the importance of the issue for reform, a lot more careful analysis should be going on in the USSR than there is evidence of, in the interest of developing a solid picture of how money holdings are split between households and enterprises, of what groups of households hold the money (as a clue to what their motivations might be), and so on.

What can be done about the overhang? One possibility is to implement a bolt-from-the-blue currency conversion like that of 1947. The leaders would find it very difficult to do that, however, because it would be taken as a betrayal of trust. Another possibility is to sell off assets. If the state sector insists on living beyond its current means (as does the United States), one solution is to sell assets to the savings sector (as the United States does to Japan). This is being done to some extent but not enough and not on the basis of the right principles. Housing is apparently sold to households at its book value rather than auctioning it off to the highest bidder. People have little motivation to hold money as a store of value—not only is it not income-producing, but its value depreciates with inflation. Thus, a third possibility might be to offer interest-bearing government securities in exchange for cash, perhaps even with the interest rate indexed.[11] Still another idea is a replay of the chervonets replacement of the 1920s. A new currency would be issued along with the old and give its holder special rights, such as trading it for foreign currency or using it to buy certain rationed goods. It would be the money of the new economy, and its stock would expand along with the new economy. Besides these proposals, a budget surplus or a contraction of bank credit has been suggested. The reformers have come up with some of these ideas—Petrakov mentioned most of them in the Soviet-Czech round-table discussion. They all present problems, however, and action to carry them out is very slow.

---

11   The authors from the NIIBank mentioned above complain that more would go into the savings accounts if the savings banks were allowed to offer interest rates "at least as high as the rate of inflation." But the money would be much more effectively sterilized if it were in long maturity bonds, rather than in the rather liquid form of savings bank deposits.

In the absence of a solution to the overhang, how well can *perestroika* tolerate inflation? Yugoslavia has tolerated inflation without stopping growth, and so has China; maybe the USSR can as well. Much is made of the danger inflation poses for popular support of economic reform, but inflation has a much more complicated relationship to reform than that emphasis suggests. One way to think about inflation is as a process that transfers income to those who serve the new markets from those whose link to the market is mediated through remnants of the old system. Keynes saw an advantage in inflation as leading to "euthanasia of the rentier." The concept of rentier is tricky to apply to Soviet society since rentier status is determined differently there, but surely most of those who work as bureaucrats are rentiers, in addition to the usual categories like pensioners. One reform strategy is to buy off the bureaucrats by retiring them on pension. Their claims on resources (and correspondingly on power) could then be further reduced by inflation. The main point to be made here is that how much trouble inflation would cause depends on what kind of a system of property relations is put in place of the old system of entitlements and insecure service-dependent emoluments. Probably some inflation is good. It offers the possibility of transferring income from those who hold old claims, those whose entitlements are based on the mistakes of the old system, to those whose current contributions are highly valued. The problem, of course, is to keep inflation low enough not to discredit current incentives and to avoid violating dominant ideas about social justice.

Mention of a budget surplus as a way of helping to solve the problem of the overhang points to the issue of the fiscal system more generally. The traditional Soviet-type economy was able to manage with a very rudimentary fiscal system, but that system is incapable of making a serious contribution to meeting the requirements of the new situation. A full fiscal policy instrumentarium must be equipped to deal with both sides of the state budget—with choices about borrowing versus taxes on the revenue side, with regulating both purchases of goods and services and transfer payments on the expenditure side, and with manipulating the totals on the two sides to achieve a surplus or deficit. In his concluding speech at the plenum of the Central Committee in April, 1989, Gorbachev bemoaned "the lack of a tax policy" that would permit the leaders to regulate incomes and deal with the financial disorder into which the system has fallen.[12]

One reason for complexifying the fiscal system is that it can provide an auxiliary tool for macrostabilization. The managers of the socialist economies are now handicapped by the fact that there is no distinction between fiscal and monetary policy—the two always work in the same direction. A budget deficit always leads to an increase in the supply of

---

[12] *Ekonomicheskaya gazeta*, No. 18, 1989, p. 3.

money, and a reduction in the money supply is possible only by running a budget surplus. Issuing government securities could potentially keep these two tracks separate. The creation of a government securities market would, incidentally, provide a means by which a more sophisticated central bank could regulate the supply of liquidity in the system. This sounds like a recommendation that the socialist reformers create carbon copies of the market economies, and it may be objected that it is unrealistic to expect them to do so. It should be kept in mind, though, that while tremendous variation is possible in the forms fiscal and monetary arrangements take, they are the most important economic policy tools appropriate to a marketized economy. It does not make much sense to marketize the economy without having this macrocontrol instrumentarium in place as well. The experience of Yugoslavia, China, Hungary, and Poland attests to the danger of failing to create fiscal and monetary policy instruments, and if the USSR is willing to learn from their record *perestroika* can avoid some of the pitfalls they have encountered.

Making the fiscal system more complex would not only provide a fuller menu of fiscal tools for dealing with macrostability but would also permit the policymakers to deal with another major problem of a reforming economy—namely, the issue of income distribution. As control of prices is relinquished to the market, leaders lose control over the distribution of real income—some people get high incomes, others are stuck with stagnant incomes or even lose their jobs. This rouses opposition to the reform process by offending whatever ideas about distributive justice are held either by the leaders or the population at large. These phenomena, quite strongly developed in China, are also appearing in the USSR. Popular revulsion at the high prices exacted and the high incomes earned by the cooperatives has been well publicized, and there was an attempt by the Ministry of Finance (later aborted) to tax cooperatives out of existence.[13] The draft of a proposed new income tax schedule has been promulgated.[14] There is also a need to build a safety net for those who lose out under market pricing through some

---

[13] The Ministry of Finance originally enacted a tax on cooperatives with a marginal rate of 90 percent. One of the motivations for tightening restrictions on cooperatives at the end of 1988 was popular resentment at their high prices and high profits.

[14] The Council of Ministers has proposed a new income tax law, which is now to be discussed generally and then acted on. See *Ekonomicheskaya gazeta*, No. 17, 1989, p. 3. It is moderately progressive, starting with incomes of about 740 rubles per month (about 3 times the average pay in industry) and rising to a marginal rate of 50 percent at 1,540 rubles per month. The tax will apply to all personal incomes, although taxes on cooperative profits are still to be taxed differently from state enterprise profits and depending on field of activity.

combination of disadvantage with regard to income and cost of living. It should be the task of the tax system to deal with the equity issues that marketization raises. This is partly a matter of understanding fiscal policy and partly a matter of creating a political process that will involve the public in the determination of fiscal policy and do so in a way that wins its support for the process of change.

The Soviet reformers will probably have a hard time dealing with fiscal policy. As the economy becomes marketized, incidence and shifting of the tax burden become important. Under the old system, which depended heavily on the turnover tax, it was clear who paid the tax—i.e., households. The only issue was interpersonal welfare incidence (the tax burden was heavier on those who liked vodka than on those who bought children's shoes). Even when Soviet tax policy deemphasized the turnover tax to collect more taxes from enterprises in the form of profit deductions,[15] there was little shifting, since prices were administered and input menus determined administratively. But in a reformed system in which price and cost interact with allocation, the shifting and final personal incidence of taxes is likely to be much more difficult to gauge. What is most intriguing about this is that Soviet economists evidently do not know the issue exists. The ideas of shifting and incidence are central enough to any notion of fiscal policy that they are introduced in a sophomore economics course in the West, but they never even seem to be mentioned in Soviet writings. For their part, the Hungarians, in reforming their tax system, relied mostly on a value-added tax (VAT) and a personal income tax, giving the impression that they understand and are trying to deal with the incidence problem.

CREATING A COMPETITIVE STRUCTURE

Mention of the policy tools appropriate to a marketized economy points to another issue that needs to be resolved—that of industrial concentration and market power. The socialist economies are highly concentrated.[16] If enterprises are turned loose to maximize profits, they will have the market power to distort allocation. It is very likely that such freedom would also add to the inflationary process by creating a cost-

---

[15]   In 1960 the turnover tax was 1.78 times the collections from enterprises, but by 1986 that ratio had fallen to 0.70.

[16]   There are some puzzles about how the industrial structure of these economies might affect market power. The Soviet economy is characterized by very large enterprises, often because of a high degree of vertical integration. A safe guess is that production profiles for final products are rather specialized but that the high degree of vertical integration means lack of concentration at the level of intermediate products. There are a lot of considerations involved here, though, that have not been studied well.

push pressure in addition to the demand pull of the monetary over-hang. One objection of the antireformers to marketization is the high prices and high profits of firms not under central control. A better way out than following their counsel, which is to reintroduce and strengthen central control, would be to make entry to the market easier.

Again, the experience of the East European pioneers is useful. The Poles broke up industrial concentrations. Control of market power through opening the domestic economy to foreign pressure is another option. Marketization of foreign-trade decisions would help not only to improve allocation but also to create a climate of competition. Besides this, an important step would be the easing of conditions for the forma-tion of new enterprises, to which there are many approaches: some self-organizing initiative could come from cooperatives and joint ventures, and leasing could also provide a backdoor for new entrants. Finally, removing artificial constraints (that exist de jure or because of admin-istrative pressure from above) on production profiles of enterprises and allowing assets to be transferred (maybe bought and sold) between enterprises would likewise be important steps. A recent report tells how an insolvent enterprise in one ministry was taken over by another ministry. The ministry doing the acquiring assumed the enterprise's debts and undertook to provide investment to reequip it and change its production profile. It will thus have furnished itself with a supplier for much less than building a new plant from scratch would have cost.[17] This kind of action leads to vertical integration, which may pose dan-gers to competition, but on the whole is no doubt beneficial. The ratio-nale for buying and selling enterprises and facilities is to encourage po-tential entrants to scout out underutilized assets that could be em-ployed more effectively. This will be helpful in itself (an abundance of underutilized assets is a major feature of the centrally planned econ-omy), but it is also a method of encouraging entry to counter market power.

THE ENCLAVE STRATEGY

One of the discouraging problems for the reformers is that it seems impossible to redesign the Soviet dinosaur completely, all at once, or with a phasing that does not create too many contradictions. The idea of turning all industry loose, dropping all controls on consumer-goods prices, and all that is pretty scary, both because of the supply-demand issues it raises and because of the uncertainty and, hence, opposition it creates. One compromise that always suggests itself is to shift only a part of the economy to new principles, while postponing or temporiz-ing on their introduction in other parts of the economy. The definition

---

[17] "Manevr autsaidera," *Ekonomicheskaya gazeta*, No. 15, 1989, p. 8.

of this "enclave" might be based on a functional principle (marketizing current output but keeping administrative control of investment), a territorial principle (free enterprise zones), or a sectoral principle (privatizing agriculture through leasing while leaving the rest of the economy socialist). The choice of the enclave would be based on the criterion of urgency—quick results are needed in producing food and consumer goods or in turning out high-tech producer goods—or on some principle of adaptability—certain kinds of activities can adjust faster to a new regime than others. Variants of the enclave strategy have been popular in reforming the other planned economies and in economic development everywhere. The USSR has not done much along these lines so far, but it is likely to happen. Legislation has been promised concerning a special economic zone for Siberia, there may be regional *khozraschet*, and there is likely to emerge a more carefully designed "open sector" for foreign enterprise.

The trickiest part of such an approach is the interface with the rest of the economy. The enclave must not disrupt the traditional economy or be hamstrung by dependence on it but must at the same time become an *ochag* (hotbed) of progressivism. That is not easy to do. Cases that satisfy the first goal—tourism, services, etc.—do not satisfy the second and vice versa. The proposals floated so far seem to lean too far in the first direction.

STEWARDSHIP OF SOCIALIST PROPERTY

The socialist system has primitive arrangements for stewardship of "property" or, as a Marxist would call it, "the means of production." In a socialist society, the means of production are owned by the state on behalf of, and in the name of, the working class. Unfortunately, the state and its agents have proved to be feckless stewards in managing that property. The worshipers of socialist thought have an ideological fixation about state ownership, having always treated nationalization or socialization of the means of production as the *sine qua non* of the socialist order. But many reformers in both Eastern Europe and the Soviet Union have come to see that the ritual assertion of the primacy of state ownership as a hallmark of socialism ignores the question of whether effective use is being made of the means of production for the good of the working class. Rights of ownership are now being intensely discussed in the Soviet Union, and a better understanding of these rights could result in improved institutional and policy reforms.[18]

---

[18]   Nearly every issue of any economic journal has an article or so on the question of property, and proponents of a private-property approach frequently have their say in articles in the central press. There has been a series of such articles in *Ekonomicheskaya gazeta*. A conference to try to work out a position

There are also discussions of charging rent on urban land and even of letting some agent of the state auction the right to use it.[19]

The key to any sensible resolution of this issue lies in recognizing that ownership is a bundle of rights—the right to receive income from productive assets, the right to make decisions about their use, the right to dispose of property through sale or transfer or inheritance, and so on. Abalkin and Petrakov distinguish clearly between the right to appropriate the surplus value created by capital and the right or function of "control,"—i.e., managing the use of property.[20] These aspects of ownership can be unbundled through various forms of contract, such as leasing agreements or the more complicated forms of agreement that are characteristic of capitalist countries and that distinguish between debt contracts, voting and nonvoting stock, and alternative tenure arrangements for land. Moreover, it is possible to formulate most of these rights in the form of contracts that can be traded, so that various functions of ownership can be marketized. As has been learned in the West, an important distinction exists among the various members of the coalition with a stake in the economic activity of a productive entity (the customers for its output, the suppliers of produced inputs, the contributors of land, the workers, the different classes of owner). This is the distinction between those whose contract terms are determined in a market and the party who is a residual claimant on the income of the entity. That party is sometimes also described as "a rent-seeker." With most of the interactions with the rest of the economy settled at market prices, the "owner's" income is the residual—positive or negative; therefore he has the greatest incentive to use the property in the most productive way. Abalkin sees this clearly enough: he goes so far as to say that the difference between managerial income (one of the routine market-valued payments) and entrepreneurial income familiar in the analysis of market economies can have an analogue in socialist economies.

Decades of experience have demonstrated that the socialist state with all its bureaucracy for administering the economy is not capable of fulfilling its stewardship function—it is short on information, and its stewards are not motivated to ensure that property is used in the most

on property issues is said to have been held early in the spring of 1989. Zaslavskaya says there are to be many forms of property. Bogomolov asks what is wrong with the desire of an individual to have a bit of land on which to build a house. Again, one of the most direct and clearly stated set of ideas by the reformers is what Abalkin and Petrakov said in their discussion with the Czechs in the article in *Kommunist* (see Note 5).

19 "Tsena zemli moskovskoi," *Ekonomicheskaya gazeta*, No. 12, 1989, p. 18, and other articles in earlier issues—e.g., Nos. 33 and 49, 1988.

20 See Note 5.

productive way. Current Soviet discussions are not very clear about what to substitute for state ownership. Some reformers suggest that the role of "owner" might be vested in lower-level organs of government—a city government, a ministry, or others. The Estonians want the right of property on the territory of their republic to be vested in the Estonian people. The idea is now very common that elements of ownership may be transferred to individuals or private entities for fairly long periods of time through various kinds of leasing. It is also recognized that the claims of the various parties under these contracts might become badly tangled over time. A cooperative might lease property from the state but then invest its own resources to expand or improve it, confusing ownership rights in the entity as a whole. The Soviet draft leasing law now proposes to recognize the ownership right of the lessee in lessee-made improvements.[21]

Plainly, "state ownership of the means of production," the last bulwark of the administrative-command system, is coming to be seen in a new light by socialist economists, and arrangements are being proposed that will permit the marketization of property rights along with the marketization of other valuables. The semireformed economy that marketizes everything except property rights will find that one of the crucial tools for effective production (i.e., rent-seeking by an active residual claimant) is still missing. "Privatization," understood in this way, is one of the necessary conditions for effective reform.

MOVING TO AN OPEN ECONOMY

No attempt will be made here to elaborate on the problem of opening the Soviet economy to the world economy. Suffice it to say that the message to be conveyed is the same. The Soviet Union will get better performance when it lets market principles govern foreign trade. Export and import decisions need to be left to individual firms, guided by and participating in a market process that determines the most important price governing this class of transactions—i.e., the exchange rate. Only then will the Soviet Union get what it wants from foreign trade—the stimulus of external competition, gains from comparative advantage, a climate that will encourage foreigners to engage in joint ventures and invest significant amounts of capital. On the other hand, convertibility and its crucial foundation, "goods convertibility," cannot come until the rest of the economy is marketized. Again, it appears the reformers have a vision of a reformed economy in which these conditions would be satisfied, and some well-publicized actions have been taken, but so far these add up only to half-measures, maybe quarter-measures.

---

[21] See draft law on leasing in *Ekonomicheskaya gazeta*, No. 16, 1989, p. 4.

CONCLUSION

How should all this be summed up? The experience of socialist economic reform has given us the concept of "the semireformed economy," a kind of "halfway house" represented in variant forms in Yugoslavia, Poland, China, and Hungary. It is clear that the semireformed economy is still burdened with much of the ineffectiveness of allocation and the weakness of incentives that were part of the old system, along with some special problems all its own. These problems can only be solved by moving further in the direction of reform. On a reform thermometer calibrated in terms of the experience of the other socialist countries, economic *perestroika* in the USSR has not yet brought the system much above the freezing point. Put somewhat differently, it is not yet to the halfway house. At the same time, it is clear the Soviet reformers are determined to reach a goal well above the present reading, and the next question is what are their prospects for moving in that direction.

There is a classic process at work in socialist economic reform, one that has come to be understood and generalized in a large literature on East European reform.[22] The experience of reform has consistently been that it creates new problems even as it is producing some improvements in the use of resources. Various components of the reform package are inconsistent and work at cross purposes. Because reform upsets established ways of doing things, it results in confusion and economic disruption. The reforms are hindered by those individuals or groups whose special interests they contravene. As defects in performance are revealed, the enemies of reform renew their attack, and the leaders face a choice between going forward or retreating. If the choice is to go forward, towards loosening central control still further, the intensified reform measures usually lead to new undesirable side effects, such as inflation and inequitable distribution of income. This process may continue through several iterations. It has been seen over and over again in Eastern Europe and in China. Since the advent of reform in the USSR under Khrushchev, there have been several important junctures at which decisions of this kind have had to be made, and until the Gorbachev period the decision was usually to retreat. Gorbachev's renewal of the push for reform has exhibited some instances of the pattern "two steps forward, one step backward," but the general movement ahead has continued. As Gorbachev encounters obstacles, either in the form of political opposition or failure to improve performance because of inconsistency and incompleteness in the reforms, he has usually found

---

22   One example is Benjamin Slay, *Reform of the Soviet-Type Economy: A Comparison of the Hungarian and Polish Reform Experience*, a dissertation at Indiana University, March, 1989; another is Judy Batt, *Economic Reform and Political Change in Eastern Europe*, London, Macmillan, 1988.

a way to confound the enemies of change and to impel reform to the next stage. He dislodges the opponents of reform from the top by classical power moves. Where that does not work, he tries to get at them from below, with tactics like election of directors by workers. If he cannot vanquish particular individuals, he neutralizes them by reorganizing them out of influential positions. If he cannot win on some issue, he shifts the struggle to a different battleground. When he was unsuccessful in getting the military-industrial complex (VPK) to help with the job of reequipping the food and light industries, he responded by dumping the whole problem directly in the VPK's lap. The big question is whether the process will keep going. The reformers seem to believe that if they do enough fast enough the system can never go back. Whether Gorbachev has gone far enough to make the process irreversible is hard to say. Brezhnev introduced the notion of irreversibility with respect to détente, and how incompletely he succeeded is well known.

Bright spots are hard to find in the performance of the economy to date under *perestroika*. A review of the whole economic situation would have to conclude that it is fairly grim. The line taken on this by the CIA and the DIA in their testimony to the Joint Economic Committee of the US Congress in April, 1989, seems more or less justified.[23] As Gorbachev found out last fall in Krasnoyarsk and from criticisms at the Central Committee plenum in April, 1989, made by the defeated Party people, the consumer-goods situation is disastrous and is generating widespread popular dissatisfaction. Gorbachev is temporizing, focusing on the most urgent things first. He has backtracked on the anti-alcohol campaign, and he is going to import more consumer goods. Understanding that the budget deficit is leading to an intolerable inflationary situation, he is going to make some budget cuts. He is going to put more pressure on the defense industry to produce consumer durables. Well into the year, it was decided to cut investment in 1989 below the original plan approved in the fall of 1988, and in the plan for 1990 these expedients have been intensified. As for institutional reforms, Gorbachev made the new law on leasing his highest priority item in the hope that this would help with the most urgent problem in keeping *perestroika* alive—i.e., production of more food soon. What he is going to do about the problem of regional claims, which is another obstacle threatening the emergence of a viable new system, is not yet clear.

Over the last three years the reformers have made some big mistakes and lost valuable time. One of the most interesting things that has emerged is how poorly they understand their own system.

---

[23] *The Soviet Economy in 1988: Gorbachev Changes Course.* This is a study presented by the Central Intelligence Agency and the Defense Intelligence Agency to the National Security Economics Subcommittee of the Joint Economic Committee, Congress of the United States, April, 1989.

Zaslavskaya tells us that; the historians tell us that; and Gorbachev offered that as part of his excuse for financial disorder and the inflationary pressures in the consumer-goods markets. Are they learning fast enough? Can they stay in control of this monster they have unleashed? Will things get worse before they get better, and how long can Gorbachev survive their getting worse?

It would be foolish to offer a definitive answer to this set of questions. Rather, it may be useful to try to imagine how an optimistic prognosis might work. The greatest problem is the monetary overhang, but it might be handled by a variety of palliatives. Prices for consumer goods could be allowed to rise a bit. Inflation means a higher transactions demand for money. Some of the overhang could be channeled through banks to cooperatives, so that it would appear not as consumer-goods demand but as demand for real estate and existing assets. A contribution to consumption could be taken from foreign trade and from the defense industry. Production in the defense industry would take the form not of defense goods that have to be financed through the budget by collecting revenue somewhere but of consumer goods that can be sold to households, mostly at high markups over cost. Some of the alcohol revenue could be regained. Offering government bonds or higher interest rates on deposits would help to whittle away the overhang. It is not that consumer-goods production has broken down—output is growing slightly, and it will continue to do so. On reform, consistency in opening the gates for enterprise formation via numerous channels would be essential. A response from leasing in agriculture will probably make itself felt within a couple of years. Consumption could be increased by canceling a lot of expensive and unproductive capital investments. By careful distinctions between sectors and tasks, Gorbachev could keep enough of the old system functioning, say in energy production and exports for hard currency, to avoid a breakdown and to achieve some reallocations, as in reorienting the defense industry. Soviet observers report that the atmosphere within the enterprise has changed significantly for the better, and they might find that managers in the state sector begin to take responsibility.

Would this happen soon enough to make a difference? It is not implausible to consider the possibility of *perestroika* surviving into the 1990s anyway, by which time it could turn the corner. Between now and the year 2000 there is no way of achieving the kind of *uskorenie* (acceleration) of growth Gorbachev originally promised. But in the 1990s there may be enough change to begin to show some effect on the ability of the Soviet economy to serve consumers better and to reveal the capabilities of a modern economy to attain growth through structural and technical change.

2

Redefining Socialism in the USSR

Elizabeth Teague

ALONGSIDE all the discussion about what is to be *done*, there is under way in the USSR a more abstract debate about what is to be *thought*. Soviet leaders now openly acknowledge a truth the population has long known from personal experience—namely, that the Soviet system is a failure. As two leading Soviet spokesmen have put it: "The all-embracing 'total' state is not only difficult and expensive to manage but ineffective and even counterproductive."[1] Soviet social scientists are, accordingly, attempting "to redefine socialism" in order to decide where the USSR is going and how it should get there.

Perhaps reform does not, or should not, require this. Perhaps the Soviet Union is in the process of ceasing to be a society with a formal and articulated ideology—what has been called an "ism" society. Indeed, a number of the reformers seem simply to be saying that it is time for the USSR to become what they term "a normal society"—in effect, a Western society.

Some of the ideas being put forward by the reformers about what is wrong with the Soviet model of socialism and what kind of society should be built in its stead will be examined here. Because it is at the most fundamental level that the Soviet model is perceived to have failed, the discussion touches on the most basic questions of political philosophy: how the claims of the individual are to be balanced against those of the community; what should be the relationship between the individual, society, and the state; and how a regime that has long relied on the use of coercion can move towards greater reliance on popular consent while, at the same time, maintaining social stability.

---

[1] G. Arbatov and E. Batalov, "Politicheskaya reforma i evolyutsiya sovetskogo gosudarstva," *Kommunist*, No. 4, 1989, pp. 35-64 at p. 43.

IN SEARCH OF TRUE SOCIALISM

One of the explanations Soviet reformers are offering for the failure of the Soviet system is that it is not truly socialist. The more radical the reformer, the more likely he or she is to mock the existing system under such epithets as "barracks socialism," "bureaucratic socialism," or "the socialism of War Communism." Of course, a lot depends on how "socialism" is defined. If all that is meant is public ownership of the means of production, then the USSR qualifies. The economist (and deputy prime minister) Leonid Abalkin argues, however, that socialism means more than that. He has advanced two criteria to determine whether or not a system is socialist. First, there is the economic criterion: "If socialism is a higher stage of social development [than capitalism], it must outdo its predecessor in efficiency, quality, productivity, and rate of innovation." The Soviet economy does not, of course, outstrip the capitalist world in these respects. Abalkin's second criterion is social, and in this respect too the USSR fails the test. Socialism, he says, should "guarantee everyone a minimum standard of living, a lower limit of social well-being." If a system "fails to make the individual feel master in his own workplace," Abalkin concludes, "then the system is not socialist."[2]

Along with other reformist economists, Abalkin argues that the Soviet system of property relations is at the root of the problem, since it is held to be property relations that primarily distinguish socialism from capitalism.[3] He would doubtless agree with the Polish economist Wlodzimierz Brus that "socialism entails a particular concept of property rights—a system of ownership whereby *society* is genuinely in control of the means of production and benefits from their use." Brus goes on to fault official Soviet ideology for automatically equating "nationalization," or the taking of capital into *public* or *state* ownership, with "socialization."[4] On this too Abalkin would be likely to concur. He blames centralized and authoritarian state control for "deforming socialism" in the USSR and "alienating the masses from property and economic management."[5]

A number of radical reformers argue that the introduction of state-monopoly ownership in the USSR created a bureaucratic "caste" that staged a "counterrevolution" and "expropriated" the workers in whose

---

[2]   *Financial Times*, December 13, 1988.

[3]   See the three-part series, to which Abalkin and other leading Soviet reformers contributed, "Kakim byt' sotisalizmu?" *Pravda*, July 14, 16, and 17, 1989.

[4]   Wlodzimierz Brus, "Socialism—Feasible and Viable?" *The New Left Review*, No. 153, 1985, pp. 43-62 at pp. 44-5.

[5]   L. Abalkin, "Opirayas' na uroki proshlogo," *Kommunist*, No. 16, 1987, pp. 9-17 at p. 11.

name the revolution of 1917 was supposedly made. The sociologist Tat'yana Zaslavskaya argues that the Soviet elite constitutes a separate social class. The *nomenklatura*, she asserts, has "all the necessary attributes: control over the production apparatus, privileges, a separate way of life."[6] In the words of writer and critic Andrei Nuikin:

> What we habitually called "public property" was, in fact, state property. And the state, as Marx put it, is the private property of the bureaucrats. Socialization, people's rule, and other substantive attributes of socialism are ruinous to them as private property owners. In our case, the "state" means not only nationalized means of production but, as elsewhere, the judiciary, the army, the law-enforcement and state security agencies, schools, the information and propaganda media. . . . All this has also been the "private property" of our bureaucrats.[7]

The young Soviet writer Sergei Andreev has taken the argument to its logical conclusion and asked how the power of the bureaucracy can be broken.[8] Andreev categorizes the USSR as a dictatorship of a "new class" consisting of fourteen million manager-bureaucrats who stand to lose from any change in the existing system and therefore undermine all attempts at reform. Unless its power is broken, Andreev writes, this class will bring about "the failure of socialism as a societal form." The Communist Party, he says, has ignored the interests and will of the public and become fused with the bureaucracy; it is now a tool in the hands of powerful forces opposed to change. To break this symbiosis, the Party must be subordinated to the public and made answerable to the "non-Party majority" as well as to its own membership. This will not, Andreev concludes, be achieved without "a most desperate struggle."

As Gorbachev's supporters see it, the purpose of his political reform is to move away from what the historian Yurii Karyakin calls "the myth of the monolith"—that is, the idea that socialist society is homogeneous and that there exists in it a single "social interest" in pursuit of which the interests of the individual and of the minority may legitimately be subordinated to those of the collective. The CPSU has justified and justifies its monopoly on political power by claiming to be uniquely qualified to determine and administer "the general interest." Under this system, Gorbachev has acknowledged, the people were "degraded and insulted. . . . The way we behaved in recent years meant keeping them out of politics."[9]

---

[6]   *Le Nouvel Observateur*, March 1, 1989.

[7]   *New Times*, No. 26, 1988, p. 20.

[8]   S. Andreev, "Struktura vlasti i zadachi obshchestva," *Neva*, No. 1, 1989, pp. 144-73.

[9]   *Central Soviet Television*, July 14, 1987.

The journalist Aleksandr Bovin says the Soviet Union is rejecting this model of "early socialism . . . weighed down by authoritarianism, the deification of leaders, the dominance of the bureaucratic apparatus, economic inefficiency, and low living standards for the working people."[10] Gorbachev's Politburo ally Aleksandr Yakovlev says that the root of the problem is that, when the USSR was building socialism, "the main principle" was violated—that is, "that socialism must be built by the people themselves and not by the leaders."[11] *Perestroika*, Yakovlev has said, "means the dismantling of the economic and political structure that was created over the course of decades and that assigned to the individual the role of a building material that could be used to cobble together anything—while the individual's own hopes and interests were ignored."[12]

IN RETREAT FROM TRADITIONAL SOCIALISM

The traditional model of socialism was encapsulated in "general laws" for the construction of socialism promulgated by Party ideologist Mikhail Suslov in November, 1956, in the aftermath of the Soviet invasion of Hungary.[13] They specified: (1) the leading role of the Communist Party; (2) centralized control of all aspects of social activity; (3) nationalization of the means of production and central planning of the economy; and (4) defense of the gains of socialism ("proletarian" or "socialist internationalism"). A brief review of these "laws," held by Suslov to be universally applicable to Communist Parties everywhere, reveals the extent to which the Gorbachev leadership is departing from traditional doctrines.

(1) The dogma of "the leading role of the Party," which has in practice never meant anything other than the Communist Party's monopoly on power, is perhaps the only one of Suslov's prescriptions to which the Gorbachev leadership still professes adherence, with Gorbachev dismissing as "nonsense" the idea that the USSR might move towards a multiparty system.[14] Realizing, however, that the Party's stranglehold on all branches of political and economic activity has proved counterproductive, Gorbachev has in reality made strenuous efforts to streamline the Party bureaucracy, to separate its functions from those of the state, and to remove it from day-to-day involvement

---

10   *Izvestia*, May 11, 1989.

11   Yakovlev interviewed by Seweryn Bialer, *Journal of International Affairs*, No. 2, 1989, pp. 333-55.

12   *Pravda*, June 23, 1989.

13   *Pravda*, November 7, 1956.

14   *Central Soviet Television*, February 15, 1989.

in the management of the economy. He is shifting executive power from the Party to the organs of local government (the soviets) and legislative power to new parliamentary bodies which are beginning to act as counterweights to the Party apparatus.

In 1987, Gorbachev became the first Soviet leader to use the term "pluralism" in a positive sense.[15] To be sure, Gorbachev prefaced it with the adjective "socialist" without explaining what he meant by that, and he has since explicitly ruled out the possibility for the USSR of "political pluralism" (generally understood to mean a multiparty system, not just the existence of different factions within a single ruling Communist Party.)[16] (The term "political pluralism" has, however, subsequently been employed in a favorable sense by the political scientist Anatolii Butenko in the pages of *Pravda*; Butenko also did not make it clear precisely what he meant by the term he used.)[17]

This lack of clarity notwithstanding, Gorbachev's political reforms are having a greater impact on the Communist Party than on any other Soviet political institution, provoking a crisis in the Party and a steep drop in its authority and self-confidence. The Party is now divided into conservative and progressive wings, and the possibility of its splitting into two or more warring factions can no longer be ruled out. A move to a multiparty system may not be on the Party's agenda, but it looms large on that of the general population, and Popular Fronts in the Baltic republics and other regions, as well as the Interregional Group of parliamentary deputies, show the potential to develop into alternative political parties at some future date.

(2) There has been a sharp departure from Suslov's demand for central control of all aspects of social activity. In particular, Gorbachev's policies of *glasnost'* and *demokratizatsiya* seek to liberalize Soviet society and to provide incentives for ordinary people to participate in the political process. The Soviet population, Gorbachev seems to be saying, must be allowed more freedom to govern themselves. Censorship of the mass media has been eased (though not abolished); and, while not officially encouraged, the publication of numerous unofficial newspapers and magazines is now tolerated. A multitude of informal citizens' action groups has sprung up, while the unofficial "workers' committees" formed in the course of miners' strikes in the middle of 1989 show the potential to develop into independent trade unions.

---

[15]   *Pravda*, July 15, 1987; see also Archie Brown, "The Soviet Leadership and the Struggle for Political Reform," *Harriman Institute Forum*, April, 1988, p. 3.

[16]   *Izvestia*, June 10, 1989.

[17]   *Pravda*, August 8, 1989.

(3) As for state control over the economy, Gorbachev is attempting to reform the planning apparatus to increase the influence of market forces. So far, his economic reforms are lagging far behind his political reforms; he speaks of establishing "a socialist market," but shows no sign at this stage of wanting to jettison central planning altogether. Under his leadership, however, the USSR is making a significant move towards greater diversity of ownership forms. To cite Yakovlev again, the problem is that state property belongs to no one: *"nashe, eto ne moe, eto—nich'e."*[18] That is to say, no one is responsible or accountable for its proper use. In an attempt to correct this situation, the Gorbachev leadership has officially declared cooperative property to be equal in value to state property, is encouraging leasing and family farming, and has legalized some forms of private enterprise. The lion's share of the means of production will, though, remain in the hands of the state; and, to guard against "the restoration of capitalism," Soviet leaders insist that "exploitation" must be ruled out—that is, mechanisms must be built into the system to ensure that no one is able to profit unfairly from the labor of another.

(4) Finally, with respect to the USSR's socialist neighbors, Gorbachev has all but renounced the "Brezhnev Doctrine"—the Soviet Union's self-proclaimed right to intervene militarily where it judges the socialist orientation of an allied country to be under threat. In many other respects too, Soviet foreign policy under Gorbachev has undergone startling changes. The Soviet leader attracted world attention when he told a visiting delegation of Yugoslav Party leaders in Moscow in late 1986 that he recognized "the diversity of the revolutionary process" and that no Communist Party had a monopoly on the truth,[19] and his leadership appears to be looking with equanimity on the reforms under way in Eastern Europe. In a sharp departure from Leninist doctrine, Gorbachev has asserted the superiority of "all-human" values over class values,[20] while his foreign minister, Eduard Shevardnadze, has disavowed Suslov's definition of "peaceful coexistence" as a form of the class struggle.[21] Bovin has praised Gorbachev's "de-ideologizing approach," under which, he says, socialist and proletarian internationalism "take second place to the principle of peaceful coexistence as the universal norm of state relations."[22]

---

[18] Literally translated, "What's ours isn't mine—it's nobody's." "Dostizhenie kachestvenno novogo sostoyaniya sovetskogo obshchestva i obshchestvennye nauki," *Vestnik Akademii Nauk SSSR*, No. 6, 1987, pp. 51–80.

[19] *TASS*, December 10, 1986.

[20] *Literaturnaya gazeta*, November 5, 1986.

[21] *TASS*, July 25, 1988.

[22] *Izvestia*, May 11, 1989.

The abandonment of traditional doctrines is not unprecedented: debates over the nature of socialism and how it should be built run throughout the history of the Left, and present-day disputes are reminiscent of those between Lenin and Bernstein; between Stalin, Bukharin, and Trotsky; and, closer to the present, between the CPSU and the "Eurocommunist" Parties of Western Europe. All Soviet leaders have tended to adapt their ideological precepts to the needs of the moment. But Gorbachev's doctrinal innovations are extremely controversial, and the old definitions still have their supporters; he himself has complained of "a widely held tendency to view any change in the economic mechanism as if it were a deviation from socialist principles."[23] More recently, Prime Minister Nikolai Ryzhkov and other senior Party leaders have sounded the alarm about the "de-ideologization" of Soviet society set in motion by Gorbachev's reforms.[24]

It is not only state and Party officials, afraid of losing the privileges that go with their cozy jobs, who are putting up resistance to Gorbachev's reforms. Many ordinary people have been alarmed by talk from reformist economists about the need for wider wage differentials, food price hikes, tighter labor discipline, relocation, retraining, and possible unemployment of the work force. If the leadership bites the bullet of a radical economic reform, large numbers of the Soviet population will face a difficult and painful adjustment. As in any major reform, there will be losers as well as winners. Those who stand to profit include the intelligentsia and those who can reveal latent entrepreneurial skills. In the long run, a successful reform will improve material prosperity for most, if not all, the population. In the short run, however, significant sections of the industrial working class stand to lose, and even the promised long-term improvement will be accompanied by a regime of greater individual financial uncertainty—a prospect that strikes fear in many hearts. It is little comfort to think that the consequences of a failure to reform would be even more unpleasant for ordinary people.

Many elderly people are shocked too by revelations about the ills of Soviet society appearing daily in the official press. For seventy years, the Soviet population was told the deprivations they suffered were justified because the USSR was building the most humane society in the world. In Gorbachev's words:

> We proceeded from the premise that the social structure we had created was the best one possible. This conclusion stemmed from our idea that there was a single socialist model. . . . Now we know that this is not so.[25]

---

[23] *Pravda*, February 26, 1986.
[24] *Pravda*, July 21, 1989.
[25] *Pravda*, June 10, 1989.

It is hard for people to abandon the certainties on which they were brought up and the values in whose name they have been called upon to make sacrifices. In the eyes of many people, *glasnost'* has already gone too far and too fast. At the beginning of 1988, Gorbachev spoke of those who were warning that "democracy may turn into chaos" and asking: "are we not retreating from socialist positions, particularly when we introduce new, unaccustomed forms of economic management and social life?" He said "defenders of Marxism-Leninism and mourners of socialism" were warning that both were "under threat."[26]

How right Gorbachev was became evident with the publication in *Sovetskaya Rossiya* on March 13, 1988, of that now notorious defense of Stalinism: Nina Andreeva's open letter "I Cannot Renounce Principles," which was lambasted by *Pravda* three weeks later as "a manifesto of the anti-*perestroika* forces." Andreeva complained that criticism of Stalin in the Soviet press and discussion of the problems of Soviet society were causing disorientation and nihilism among young people. She was particularly incensed by the trend she discerned towards a reevaluation of the role of the individual, which she described as "some sort of left-wing liberal intellectual socialism that allegedly expresses the most genuine humanism, 'cleansed' of class accretions." Its champions, Andreeva stated with indignation, "counter proletarian collectivism with the 'intrinsic value of the individual,'... [claiming] that what we have built is supposedly not proper socialism."

ASSERTING THE HUMAN FACTOR AND ADVOCATING A CIVIL SOCIETY

Gorbachev's reforms do indeed center on what he calls "activating the human factor"—that is, reinserting the individual into the political process and reinvigorating the economy by rewarding individual effort. In his eyes and those of his fellow leaders, the orthodox Soviet model of socialism has discredited itself because it has defaulted on its promise to create "the new man." Today's Soviet work force conspicuously lacks the qualities of adaptability, enterprise, and creativity essential for the successful running of a complex modern economy. The agricultural expert Aleksandr Nikonov says that "bureaucratic management of the economy ruined a great deal. In the first place, it ruined people."[27] Abalkin laments the destruction of the "topsoil" of Soviet society. " Social humus," he says, "is the culture of labor and everyday life, ... knowledge carefully passed from generation to generation." Describing contemporary Soviet society as "a lunar landscape," Abalkin says "no prescriptions exist for the dramatic moment when seeds have to be

---

26   *Pravda*, February 19, 1988.
27   *Central Soviet Television*, July 19, 1987.

cast not onto soil but onto stones." He estimates that it will take one or two generations for the "topsoil" to be recreated.[28]

Gorbachev's interest in "the human factor" seems to have been stimulated by the ideas of Tat'yana Zaslavskaya. In her "Novosibirsk Report," delivered at a closed conference in 1983, Zaslavskaya called into question the monistic view of socialist society that is a crucial component of orthodox Soviet Marxist thought.[29] Even under social-ism, Zaslavskaya argued, society is heterogeneous, and individuals and groups retain vital and often conflicting interests. If these interests are denied or neglected, they find an outlet in a corrupt or perverted form. The official Soviet attitude, Zaslavskaya said, of pretending that individual and group interests did not exist meant, first, that workers were deprived of individual incentives to work conscientiously and, second, that members of the bureaucratic apparatus were free to pursue their interests at the expense of those of the rest of society. (The logical conclusion of Zaslavskaya's demolition of the assumption of a single national interest and her focus on the existence of a multitude of individual and group interests was that there exists a need for orga-nized representation of these interests. Zaslavskaya did not explicitly draw this conclusion, but her argument destroyed the claim of the CPSU to represent the "real" interests of society and laid the ground-work for an eventual move to a multiparty system.)

Zaslavskaya focused on the need for effective economic incentives to reward effort and stimulate conscientious work. Her influence can be seen in the (so far unsuccessful) attempts of the Gorbachev leadership to widen wage differentials and introduce self-management in the workplace. The essence of these policies has been summed up by the economist Oleg Bogomolov, who heads Moscow's Institute of the Economics of the World Socialist System, a powerhouse of reform-oriented ideas. He says that, in his opinion,

> Socialism tomorrow will be qualitatively different from its present form. We no longer regard giving orders as the major method of managing the economy. Economic management under socialism must be mainly carried out through stimulating people's economic inter-ests. Commodity-money relations, the law of value, the market under conditions of the socialist economy are beginning to play new roles.[30]

Bogomolov asserts that what the USSR and other societies of the Soviet-type such as Poland and Hungary are experiencing is not a crisis of "socialism and its ideals" but a crisis of "the Stalinist embodiment of

---

28   *Komsomol'skaya pravda*, February 8, 1989.
29   *Arkhiv Samizdata*, No. 5042.
30   *Moscow News*, No. 45, 1987.

those ideals."[31] Recently, however, the theoretician Aleksandr Tsipko and the sociologist Vladimir Shubkin have argued that the now standard position of blaming Stalin for "deforming" socialism fails to get to the root of the problem. The fault, these writers argue, goes deeper and lies "not just with the mustaches but with the beards"—that is, not only with Stalin but also with Lenin's interpretation of Marxism and with certain doctrines of Marxism itself.

Tsipko faults Marx's belief in human perfectibility and "the pure new man."[32] He says that, because he misunderstood human nature, Marx failed to understand the sources of human behavior. Furthermore, Tsipko argues, Marx's mistaken assumptions made the use of repression by the Soviet state against its citizens not only possible but even probable, for they led the leaders of the Russian revolution to despise "the masses" in whose name the revolution had supposedly been made. The Bolsheviks came to power with little understanding of human motivation; unable to create incentives that would stimulate the population, they fell back on terror and violence. Tsipko says the Bolsheviks believed that, in the interests of building an ideal society, they had the right to destroy everything that had been created in the past, regardless of the suffering of individual citizens who got caught in what the sociologist Igor' Klyamkin has called Stalin's "meat-grinder."[33]

Tsipko goes on, "We have paid dearly . . . for our neglect of man's true nature." It is, he argues, the application of Marx's mistaken ideas that has led the USSR into its present economic and social crisis. Now, the recognition that the Soviet approach was wrong "is forcing us to rethink what is man and what is society. . . . On the one hand," he says,

> we say that man is born good and pure and made to live in a collective and that he can be corrupted only by evil circumstances and "bad" economic relations. On the other hand, we do not trust him; we deprive him of choice from childhood and fence him around with bans and restrictions.

By "telling man he is an angel but treating him like a child," Tsipko goes on to say, Soviet ideology has absolved citizens from the duty of

[31]   *Moscow Radio*, February 8, 1989.

[32]   Aleksandr Tsipko, "Istoki stalinizma," *Nauka i zhizn'*, Nos. 11 and 12, 1988, and Nos. 1 and 2, 1989; *idem*, "Chelovek ne mozhet izmenit' svoei prirode," *Politicheskoe obrazovanie*, No. 4, 1989, pp. 68-78. See also Paul Bellis, "Ditching the ISM," *Detente*, No. 13, 1988, pp. 29-30; and Vera Tolz, "Soviet Scholar Sees Roots of Stalinism in Bolsheviks' Terror and Marxist Theory," *Report on the USSR*, No. 8, 1989, pp. 1-3.

[33]   Igor' Klyamkin, "Kakaya ulitsa vedet k khramu?" *Novyi mir*, No. 11, 1987, pp. 150-88.

heeding the voice of individual conscience and relieved them of personal responsibility for their actions. The result is a state of what he calls "moral infantilism." Moreover, their false idea of human nature rendered Soviet leaders unable to deal with the real faults and failings of flesh-and-blood people—greed, envy, lust for power, wanton aggression. The costs of their failure, Tsipko says, have been high.

Tsipko criticizes Marx's monistic, "nonmarket," and "noncommercial" concept of socialist society. "In all cases without exception," he writes, "the struggle against the market and against commodity-money relations has led to adventurism, to encroachments on the rights and dignity of the individual, and to the unrestricted power of the administrative and bureaucratic apparatus." This was possible, he suggests, because of the state's monopoly on economic activity. "Where are the guarantees of personal freedom if everyone has to work as the state's hired labor, deprived of the right to own property and therefore of a livelihood independent of the state?" Tsipko blames "the deification of the collective" for placing greater value on the public than the private interest, and he deplores the unlimited power such thinking vests in the Party, which claims to represent "the general interest":

> We now know how dearly the Communist Party pays for its right to control all facets of life, all aspects of social existence. This excessive power undermines the independence of the population and engenders a universal unwillingness to take independent decisions or to accept responsibility; it removes the Party leadership from the control of the people and makes possible the feudalization of society and the corruption of the agencies that manage it.

Tsipko's conclusion is that the Soviet leaders must find new ways of motivating the population. He rejects the idea that the Soviet Union should be trying to build "a new man" and says that, instead of attempting to mold people to fit an ideal society, it should try to make society fit men and women as they are.

Tsipko's ideas are of particular interest since he holds a post in the CPSU Central Committee and is believed to act as an adviser to both Yakovlev and Gorbachev's aide, Georgii Shakhnazarov. Until two years ago, Tsipko worked under Bogomolov at the Institute of the Economics of the World Socialist System. Vladimir Shubkin, who is on the staff of Moscow's Institute of the International Working Class Movement, also focuses on the impact of the Soviet state on the individual citizen.[34] Shubkin dates the use of force as a normal tool of government to the earliest days of Soviet power and asserts that, even today,

---

[34]   Vladimir Shubkin, "Trudnoe proshchanie," *Novyi mir*, No. 4, 1989, pp. 165-84.

the Soviet citizen is defenseless before the arbitrary power of the state. Like Tsipko, Shubkin wryly observes that the Soviet system is founded on the assumption that human nature is perfect; that Soviet leaders are just and good and that there is, therefore, no need to create mechanisms to protect the citizenry against stupid, wicked, or mad leaders.

Shubkin says man can be evaluated according to three dimensions: biological, social, and spiritual. In a damning indictment of the Soviet polity, he says it has destroyed in its citizens all save the biological dimension. Soviet man, Shubkin says, thinks only of how to feed, house, and reproduce himself; his moral capacity has been eliminated by what Shubkin terms "the totalitarian system," and he has ceased to function as a social animal. Shubkin goes so far as to ask whether the Stalin Terror may not have done lasting genetic damage to the Soviet population.

Shubkin's solution is the creation of "a civil society." Like Tsipko, he rejects the idea that the formation of "the new man" is realistic or even desirable. The population, he says, should no longer be required to exist for the benefit of the state: the state and the Party should be made to work for the good of the people. Then, in Shubkin's opinion, it will be possible to call the USSR "a normal society." Like Tsipko, Shubkin believes a precondition for such a change in the balance of power to be a reform of property relations that would deprive the state of its monopoly on the means of production and allow cooperatives and private enterprises to develop and flourish. "A mixed economy," Shubkin states, "is essential." Even more important, in Shubkin's opinion, is recognition of the freedom of conscience of the individual citizen. "The Kingdom of Heaven," he recalls, "is within us."

URGING CONTROL BY SOCIETY INSTEAD OF CONTROL BY THE STATE

While writers such as Tsipko and Shubkin have examined the role of the individual in the USSR, other theoreticians have turned the spotlight on the exercise of state power. Georgii Arbatov and Eduard Batalov, for example, of Moscow's Institute of the USA and Canada, date what they call the "state-ization" of Soviet society to the early 1920s (that is, to the time when Lenin was still alive.)[35] The subordination of all aspects of social activity to the "Party-state apparatus" or "hyperstate" was made possible, Arbatov and Batalov say, by a massive build-up of the coercive apparatus. All avenues of political participation were blocked to the population, among whom fear of repression spawned "passivity, lack of principles, loss of initiative, alienation from social activity," and an attitude of psychological dependency on the state akin to the orientation known in the West as "learned helplessness."

---

[35] Arbatov and Batalov, *op. cit.*

Arbatov and Batalov lay some of the blame on the lack of democratic traditions in pre-revolutionary Russia. In this, they echo the American historian Edward Keenan, who has analyzed the political culture of the pre-Petrine period and argued that the patterns of political behavior formed then survived intact into the Soviet period.[36] As described by Keenan, the dominant characteristic of both Russian and Soviet political culture was and is aversion to risk. Shaped by inhospitable terrain and a hostile natural environment, the culture was deliberately designed to minimize the threat of danger and maximize the chances of survival of the largest number of members of the community (village, commune, or collective). Under such a system, the interests of the individual were inevitably, Keenan says, subordinated to those of the group.

Arbatov and Batalov suggest that, in order for the Soviet government to evolve from reliance on force to reliance on the consent of the governed, it is necessary to rehabilitate Marx's concept of the withering away of the state. Recalling that Marx envisaged that this process would begin under socialism, they say that it should not be put off until some time in the distant, "communist" future but that an immediate start should be made to involve the population in the political process. The authors stress they are not suggesting that state institutions should be abolished overnight: that would be utopian. But they do argue that the state's all-embracing powers must be reduced; the aim, they write, is to replace state control of society with society's control over the state. (Arbatov and Batalov do not use the term "civil society," preferring to speak of "social self-management"—itself a term that was taboo until quite recently—but this is clearly the kind of idea they have in mind.) Towards this end, they call for concrete legislation to institutionalize in the USSR changes that are already taking place or have been promised—e.g., increasing the powers of local government; diversifying forms of ownership; legalizing independent centers of activity such as Popular Fronts and political clubs and authorizing them to propose "popular alternatives" to official policies; and, last but not least, expanding individual freedoms to encourage a sense of citizenship among the population.

Both Yakovlev and Gorbachev have spoken of the emergence of "civil society" as the best hope for the reform of the Soviet system. "We are moving," Yakovlev has stated, "from an autocratic, authoritarian society to a civil society."[37] As this term is generally understood, at least in the West, it denotes the existence of autonomous social

---

[36] Edward L. Keenan, "Muscovite Political Folkways," *The Russian Review*, April, 1986, pp. 115-82.

[37] For Yakovlev see *Novoe vremya*, No. 24, 1989, p. 6; for Gorbachev see *Pravda*, July 19, 1989.

organizations strong enough to monitor the activities of the state and to act as mediator between the state and the individual citizen. Such a concept is a sharp departure from traditional Soviet orthodoxy which, as already stated, has long portrayed the interests of the individual as insignificant in relation to those of the collective, a strong state as the surest guardian of "the general interest," and a monolithic Communist Party as the sole legitimate interpreter of where that interest lies.

The first Soviet scholar explicitly to argue the case for the creation of a civil society in the Soviet Union was Andranik Migranyan, an historian who is on the staff of the Institute of the Economics of the World Socialist System.[38] Writing in August, 1987, Migranyan argued that political regimes in which the interests of the individual and society were securely defended against the encroachments of the state were more stable than systems in which such defense mechanisms were weak. The reason for this, Migranyan asserted, was that the former were better able both to elaborate effective policies and to set up feedback channels to correct in good time any mistakes that were made. A state that was counterbalanced by a strong civil society was obliged to govern by consent; one in which civil society was weakly developed or nonexistent would inevitably resort to force against its citizens.

Migranyan argues that Marx assumed the transition to socialism would take place in advanced industrial nations in which a vigorous civil society had already developed; after the revolution, indeed, this civil society would eventually replace the state altogether. This was not the case in Russia in 1917, however; nor was it the case, Migranyan says, in other countries such as China and Cambodia that tried to leap directly from backwardness to socialism. In these instances, Migranyan argues, the roles of state and society have become reversed: "The state takes on not only its own functions but also those of society. The state 'swallows up' both society and the individual, in the sincere belief that the essentially bureaucratic solutions it has adopted best reflect the interests of individuals and of society."

Migranyan argues that it is in the interests of the state itself in such circumstances to create a network of strong and healthy "intermediate" associations of independent citizens and gradually to reduce its own economic and social activity. Migranyan's model is liberal democracy. In renouncing "bourgeois individualism," he laments, the Soviet Union "threw the baby out with the bathwater" and reduced the scope for independent initiative "almost to zero." In

---

[38] A. M. Migranyan, "Vzaimootnosheniya individa, obshchestva i gosudarstva v politicheskoi teorii marksizma i problemy demokratizatsii sotsialisticheskogo obshchestva," *Voprosy filosofii*, No. 8, 1987, pp. 75-91.

the West, on the other hand, state power is held in check by "various social institutions under the active control of individuals." Migranyan's conclusion is that some degree of individualism is essential for the efficient functioning of any democratic society—capitalist or socialist.

Analyzing Migranyan's ideas, the American scholar James Scanlan has expressed doubt concerning "the paradox of expecting the state to create civil society—that is, expecting the power that is said to need control to yield its power so that such control can be established."[39] Scanlan notes that, "on Migranyan's own analysis, it is capitalism that historically has created civil society." Is it realistic, he wonders, to hope for such a development under socialism?

In his search for "a new model of democratic Soviet socialism," the prominent Soviet Party theoretician Fedor Burlatsky has shown an appreciation of this paradox. Burlatsky's definition of socialism is simple: "that which really ensures prosperity and culture for working people." Like Migranyan, he is a proponent of a vigorous civil society in the USSR. In his recent writing, he has begun to suggest that this will be attainable only if individual rights include property rights.[40]

Burlatsky agrees with Migranyan that relations between the state and the citizen are distorted in the USSR because the state has taken on itself responsibility for functions that rightfully belong to society. He speaks of the need to subordinate the state to civil society; this, he implies, would involve the creation of many independent sources of political decision-making and economic activity. To Migranyan's emphasis on autonomous social organization Burlatsky adds the concept of private property. "We have not yet understood," he states, "what has long been understood in civilized countries: the wealth of the people is formed first and foremost from the property of each, and the freedom of all is made up of the freedom of each." The total abolition of private property in the USSR, Burlatsky says, "led to the total dependence of the individual on the state." The individual, he writes, became "more and more that of which Stalin dreamed: a cog in a gigantic state wheel and often the object of unjust coercion and state exploitation." So, as Tsipko and Migranyan advocate the reevaluation of Western concepts of the role of individual, Burlatsky seems to be moving towards an assessment of at least small-scale private enterprise as an essential condition of civil society and the personal freedom of the individual citizen. Similarly, Shakhnazarov has called for the develop-

---

[39] James P. Scanlan, "Reforms and Civil Society in the USSR," *Problems of Communism*, March-April, 1988, pp. 41-46.

[40] "Kakoi sotsializm narodu nuzhen," *Literaturnaya gazeta*, April 20, 1988; "Zametki deputata. Pervyi, no vazhnyi shag," *Literaturnaya gazeta*, June 14, 1989.

ment of "a socialist theory of checks and balances" to ward against "concentration of all political power in the hands of one body (or individual)."[41]

Meanwhile, some reformers have begun to advocate Western social democratic forms (generally understood to combine a mixed market-oriented economy with an extensive welfare-state safety net and a multiparty system). The Kirgiz writer Chingiz Aitmatov called on the Congress of People's Deputies not to make "a fetish" of socialism and to see it less as an aim in itself than as a means to make a better life for humanity:

> While we are arguing about what socialism should or should not be, other people have already built it and are enjoying its fruits. Moreover, we with our experience have done them a service in showing them how *not* to build socialism. I am thinking of such prosperous, law-based societies as Sweden, Austria, Finland, Norway, the Netherlands, Spain, and Canada . . . , to say nothing of Switzerland, which is a model. Workers in those countries earn on average four or five times as much as our workers. We can only dream about the social security and prosperity enjoyed by workers in those countries. That is indeed real trade-union socialism if you like, and, even though these countries do not call themselves socialist, they are none the worse for that.[42]

PROBLEMS AND PROSPECTS

Over the past couple of years, the Gorbachev leadership has jettisoned some of the most cherished dogmas of Marxism-Leninism.[43] The changes being introduced—moving from an economy controlled by bureaucratic decree to one managed to a far greater extent by market forces—seem to be bringing the USSR closer to Western social democracy. Indeed, writes the Western specialist Francis Fukuyama, "if the bulk of

---

[41] *Sovetskoe gosudarstvo i pravo*, No. 17, 1987, pp. 118-20, as cited by Archie Brown in *World Policy Journal*, Summer, 1989, p. 478.

[42] *Central Soviet Television*, June 2, 1989.

[43] See Julia Wishnevsky, "Aleksandr Yakovlev to Regain the Ideology Portfolio?" *Report on the USSR*, No. 30, 1989, pp. 9-12; Alfred Evans, Jr., "Redefining Soviet Socialism," chapter prepared for inclusion in Stephen White, Alex Pravda, and Zvi Gitelman (eds.), *Developments in Soviet Politics*, forthcoming; Archie Brown, "Political Change in the Soviet Union," *World Policy Journal*, Summer, 1989, pp. 469-501; Marc Zlotnik, "Rethinking Soviet Socialism: The Politics of Ideological Change," unpublished manuscript, 1989. Zlotnik points out that, although muted, revisionist ideas could already be found in the Soviet press during the Brezhnev years and are not, therefore, dependent on Gorbachev alone.

the present economic reform proposals were put into effect, it is hard to know how the Soviet economy would be more socialist than those of other Western countries with large public sectors."[44] Shakhnazarov has said that, until *perestroika*, the Soviet authorities considered it impermissible to borrow from Western experience but that this attitude has changed since Gorbachev's rise to power.[45] Even the most liberal Soviet reformers, however, feel obliged to go on using the word "socialism" even if, like Aitmatov, they have to define capitalist countries as socialist in the process.

Other Soviet theoreticians are seeking to place the reform process within a framework that will still be Marxist-Leninist, or at least Marxist. Perhaps this is due in some cases merely to force of habit—a continuation of the kind of thinking that produced the concept of "developed socialism" (a term Gorbachev has abandoned in favor of the far more modest "developing [*razvivayushchii*] socialism"[46]). Quite likely, though, the leadership still feels it needs some such explanatory schema.

The maintenance of a single-party state remains the professed aim. It would not be surprising if that is what Gorbachev, Yakovlev, and other reformers in the Kremlin leadership really want. Even if it is not, they can hardly come out and say so, for that would mean alienating the Party *apparat*. But if the Communist Party is to exercise its self-proclaimed leading role by something other than—or in addition to—coercion, it needs to be associated with a doctrine that can with some plausibility be used to legitimate its position. For this reason, Gorbachev is careful always to describe his reforms as socialist. Thus, he says the aim of his policy of *perestroika* is "the renewal of socialism" and the discarding of "wrong ideas and primitive concepts" that are inconsistent with it. What he wants for the USSR, he declares, is "more socialism, more democracy, and more freedom."[47]

Attempts to maintain the Party's special status may eventually prove to be incompatible with effective reform. Some of the participants in the ideological debate certainly do not seem to share the perspective of a one-party state, and it may well turn out that, as many Western observers believe, the final destination of a successful reform will be a Western-style mixed economy and a multiparty political system. Once it is accepted that conflicting interests occur in socialist as well as capitalist society (as the reform lobby appears to have done), then the official assumption that there exists a single national interest is under-

[44]   Francis Fukuyama, "The End of History?" *The National Interest*, No. 16, 1989, pp. 3–18 at p. 13.

[45]   *Central Soviet Television*, August 1, 1989.

[46]   *Pravda*, October 2, 1986.

[47]   *AFP* and *DPA*, June 15, 1989.

mined, the right of a single party to monopolize power crumbles, and it becomes logical to move towards organized representation of individual and group interests—that is, to a multiparty system.

Shakhnazarov told Soviet television in August, 1989, that the main thing at the present stage was to establish a system capable of providing for the welfare of the population.[48] Later on, he said, it would be time for the theoreticians to come along and declare whether or not the new society was socialist. While the evidence suggests that, as far as Gorbachev's leadership is concerned, policies are being adopted that are bringing the Soviet Union closer to the Western social democratic model, there apparently exists no precise blueprint for the new society. Opposition to change is strong, and it is unclear how deliberate the process of "convergence" is or how far it will go. The way in which Soviet leaders are casting about, with some signs of desperation, for a definition of socialism that will enable them to overcome the country's social and economic problems is somehow reminiscent of the old Russian folk saying: *"Idi tuda, ne znayu kuda; prenesi to, ne znayu chto"*— "Go I know not where; bring back I know not what."

If the purpose of the debate is to provide a rationale for continued single-party rule, then this exercise in redefining socialism is unlikely to be helping *perestroika*, because a single-party system is probably not compatible with radical economic reform and because its maintenance will only postpone the day when real economic reform can no longer be put off. If, however, all this is gradually leading to a situation where there is no single guiding doctrine, where no single national interest is claimed, and where the existence of competing political platforms and parties becomes the norm, then it is just a series of steps—a dance of the seven veils—in the process of the secularization of Soviet society. That could well help the USSR become a modern society.

---

[48]   *Central Soviet Television*, August 1, 1989.

3

The NEP, *Perestroika*, and the Problem of Alternatives

Mark von Hagen

HARDLY a week passes without one or more Soviet commentators, scholars, or political leaders invoking the New Economic Policy (the NEP) of the 1920s as the legitimate socialist precursor of the reforms currently taking place in the USSR. Early in 1989, at a round-table discussion hosted by the editors of *Moscow News*, Lev Karpinsky, Georgii Kunitsyn, and Yurii Goland characterized the NEP as "the first *perestroika*, a radical socioeconomic reform."[1] Soviet leader Mikhail Gorbachev himself has not only sharply contrasted the NEP with the Stalin period, the 1930s and 1940s, but also with "the period of stagnation," as the Brezhnev years are now pejoratively labeled.[2] All this talk of the NEP has to do with the meaning of Stalin and the Stalin period for the future of socialism; both the leadership and the reformist intelligentsia in the USSR seek to save Soviet socialism from Stalin and to locate a purer, more humane, and more high-minded experiment in the politics, society, economy, and culture of the 1920s.

---

[1]   "The Fate of Lenin's NEP," *Moscow News*, No. 6, 1989, p. 10. For more on the uses of the NEP in the current political discussions, see Lars T. Lih, "NEP: An Alternative for Soviet Socialism," in *The Soviet Union under Gorbachev*, Festschrift for Robert C. Tucker, edited by Stephen F. Cohen and Michael Kraus (forthcoming).

[2]   A typical example of Gorbachev's repudiation of these periods in the Soviet past is his statement in a speech given in February, 1988: "We must build and renovate socialism. We must advance our society by relying on and using all the sap that comes to us from roots that go deep into our history, especially into socialist history, and by chopping off everything negative that comes from the 1930s and 1940s and from the recent stagnant period." See Lih, "NEP: An Alternative for Soviet Socialism."

LOOKING BACKWARDS FOR A NOBLER VISION OF SOCIALISM

Soviet publicists and historians have revived a Bukharinist view of the NEP as Russia's last chance to avoid the terrors of Stalinism. In retrospect, they prefer an alternative path of moderate, evolutionary economic change, whereby socialism would grow out of a mixed system of state sector and private market; peasants would come willingly to cooperative forms of agriculture, with coercion and administrative methods replaced by education, persuasion, and example. As today's leaders and reformist intelligentsia begin a tortuous reevaluation and reconstruction of the Soviet and Russian past, the Bukharinist alternative has emerged as a new orthodoxy in the Soviet Union. These same intellectuals and politicians have found successors to the Bukharinist heritage in the premature reformism of the Khrushchev era and in the relatively mixed market socialist economies of Eastern Europe, especially Hungary, Poland, and Yugoslavia.

In the West too, the Bukharinist position has had its defenders, most passionately in Stephen Cohen, the noted biographer of Nikolai Bukharin, and in Robert Tucker, Moshe Lewin, and others.[3] These revisionists have profoundly challenged the old totalitarian school's consensus of a monochromatic communist ideology and a monolithic communist bloc. They have stressed the diversity among socialist systems adapted by ruling elites to specific national traditions, even within the constraints of the Soviet socialist commonwealth. In so doing, they have made an important and positive contribution to studies of East European politics and have foreseen a good many of the debates over socialism's future as well as many of the reforms that have actually been occurring in these countries.

Inside the Soviet Union, however, the search for alternatives to the Stalin era—all the very important intellectually liberating aspects of that search notwithstanding—reveals a crisis of confidence among the cultural and political elites that has assumed increasingly strident forms as each political faction works out its own version of the Soviet past. Outside the Soviet Union, the closest contemporary analogies to the Soviet reassessment of the Stalin years are the *Historikerstreit* in Germany over the Nazi legacy and the post-Hirohito confrontation in Japan with that nation's past, especially its brutal conquest of much of Asia and the Pacific in the 1930s and

---

[3] See Stephen Cohen, *Bukharin and the Bolshevik Revolution: A Political Biography, 1888-1938,* New York, Vintage Books, 1973; Moshe Lewin, *Political Undercurrents in Soviet Economic Debates,* Princeton, New Jersey, Princeton University Press, 1974; and Robert Tucker, *Stalin as Revolutionary, 1879-1929,* New York, W. W. Norton, 1974.

1940s.[4] As in Germany and Japan, so in the Soviet Union, the reformists explicitly link their political agendas to what they see as alternative paths of historical development and implicitly repudiate several decades of the recent national past. As elsewhere, so too in the Soviet Union, the discussion of alternatives has called forth a defense of the past from conservative circles.

The most notorious apologist for Stalin's legacy has been Nina Andreeva, the chemistry teacher whose letter was published in *Sovetskaya Rossiya* in 1988. She defends a determinist reading of the past; in her view, no other path of development but the Stalinist one was possible. In a similar vein, Igor' Klyamkin proposes a version of socio-economic determinism that resembles the arguments about modernization most forcefully made by Theodore von Laue in the West. In Klyamkin's account, backward Russia faced unprecedentedly ambitious tasks of transformation, which practically ruled out the development of a vital democratic, liberal tradition.[5]

The publicists and scholars who oppose this deterministic reading of history look to free contemporary social consciousness from a passive acceptance of the past. Here, too, a variety of strains have surfaced. Viktor Danilov, the respected historian of collectivization and the peasantry in the 1920s, identifies two "utopian alternative fantasies" that are currently popular in the Soviet mass media. The first he ironically labels "the wonderful peasant Atlantis" (*prekrasnaya krest'yanskaya Atlantida*). Its most notable proponents are the conservative writers associated with the *derevenshchiki* movement; a typical example is the novel *Muzhiki i baby* by Boris Mozhaev. The "peasant utopians" present an idyllic picture of the Russian rural world before the intelligentsia began to take up the peasant cause. Beginning with Turgenev and culminating in collectivization, they argue, the anti-peasant forces destroyed a healthy and prosperous world of joyous labor and family ties. This radical conservative utopia implicitly calls for a repudiation of socialism and Marxism and a return to pastoral preindustrial life. The second alternative fantasy, the NEP utopia, is

---

[4] On the *Historikerstreit*, see a recent, special issue of *New German Critique*, No. 44, Spring/Summer, 1988; and Charles S. Maier, *The Unmasterable Past: History, Holocaust, and German National Identity*, Cambridge, Massachusetts, Harvard University Press, 1988.

[5] Igor' Klyamkin, "Kakaya ulitsa vedet k khramu?" *Novyi mir*, No. 11, 1987, pp. 150-88. For Theodore von Laue's views, see his *Why Lenin? Why Stalin?*, 2d ed., Philadelphia, J. B. Lippincott Company, 1971. Another argument with a different agenda has been that of Aleksandr Tsipko, who asserts that Stalinism is in fact Marxism in action, a version of ideological determinism that resembles the work of the philosopher and historian, Leszek Kolakowski. Tsipko's articles have appeared in *Nauka i zhizn'*.

encapsulated in the formulation "America would be trying to catch up with us now" and is most vigorously defended by the economist Nikolai Shmelev. Shmelev believes that were it not for Stalin, Soviet Russia could have experienced at least two successful periods of industrialization and far outstripped both Germany and the United States in economic development. Shmelev presents the most optimistic vision of the NEP as a political economy of unlimited but unrealized growth potential.[6]

Even those who do not indulge in such ahistorical, utopian fantasies of the past, however, often hold up the NEP as a political, economic, and ideological alternative to Stalinism and as a model for present-day reformers. In large part, this heightened consciousness of the past— especially the Soviet past—is a consequence of the peculiar nature of the Soviet political system. As long as the Soviet state claims its legitimacy primarily on the basis of the historical laws of an ossified Marxist-Leninist doctrine, interpretations of the past will remain highly politicized and extremely susceptible to mythologizing. As a consequence, the reformists have identified as the very nature of socialism a particular group of what are in effect makeshift compromises in the organization of political and economic institutions. So far, these publicists and historians have demonstrated that an alternative order was at least conceivable to some political actors in the 1920s, but this is not enough if history is to offer any lessons to the current generation. For all the attractiveness, or seeming attractiveness, of these alternatives, the question remains why none of them survived and developed. Or, in other words, how is the triumph of Stalin and his "alternative" to be explained? If it is possible to answer this question, it must then be asked how relevant the answer is for the current reformist agenda. Can a time be conceived when mythical historical analogues will no longer constrain the imaginations of political reformers and the reformist intelligentsia in the Soviet Union?

THE IDEA OF "A CRISIS OF THE NEP"

The NEP certainly has lessons for today's reformers, but those lessons are, it may be argued, more negative than positive. First of all, it needs to be pointed out that the NEP itself appears attractive only from the perspective of the Stalinist 1930s; those who lived during the 1920s did not view the NEP as "the golden age" that it has come to represent for so many reformers in the Soviet Union and their allies in the West. The

---

[6] Viktor Danilov described the current debate over alternatives in a lecture delivered at Columbia University on April 21, 1988. Shmelev's views have appeared in a new journal entitled *Studentchesky meridian*, in many scholarly economic joournals, and in the Soviet popular press.

explanation for the negative attitude towards the NEP among its contemporaries lies not only in the ideological convictions of belligerent Bolsheviks but also in the real economic and social hardships and the political disabilities that afflicted large segments of Soviet society. After all, those who lived through the 1920s could have no idea how much worse things would become in the 1930s; the fact is that among those who were politically influential in Soviet politics the NEP had far fewer defenders than it had enemies. As one ex-Stalinist put it, "The NEP favored the strong, but did nothing for the many."[7] The uneasy compromise that contemporaries understood as the NEP sowed many of the seeds of its own destruction, and the Stalinist leadership uprooted the few reformist alternatives that had, by the end of the 1920s, managed to send forth their first fragile shoots.

Second, it has to be recalled that the socioeconomic NEP was never accompanied by a political NEP; in other words, the Party leadership under Lenin believed that in conditions of economic liberalization it had no choice but to tighten the reins on political activity and discussion. The same Tenth Party Congress that inaugurated the turn away from War Communism in March, 1921, also adopted resolutions banning political factions; subsequently, the surviving non-Bolshevik socialist parties, the Mensheviks and Socialist Revolutionaries, were subject to increasing legal disabilities and police repression. Because the arena of public political discourse was thus formally constrained, today any discussion of the alternatives must unavoidably address the

---

[7]   Abdurakhman Avtorkhanov, *Stalin and the Soviet Communist Party: A Study in the Technology of Power*, Munich, Frederick A. Praeger, 1959, p. 48. The image of NEP as "a kind of golden era of Soviet development" entered the literature of Sovietology most likely from the Soviet refugee interview project of the 1950s. The defectors, probably an unrepresentative sample, certainly would highlight the positive features of the 1920s from their longer perspective of the 1930s and 1940s. See Raymond A. Bauer, Alex Inkeles, and Clyde Kluckhohn, *How the Soviet System Works*, Cambridge, Massachusetts, Harvard University Press, 1956, p. 138. Other memoirs focus more on the opposition to the NEP. See, for example, Victor Serge, *Memoirs of a Revolutionary, 1901-1941*, London, Oxford University Press, 1967, pp. 196-99; Ilya Ehrenburg, *Memoirs: 1921-1941*, New York, The Universal Library, 1966, pp. 66-70; William Reswick, *I Dreamt Revolution*, Chicago, Regnery, 1952, pp. 53-54, 56, and 231; and Walter Duranty, *I Write as I Please*, New York, Simon & Schuster, 1935, pp. 145-49. The most influential argument for the NEP as a golden age comes from the explosion of cultural innovation during the 1920s, but even here sectarianism and intolerance became increasingly pronounced with each year. On intolerance in the world of literature of the 1920s, see S. Sheshukov, *Neistovye revniteli: iz istorii literaturnoi bor'by 20-kh godov*, Moscow, Khudozhestvennaya literatura, 1970, pp. 3-4.

nature of the Party's political culture. In brief, that political culture was by the mid-1920s not conducive to the moderate evolutionary approach advocated by the Bukharinists. Although much more needs to be known about the support that existed for Bukharin's alternative, just as important—and, quite likely, far more important—are the institutional and social supports of the Stalin system, its genesis and evolution. Over the greater part of Soviet history, the conservatives have proved to be more influential than the reformers. Why? Part of the reason the Stalinists were successful, at least during the 1920s, was that their sense of the character and dynamics of postrevolutionary society probably found greater resonance among the Party faithful than the alternative analysis offered by the Right Opposition.[8] Among their most important claims was that Soviet Russia was in the throes of a deepening multi-faceted crisis. Of course, a crisis assumes political importance only if it is recognized as such by contemporary historical actors; beyond the widespread rhetoric of crisis in the 1920s,[9] though, what objective indications might support the idea of "a crisis of the NEP"?[10]

---

[8]   Traditionally, scholars have attributed Stalin's victory to his control and manipulation of the Party machine through his preeminence in patronage politics. Anti-Stalinists, beginning with Trotsky, typically have denied that Stalin enjoyed any ideological appeal among the Party elite or society; rather, they have characterized him as a creature of the bureaucratic non-entities who served as the one bulwark of his tyranny. See Leon Trotsky, *The Revolution Betrayed*, New York, Merit Publishers, 1965; E. H. Carr, *Socialism in One Country*, Vol. II, London, Macmillan, 1958, p. 224; and Merle Fainsod, *How Russia is Ruled*, Cambridge, Massachusetts, Harvard University Press, 1953, pp. 156-66. Today the organizational factor is no longer considered to be an adequate explanation for Stalin's success. Increasingly, scholars point to Stalin's political program as a factor in winning him support among the Party bosses and state bureaucrats. See Tucker, *Stalin as Revolutionary*, pp. 292, 303; and Cohen, *Bukharin*, pp. 327-28.

[9]   See, for example, the discussions in early 1921 about the "crisis" of War Communism, the "scissors crisis" of 1923, another economic "crisis" in 1925-1926, and the provisions "crisis" in late 1927. See also Moshe Lewin, *The Making of the Soviet System: Essays in the Social History of Interwar Russia*, New York, Pantheon, 1985, pp. 26-30. Lewin argues that "a kind of permanent crisis set in" with the First Five-Year Plan, what he calls *démesure* as policy.

[10]   For this discussion, I have tried to keep separate the two levels of my argument. On the one hand, the Bolshevik Party-state and the society over which it claimed to rule in the 1920s inherited a multifaceted structural crisis from the old regime and revolutionary successor states, the Provisional Government and Civil War Soviet state. This crisis mitigated any long-term policy of even partial nonintervention if the Soviet state was to survive. On the other hand, the political culture of the Bolshevik Party also posed serious dilemmas

Among Western historians, the most recent reformulation of the question "Why Stalin?" has revolved around a reconsideration of the viability of the NEP. The most articulate historian to raise and develop this theme has been Sheila Fitzpatrick, who argues that "Russian society remained highly volatile and unstable during the NEP period. The Bolsheviks feared counterrevolution, remained preoccupied with the threat from 'class enemies' at home and the capitalist nations abroad, and constantly expressed dissatisfaction with NEP and unwillingness to accept it as an outcome or permanent settlement of their Revolution." In Fitzpatrick's judgment, the NEP remained only a retreat, "and the Bolsheviks' mood remained belligerent and revolutionary."[11] A new generation of historians, largely inspired by Fitzpatrick's work, but also taking their cues from the pronouncements of the Bolshevik leaders themselves, has begun to concur that "a crisis of the NEP" very likely spelled its doom.

CONTINUITIES BETWEEN "THE CRISIS OF THE AUTOCRACY" AND THE PERIOD OF THE NEP

There is much to support the contention that the Bolsheviks inherited substantial aspects of a profound structural crisis from the old regime, and it makes sense to elaborate on this point before focusing on the Party debates at the top of the political hierarchy. Although as yet no historians have linked the historiography on the prerevolutionary "crisis of the autocracy" with the budding work on the early Soviet period, the continuities are profound and potentially very instructive.[12]

---

about the viability of a long-term accommodation with the kind of compromise settlement that the NEP came to represent. Clearly, the two levels are not neatly distinguishable, if only because Bolshevik political culture had a great deal to do with how crisis was perceived and what responses to crisis were available.

[11] Sheila Fitzpatrick, *The Russian Revolution: 1917-1932*, Oxford, Oxford University Press, 1982, for a summary of her views, especially the Introduction, and Chapters 4 and 5. In 1964, Alec Nove argued that Stalin, or a Stalin, was necessary and that in 1928 "any practicable Bolshevik programme would have been harsh and unpopular" (see *Economic Rationality and Soviet Politics, or Was Stalin Really Necessary*, New York, Frederick A. Praeger, 1964, pp. 26-27 and 32). A similar argument is put forward by Soviet historians in V. A. Kozlov and O. V. Khlevniuk, *Nachinaetsya s cheloveka*, Moscow, Politizdat, 1988.

[12] For a recent formulation of the thesis of a prerevolutionary crisis, see the collective work, *Krizis samoderzhaviya v Rossii, 1895-1917*, Leningrad, Nauka, 1984. Moshe Lewin argues compellingly that historians of the Soviet period cannot pretend that the world begins in 1917; instead, they must have a thorough grounding in prerevolutionary economy, society, and politics. See Lewin, *The Making of the Soviet System*, especially the Introduction and

In many important respects, the year 1917 was not a fundamental break in Russian history; the revolution and Civil War did not resolve the structural crises that contributed to the downfall of the old regime. On the contrary, the revolution and Civil War only exacerbated these tensions; therefore, in all likelihood, an evolutionist, moderate, non-interventionist policy, such as the Bukharinist NEP, would sooner or later face serious dilemmas issuing from the ongoing crisis. Soviet and Western historians sympathetic to the Bukharinist position have often denied or ignored the existence of any serious structural crisis; they argue instead that the problems facing the NEP were of a local and accidental character and could have been remedied by fine-tuning adjustments in state policy, particularly with regard to price formation. Furthermore, they associate the claims of "structural crisis" with the Stalinist faction in the Party and thereby seek to discredit them as another example of Stalin's hypocritical and opportunistic theoretical fictions.[13] In general, these same historians share the consensus of prerevolutionary historians about the crisis of the autocracy; curiously, however, they fail to say how the revolution and Civil War might have resolved all the tensions and contradictions that helped to bring down the tsarist political order.

The multifaceted crisis of the autocracy and its successor Bolshevik Party-state might be summarized as follows:

(1) *A crisis of the economic structure.* The Bolsheviks inherited the lopsided economy of prerevolutionary Russia, with its pattern of state-financed "late" rapid industrialization and its relatively weak domestic market. That already shaky structure suffered immense dislocation as a consequence of the years of war and revolution. The low productivity of the rural economy sunk even further as the single-family farms that had been consolidated under the short-lived Stolypin reforms were broken up and the repartitional communes resurrected. As a result, peasants farmed much smaller plots, and the surplus they returned to the markets was below prewar levels, thereby leaving the urban population and the regime in constant fear of being held hostage by the kulaks. Industry suffered severe bottlenecks and breakdowns; painful decisions about new investment were compounded by growing rates of urban unemployment.[14]

---

pp. 6-7. Although Lewin stresses the continuities across 1917, he does not argue, as I do herein, for "a continuity of crisis."

[13]   See Cohen, *Bukharin*, especially Chapter 6, "Bukharinism and the Road to Socialism" and Chapter 7, "The Crisis of Moderation."

[14]   For an excellent summary of the economic difficulties of the 1920s, see Alec Nove, *An Economic History of the U.S.S.R.*, Middlesex, England, Penguin Books, 1969, especially Chapters 4 through 6.

(2) *A crisis in the system of political rule.* In the final years of the old regime, ministerial authorities and propertied society concluded that Russia was undergoverned or underinstitutionalized, especially in the countryside.[15] The inadequate network of the state structure left Russia backward relative to other world powers, both in its capacity to mobilize resources and to police and tax its population. The crisis of underinstitutionalization intensified after 1917 as the former rural elites were swept away by peasants and by the agents of the new Soviet power—commissars, rural soviet chairmen, and Chekists. Throughout the 1920s, the rural soviet competed in an uneven struggle with a tenacious commune, which challenged Moscow's hold on the countryside.[16] Because the new ruling elite nurtured ambitious plans for social and economic transformation, it found challenges to its political power increasingly untenable.

(3) *A crisis in social relations.* Before 1917 the social order was undergoing a rough transition from a disintegrating structure of legal estates to an emerging class society.[17] After the decisive collapse of 1917, "the dictatorship of the proletariat" immediately experienced a similar change in its social structure. The proletariat was decimated during the Civil War, and nonproletarians gained access to influential positions in the new state; consequently, the ties between the proletariat and "its" dictatorship were strained and frequently challenged. A crisis of social identities persisted throughout the 1920s as already ill-fitting prerevolutionary categories were twisted and manipulated to make sense of postrevolutionary reali-

---

[15] See S. Frederick Starr, *Decentralization and Self-Government in Russia, 1830-1870*, Princeton, New Jersey, Princeton University Press, 1972. For a related argument about the weaknesses of Russian autocratic authority, see George Yaney, *The Systematization of Russian Government: Social Evolution in the Domestic Administration of Imperial Russia, 1711-1905*, Urbana, Illinois, University of Illinois Press, 1973.

[16] Y. Taniuchi, *The Village Gathering in Russia in the Mid-1920s*, Birmingham, England, University of Birmingham Press, 1968; Dorothy Atkinson, *The End of the Russian Land Commune*, Stanford, California, Stanford University Press, 1983; and George Yaney, *The Urge to Mobilize: Agrarian Reform in Russia, 1861-1930*, Urbana, Illinois, University of Illinois Press, 1982, especially Chapter 12.

[17] See Leopold Haimson, "The Problem of Social Stability in Urban Russia, 1905-1917" in *The Structure of Russian History: Interpretive Essays*, edited by Michael Cherniavsky, New York, Random House, 1970. On problems of social identity in late Imperial Russia, see Gregory Freeze, "The *Soslovie* (Estate) Paradigm and Russian Social History," *American Historical Review*, February, 1986, pp. 11-36.

ties.[18] By the end of the 1920s, workers were showing signs of growing hostility towards technical specialists in factories, to Nepmen in trade and small industry, and to bureaucrats in local state agencies. The very basis of the social contract that ostensibly provided the legitimacy for the Soviet regime—that is, the alliance (*smychka*) of workers and peasants—was strained. Workers complained of high unemployment in the cities, which was fed by rural outmigration; inadequate market deliveries from the countryside created an atmosphere of almost constant panic.[19] For a large number of peasants, especially rural hired labor (*batraki*) and the poorest category (*bednyaki*), the revolution meant little or no improvement in their material situation, despite the rhetoric about the revolutionary alliance of proletariat and poor peasants. Other peasants, who felt the growing burden of taxation and state regulations, complained that they were being unfairly discriminated against by the proletarian dictatorship.[20]

(4) *A crisis in late imperial interethnic relations.* The disintegration of national relations under imperial policy was augmented and transformed by the breakdown of central authority during 1917, by the rise of separatist movements, and by the establishment of independent governments in several areas of the former empire's periphery. By the early 1920s, after the Red Army had reconquered the North, Siberia, Central Asia, the Caucasus, and Ukraine, Moscow reconstituted power in an arrangement that was called Soviet federalism. By means of ethnic and national affirmative-action programs Moscow began to create native elites, which captured key positions in the Party and state. By the end of the 1920s, these native elites were calling for more autonomy and were resisting central attempts to impose economic plans.[21]

---

[18]   A fascinating debate on the social support for the Bolsheviks after 1917 can be found in *Slavic Review*, No. 2, Summer, 1985, with contributions by William Rosenberg, Moshe Lewin, and Vladimir Brovkin.

[19]   On this, see Fitzpatrick, *The Russian Revolution*, Chapters 4 and 5; and William J. Chase, *Workers, Society, and the Soviet State: Labor and Life in Moscow, 1918-1929*, Urbana, Illinois, University of Illinois Press, 1987.

[20]   See Moshe Lewin, *Russian Peasants and Soviet Power: Part I*, London, George Allen & Unwin Press, 1968.

[21]   On nationality policies in the 1920s, see Richard Pipes, *The Formation of the Soviet Union: Communism and Nationalism, 1917-1923*, Cambridge, Massachusetts, Harvard University Press, 1954, 1964, and 1980; Gregory J. Massell, *The Surrogate Proletariat*, Princeton, New Jersey, Princeton University Press, 1974; Ivan Dzyuba, *Internationalism or Russification?* , London, Weidenfeld and Nicolson, 1968; and James E. Mace, *Communism and the Dilemmas of National Liberation: National Communism in Soviet Ukraine, 1917-1933*, Cambridge, Massachusetts, Harvard University Press, 1983.

(5) *A crisis in military power and national security.* Although military reforms following the disastrous Crimean War had gone far towards restoring the Russian empire's international position by the eve of the World War I, the defeats in that war, combined with the devastating Civil War that lasted from 1918 until the early 1920s, reduced the young Soviet state to the position of a highly vulnerable pariah in the international community throughout the 1920s. Red Army strength, with its numbers fixed at half a million until 1930, was woefully inadequate to meet any major European or Asian foe. War scares marked nearly every year of the 1920s, culminating in 1927.[22]

(6) *A general crisis of legitimacy.* All the foregoing elements added up to a general crisis of legitimacy for the new Bolshevik regime. In large measure, that crisis was inherited from the eroded legitimacy of the old regime and the Provisional Government, but it was also exacerbated and transformed by developments since 1917. Both friends and foes charged that the dictatorship of the proletariat had lost its proletarian complexion and that the ruling Communist Party had degenerated into a bureaucratic elite with no organic ties to society. It was the ruling ideology of Bolshevik public culture that was at stake as the elite tried desperately to salvage and transform the pre-1917 revolutionary heritage and to provide ideological sense and guidelines for its new self-appointed task of "building socialism." The crisis was manifested in a furious factional struggle that reached a crescendo in the second half of the 1920s and pitted Left and Right Oppositions against one another and against the dominant Stalinist majority in the Party command. The 1920s remain seriously underresearched; nevertheless, on the basis of the excellent scholarship on the prerevolutionary period and on the relatively meager but provocative literature on the 1920s, it can be argued with a reasonable amount of confidence that Soviet society experienced "a crisis of the NEP."

BOLSHEVIK POLITICAL CULTURE IN THE 1920s

Crises are—at least in large part—in the eyes of the beholder, and it will be necessary to take a closer look at Bolshevik political culture of the 1920s in order to assess the relevance of the NEP period for Soviet reformers today. If a dominant majority of the Party believed that Soviet Russia was in the throes of a crisis, then that crisis must be taken

---

[22]   On the early history of the Red Army, see John Erickson, *The Soviet High Command: A Military-Political History, 1918-1941*, London, Macmillan & Co., Ltd., 1962; and Mark von Hagen, *Soldiers in the Proletarian Dictatorship: The Red Army and the Soviet Socialist State, 1917-1930*, Ithaca, New York, Cornell University, forthcoming.

seriously as a fact of political history. What was it about Bolshevik ideology, Bolshevik assumptions, analytical categories, and rhetoric that diminished the chances for a moderate path to modernization? Are those assumptions, categories, and rhetoric still an integral part of the political culture of Gorbachev's Soviet Union? If so, what social and institutional bases keep them alive in the radically different environment of today? Or are the forces of moderation and reformism likely to prosper in a more hospitable environment? To answer these questions, it is necessary to go beyond the traditional canon of Lenin and explore the writings and speeches of other prominent Bolsheviks. More important, it is necessary to investigate the specific diagnoses of problems and the proposed solutions to them of a much larger political elite than the duumvirates and triumvirates that alternately held power over the course of the 1920s.[23]

BOLSHEVIK ASSUMPTIONS, MILITARIZED SOCIALISM, AND "THE ORGANIC LABOR-DEFENSE STATE"

Why did Bukharin, when faced with an almost certain defeat in the Politburo, make no appeal to his many potential constituencies? Cohen concludes sadly that "Bukharin was trapped by Bolshevik assumptions, many of them mythical and partly of his own making."[24] Among those assumptions were the Party ethos of patriotism and democratic centralism that forbade Party members to air their dissent in non-Party forums; but they also included Bukharin's reliance on Bolshevik categories of social analysis. His moderate evolutionary plan for socialism was perceived by his enemies to be a defense of peasants and technical specialists, both of whom were clearly in the camp of what Bolsheviks called "the petite bourgeoisie." Bolsheviks, as Marxists, also conceived of the past in terms of the inexorable unfolding of stages of historical development. In accord with this understanding, they could and did lay the blame for the nation's troubles at the doorstep of the previous socioeconomic formations, capitalism and perhaps even feudalism, and their many vestiges, including remnants of former elites who were only lying in wait for propitious conditions in which to restore the old order. As Marxists, the Bolsheviks understood history to move by means of class struggle; the revolution and Civil War had only confirmed the harsh truth of Marx's analysis that class peace was not a "natural" condition for

---

[23] With the term political culture, I understand not only ideology, assumptions, analytical categories, and rhetoric but also practical responses to perceived problems, including central policy and the ways in which local elites tried to implement central decisions.

[24] Cohen, *Bukharin*, p. 324.

human history.[25] Prominent Bolsheviks succeeded in equating Bukharin's appeal for civil peace with social-conciliationism (*sotsial-soglashatel'stvo*), a charge that Lenin and others had leveled against the Socialist Revolutionaries and Mensheviks during 1917 for their overly cautious and defeatist attitudes towards the Revolution. Finally, Bukharin appears to have fundamentally misunderstood the new forms that Bolshevik political culture had taken since 1917—for example, in his naïve illusion that the Party would guard against the natural bureaucratic (*chinovnik*) habits of state officialdom.

Bolshevik political culture was increasingly taking on aspects of what this writer has elsewhere called militarized socialism, a development that certainly had strong roots in the Civil War experience of the Party but evolved during the 1920s as well.[26] Bukharin occasionally showed signs of understanding this transformation in Bolshevik culture, such as when he charged that the Party was becoming patterned along the lines of military command,[27] but most serious criticism of the Party's militarization ended early in the 1920s. Militarized socialism resulted from the merging of certain features of the Red Army military ethos with important aspects of Bolshevik socialism; it flowed from the rising fortunes of the army in the Soviet state's priorities, from the evolution of soldiers' status in the new social order, and from increasingly alarmist perceptions of international threats. By the mid-1920s, the defense industry had a powerful lobby that pointed to backward Russia's vulnerable position in an unstable and hostile international system. Even Bukharin, in his revision of the orthodox Marxist position on war and revolution, believed that cataclysmic war was inevitable between capitalist states and that only war would produce world revolution. This expectation of war was at fundamental odds with Bukharin's vision of a moderate evolutionary path to socialism, which required a long period of time free from serious domestic and foreign

---

[25] For a poetic statement of these militant political values, see Vladimir Mayakovsky's poem, "At the Top of My Voice," ("Vo ves' golos'," 1930): "Our dialectics/were not learned/from Hegel./In the roar of battle/it erupted into verse,/when,/under fire,/the bourgeois decamped/as once we ourselves/ had fled/from them." See also Mayakovsky's poem "Home" ("Domoi," 1925), in which he appeals to Gosplan to set quotas for poetry production and to Stalin to read out reports of the Politburo on the efficacy of poetry. In the same poem he equates the pen with the bayonet.

[26] For a more detailed development of these themes, see von Hagen, *Soldiers in the Proletarian Dictatorship*. For a recent discussion of the militarization of the Party during the Civil War, see Francesco Benvenuti, *The Bolsheviks and the Red Army, 1918-1922*, London, Cambridge University Press, 1988.

[27] See the speech by Bukharin to the Seventh Komsomol Congress in March, 1926, cited in Cohen, *Bukharin*, p. 237.

crises. The threat of capitalist encirclement, as the argument of national security was expressed in the 1920s, was used to justify universal military service, an increasingly large military budget, and "the militarization of the civilian populace." Schools and mass organizations were expected to inculcate in all citizens such virtues as self-sacrifice, obedience, and Soviet patriotism in the name of defending the gains of the revolution.

This sort of a public culture appealed to military men, who traditionally perceive themselves to be risking their lives for generally money-grubbing civilians; it also appealed to many Russian socialists, not just the Bolsheviks, who despised the philistinism of the bourgeoisie and the petite bourgeoisie and who viewed themselves as having sacrificed a comfortable personal life for the sacred socialist cause. Even before the revolution, Russian military and socialist cultures had shared a profound disdain for commercial activity, profit motivations, and the market economy, but during the revolution and Civil War, Bolshevik socialism and Red Army military culture were fused in a new set of political attitudes and behavior that persisted throughout the 1920s.[28]

The two most important bulwarks of the Bolshevik regime during the early years after 1917 were workers and soldiers; and the two most important tasks that the new regime faced were labor mobilization and defense, symbolized by the Council on Labor and Defense, Lenin's minicabinet that directed the country during the Civil War. Bolshevik political culture bore the legacy of these emphases in the prominence of industrial and military rhetoric and imagery and also in the prominent place of former soldiers and workers in the new Soviet administrative hierarchy. The peculiar form of political economy that emerged from the revolution and Civil War has been described by Neil Harding as "the organic labor state." In sharp contrast with the concept of social contract that buttresses Western political institutions and practices, Harding argues, the Soviet state confers rights to individuals and groups only when such rights tend "to promote and enhance the *state's* objectives." Furthermore, "the distribution of awards, honors and social prestige is, likewise, directly linked to functional contribution to the goals set by the state. Even the definition of citizenship is determined by the same criteria."[29] On the basis of what has been claimed about the dual nature of the state's functions in the Civil War—i.e., labor

---

[28]   See Robert V. Daniels, "The Militarization of Socialism in Russia, 1902-1946," Occasional Paper No. 200, Washington, D.C., Kennan Institute for Advanced Russian Studies, 1985.

[29]   Neil Harding, "Socialism, Society, and the Organic Labour State," in *The State in Socialist Society,* edited by Neil Hardin, Albany, New York, State University of New York Press, 1984, pp. 2-3 and 27.

and defense—and of the dual nature of the regime's social support—i.e., soldiers and workers—Harding's notion might be expanded to describe the early Soviet state as "an organic labor-defense state." From this character flows a series of fundamental features of the Soviet legal regime and political economy.

BOLSHEVIK POLICIES

As a result of the political understanding that buttressed the organic labor-defense state and its militarized socialism, discrimination was built into Bolshevik policies. Those policies favored key constituencies, particularly the industrial proletariat and Red Army men, and excluded other social and economic groups from participation in political life. For example, the first Soviet constitutions of 1918 (RSFSR) and 1923 (All-Union) denied citizenship to members of the former elite classes and their most heinous servitors, the police and the clergy. All persons who derived their income from exploiting others' labor, such as traders and owners of manufacturing enterprises, were likewise ineligible to be elected to soviets, join the Party, or otherwise take part in civic life. Beyond that, a whole series of discriminatory policies placed considerable obstacles in the way of noncitizens who sought access to education, housing, and credit.[30]

Private Traders. Throughout the 1920s, private traders and manufacturers led a precarious existence. Even in the best year for the Nepmen, 1925, taxes levied on private traders far exceeded the tax burden of prewar traders; consequently, private trade, for all its recovery following the Civil War, never exceeded 40 percent of its prewar volume. A recent historian of the Nepmen has concluded: "The Civil Code granted them the right to engage in private business, but the constitution disfranchised them if they exercised this right."[31] Despite the exhortations of Lenin and Bukharin about building communism with bourgeois hands, in Bolshevik political culture private trade was never far

---

[30]   For more information on early Soviet civil rights policy, see Elise Kimerling, "Civil Rights and Social Policy in Soviet Russia, 1918-1936," *Russian Review*, January, 1982, pp. 24-46.

[31]   Alan M. Ball, *Russia's Last Capitalists: The Nepmen, 1921-1929*, Berkeley, California, University of California Press, 1987, p. 75. Ball also quotes John Maynard Keynes who recalled that during the NEP, "the system [does not] involve the actual prohibition of buying and selling at a profit. The policy is not to forbid these professions, but to render them precarious and disgraceful. The private trade is a sort of permitted outlaw, without privileges or protections, like the Jew in the Middle Ages—an outlet for those who have overwhelming instincts in this direction, but not a natural or agreeable job for the normal man." J. M. Keynes, *A Short View of Russia*, London, L. and V. Woolf, 1925.

removed from speculation and avaricious profit-making. Even Bukharin did not envision the market as a permanent feature of his proffered path to socialism; instead, the Bolsheviks would use the market in order to establish a planned economy that would in turn permit them to eliminate the market in the future. Much of the antagonism that Party members and other social groups felt towards the NEP centered on the Nepmen and the private market, symbols of the corrupt past that had no place in a socialist order.[32] The managerial elite in Soviet factories and offices, mostly inherited from prewar society, also shared in the ambiguous status of private traders. They too were useful in the short run for building socialism, but they had no future in a communist society. As unemployment and inflation rose towards the end of the 1920s, discontented workers vented their rage on "the bourgeois specialists."[33]

The Peasantry. The political culture of the organic labor-defense state created serious dilemmas in the realm of rural policy. All political observers and spokesmen concurred that the Party's influence in the countryside was insignificant and that the Bolshevik Revolution had for the most part not reached the rural population. In Bolshevik eyes, peasants too were a suspect lot, closely linked with the petite bourgeoisie and the fragmented, anarchic market economy. Because they lacked the fundamental attributes of a firm and progressive class consciousness, they were assigned a decidedly subordinate role in the postrevolutionary social hierarchy. Again, even Bukharin, the most outspoken advocate of civil peace and social collaboration under the aegis of the worker-peasant union (*smychka*), was not prepared to admit the peasantry into political equivalence with the proletariat. Social collaboration did not translate into political democracy in the proletarian dictatorship. Rural suffrage was significantly more restricted than urban suffrage; with the important exception of those who became soldiers, peasants in general faced much tougher entry requirements for Party membership as well.

Furthermore, the Party-state, in an attempt to divide and better manage an unreliable peasantry, split peasants into socioeconomic categories that were meant to guide local authorities during the 1920s, especially in the area of income-distribution policy via discriminatory taxation and credit measures. A cursory glance at the

---

[32] For more on the negative connotations of the NEP and Nepmen, see A. Selishchev, *Yazyk revolyutsionnoi epokhi*, Moscow, Rabotnik prosveshcheniya, 1926, p. 196.

[33] On the precarious status of "bourgeois specialists," see Sheila Fitzpatrick, *Education and Social Mobility in the Soviet Union, 1921-1934*, London, Cambridge University Press. 1979; and Kendall Bailes, *Technology and Society Under Lenin and Stalin*, Princeton, New Jersey, Princeton University Press, 1978.

economic and agrarian journals of the period reveals how seriously these categories were taken, even in the face of constant disagreement on how many households qualified in each category (kulaks, middle peasants, poor peasants, hired labor).[34] A fundamental contradiction emerged by the mid-1920s between the imperative of raising agricultural productivity and the need to guarantee a reasonably egalitarian income distribution. National economic recovery depended on raising rural productivity, but the Bolsheviks shared a persistent distrust of the market, trade, and the inequalities of wealth that were the inevitable by-products of a market economy. On the one hand, the peasants were exhorted to improve farming methods and thereby restore the nation's economy. If, on the other hand, the peasants became too prosperous, they risked slipping into the category of kulaks and thereby losing their votes in rural soviets and their tax-exempt status. Thus, a peasant was encouraged to be only partially successful, and the regime hoped to channel all peasant productivity through its schemes of cooperative credit and marketing associations.

Party categories represented the peasant as an economic schizophrenic, whose essence was summed up in the middle peasant. The middle peasant had one foot in the world of the capitalists because he typically owned property and hired some labor, but he had his other foot in the world of the proletariat because he too suffered at the hands of the kulak and might at any vulnerable moment slip into the desperate situation of the rural proletariat. Party theorists agreed that the middle peasantry was both exploited and exploiter; in fact, it appears it was Party policy that was schizophrenic and unable to break out of the ambiguities of its own classification schemes. As one telling consequence of these ambiguities, a vocal and influential sector of the Party membership was accused of working towards "de-peasantization"—i.e., the unmaking or remaking of the peasantry into a "better" social category, proletarians. The "de-peasantizers," many of whom came from the peasantry itself, answered that their critics were soft on kulaks and were betraying the poor peasants, the only true allies of the working class in the countryside. When, in 1925, the Central Committee sanctioned a package of concessions to the peasantry under the slogan "Face to the countryside," the "de-peasantizers" opposed the new line and, in places, engaged in sabotage of the policy. According to one observer in the army, "you can find several thousand soldiers who in all sincerity think that the poorer a peasant is, the more good he is for the Soviet state," and "that to be a permanently poor peasant means to render the Soviet

---

[34] See also Moshe Lewin, *Russian Peasants and Soviet Power*, Chapters 2 and 3.

state a great service."[35] Such attitudes undermined any progress that central policy might have achieved in restoring confidence among productive peasants.

Women. Private traders, technical specialists, and peasants were not the only troublesome social categories for Bolshevik leaders as they tried to identify the dilemmas they faced. Women too were vulnerable, increasingly so as the NEP unfolded. The difficulties that the Bolsheviks encountered in the realm of gender politics go to the heart of many of the dilemmas that continue to affect the quality of life and the process of reform today. Though the Bolsheviks formally recognized women as equal citizens in the early constitutions of the Soviet republic and even looked to women in some regions to stand in for an absent proletariat,[36] the new political elite clearly assigned gender politics a subordinate role to class politics. In general, women were linked to peasants and private traders by virtue of their association with the domestic realm. Publicists also blamed women for adversely affecting male proletarian consciousness by their continued adherence to religious practices. Moreover, the elite shared a consensus that sex was not a dignified concern to which professional revolutionaries should devote any of their energies. Romance and romantic love were viewed as a concession to weakness, a typical philistine obsession with self-satisfaction, self-ishness, and materialism, all of which were summed up as "lack of consciousness." The official ethos of the 1920s prized a spartan life-style with an emphasis on self-sacrifice, struggle, and obedience. Interest-ingly, certain particularly hard-line old Bolsheviks warned that all the contemporary chatter about sex in the 1920s recalled the decadent period after the repression of the 1905 revolution when the workers' revolutionary energies were diverted into eroticism, the occult, and other dark areas of human activity. When confronted by women emancipationists with evidence of discrimination and repression, they argued that only economic development would solve their essentially economic problems.

The favorite cultural hero of the proletarian dictatorship naturally was a proletarian, most typically represented in mass culture as a young male Russian metalworker. (The metal industries were consid-ered by nearly all socialists, especially the Bolsheviks, to be the back-bone of industry and the major target of expanded industrial invest-

---

35   In the Red Army, the reception of the moderate policy towards the countryside met with vociferous opposition. See B. Zorin, "'Derevensky vopros' v agitatsii i progagande v Krasnoi Armii," *Sputnik politrabotnika,* No. 19, 1925, p. 4; "Eshche o derevenskom voprose v agitatsii i progagande v Krasnoi Armii," *Sputnik politrabotnika,* No. 20, 1925, p. 1; and M. Romanovsky, "O serednyake v Krasnoi Armii," *Krasnaya rota,* No. 5, 1925, p. 7.

36   See Massell, *The Surrogate Proletariat.*

ment.[37]) Additionally, because of the role played by soldiers in toppling the autocracy and defending the virtue of the revolution during the Civil War, they too were practically adopted as proletarians and thereby added to the representations of virtuous citizens in the organic labor-defense state. Of course, soldiers were young men. All other groups similarly derived their standing in the official political culture in keeping with their approximation of these ideal types. By contrast, an old Ukrainian peasant woman might be expected to be seen as a hopeless bulwark of all that stood in the way of progress.

All these definitions of citizenship and consciousness had a tremendous impact on the status of women in the new society. In the most practical sense, a whole system of benefits and privileges was enacted to favor industrial workers and soldiers in employment and education and to give them preferential access to other welfare and cultural benefits. Neither the most influential trade unions nor the Red Army and its many allied organizations devoted much attention to the plight of women in the 1920s; consequently, women were left without any protection either in their roles as mothers or workers. Female labor, until women entered the industrial work force in large numbers during the five-year plan, was viewed as nonproductive according to a system of values that equated national power with heavy and large-scale industry.[38] Initially, the state retreated drastically from involvement in the family realm by liberalizing divorce and abortion laws, but the underfunded administrative agencies were later unable to deliver on the revolutionary promises to care for children and to operate more public food and laundry facilities. For women too, as for peasants and private traders, the NEP brought little joy, but great economic hardship and legal insecurity.

Nationalities. The mention of a Ukrainian peasant woman touches upon another aspect of the fundamental tensions of the NEP, and perhaps the most explosive issue that confronts the leadership today—namely, the multiethnic nature of the Soviet state. In this area also, the Bolsheviks eventually proved unable to accommodate the demands for greater national autonomy that native communist elites began putting forward with increasing stridency during the 1920s. To begin with, Bolsheviks, both by virtue of their ideological beliefs and their recent

[37] Again Bukharin, who is often presented as an exception against the general background of public Bolshevik culture of the 1920s, appears more representative when he declared his preference for a large capital goods sector, "Metal industry . . . this is the basic spine, the backbone of our industry," quoted in Cohen, *Bukharin.*

[38] See the unpublished paper by Elizabeth Wood, "NEP and Its Discontents: Gender Politics in Soviet Russia, 1921-1924," [n.d.], for more on the plight of women in the 1920s.

Civil War experience, invariably attached disparaging connotations to nationalism; the Party condemned "bourgeois nationalism" and "national deviationism." The Twelfth Party Congress in 1923 expelled Mir-Said Sultan Galiev, a Volga Tatar, for his errors in championing expanded local Party autonomy.[39] Bolshevik prejudices against nationalism were reinforced by the fact that ethnic identity often overlapped with religious identity; and, of course, religious faith was another persistent holdover from the superstitions of previous socioeconomic formations, especially from the backward rural population. Stalin summed up what was accepted by many vocal Bolsheviks when he said, "The nationality problem is, according to the essence of the matter, a problem of the peasants."[40] Just as peasants represented an anachronistic social formation, capitalist if not feudal in character, so too nationalism and national identity were relegated to the category of vestiges of earlier socioeconomic formations that had to be overcome as humanity made its way into the world brotherhood of labor.

Clearly, not all Marxists were such national nihilists as the Bolsheviks, and few Bolsheviks were as consistently antinationalist as was the anti-Bolshevik German Social Democrat Rosa Luxemburg. The Marxist solution most accommodating to the dilemmas of nationalism came from the Austrian Social-Democrats, who were prepared to live with national identities for decades, if not longer. The Austrians were, though, tainted with the sin of revisionism and social-conciliationism, so their theoretical writings could not sit well with the impatient believers in radical transformation of humankind among Bolshevik ideologues. Although Lenin took an increasingly conciliatory attitude towards the survival of national identities near the end of his life, his polemics with the Central European Marxists before the Great War later provided powerful ammunition to those Bolsheviks who opposed any concessions to "petit-bourgeois" Austro-Marxism by the mid-1920s. Moreover, during the Civil War, the Bolsheviks had developed a taste for strong central control and a suspicion of everything that reeked of regional or local loyalties. Especially small nations (Marx's *Völkerabfälle*) were considered impediments to the progress of socialism. In a telling conflation of attitudes, commissars during the Civil War equated local claims for autonomy (*mestnichestvo*) with cottage-industry methods (*kustarnichestvo*) in the economy, with guerrilla warfare (*partizanshchina*) in military thinking, and with "kulak-Left Socialist Revolutionaries anarchism" in political matters.

---

[39] Alexandre A. Bennigsen and S. Enders Wimbush, *Muslim National Communism in the Soviet Union: A Revolutionary Strategy for the Colonial World*, Chicago, University of Chicago Press, 1979, Part Four.

[40] Joseph V. Stalin, *Works*, Vol. 7, Moscow, Foreign Languages Publishing House, 1953, p. 72.

Great Russian Chauvinism. During the early 1920s, Lenin and a few other leading Bolsheviks waged a determined struggle against Great Russian chauvinism. Marxist historians pilloried the Russian empire as the prison house of nations; special attention was paid to restoring non-Russian national cultures to a more prominent place.[41] Beginning in the mid-1920s, however, discussions about the Russian character of literature and culture began to appear in the press. The parameters for discussing national problems were noticeably shifting in the direction of a more tolerant attitude towards expressions of Great Russian nationalism. Some historians have attributed the resurgence of Great Russian nationalism to the influence of the Changing Landmarks (*Smena vekh*) movement among Soviet bureaucrats, especially those who were holdovers from the old regime and particularly those who were in the army; but other factors were at work as well. Following the failed attempts at proletarian dictatorship in Europe, world revolution faded into the realm of distant, frustrated dreams. As the European economies temporarily stabilized, the Stalin leadership, to whom Bukharin through his writings and speeches gave a certain measure of ideological legitimacy, appealed to the patriotic sentiments of bureaucrats and rank-and-file Party members with the doctrine of "socialism in one country." The constitutional settlement of 1924 was the result of a heated battle between Stalin and his allies, on the one hand, and non-Russian Party leaders, on the other.[42]

Ultimately, the Party repudiated pluralism and multiculturalism for a monistic ideology of Great Russian chauvinism under the guise of proletarian internationalism.[43] Most often with arguments of national security and greater economic productivity, the center stripped the national republics of their powers and reduced native elites to the position of Moscow's agents. A short-term experiment in the creation

---

[41] See Ivan Dzyuba, *Internationalism or Russification?* for more on the early history of Soviet nationality policies.

[42] See the debates at the Twelfth Party Congress in 1923, where the majority defeated nearly every proposal for greater genuine autonomy for the non-Russian republics. Stalin's enemies accused him of using his considerable powers of appointment to stack the congress against more accommodating resolutions of the national question.

[43] For more on the coopting of Russian patriotism and great-power ideology, see Nicholas Timasheff, *The Great Retreat: The Growth and Decline of Communism in Russia*, New York, Dutton, 1946. See also Lowell Tillett, *The Great Friendship of Peoples: Soviet Historians on the Non-Russian Nationalities*, Chapel Hill, North Carolina, University of North Carolina Press, 1969, and Konstantin Shteppa, *Russian Historians and the Soviet State*, New Brunswick, New Jersey, Rutgers University Press, 1962, for discussions about the change in Soviet historians' treatment of non-Russian nationalities.

of native elites that exercised substantial power in key areas, the policy of indigenization or nativization (*korenizatsiya*), came to an abrupt halt in the early 1930s, almost simultaneously with the collectivization of the countryside and the assault on private trade.[44] The contradictions between centralization and the empowerment of ethnic groups were suppressed in favor of the former. The idealistic visions of an international socialist commonwealth, such as the programs conceived by Myhailo Volobuev in Ukraine, remained paper visions; and even those faint dreams disappeared after men like Volobuev were expelled and arrested for national deviationism.[45] The Stalin leadership came to equate non-Russian national autonomy with a weakened Soviet state, and a period of relative acquiescence to national demands was succeeded by ruthless state intervention in local politics, economy, and culture.

Dissent. One final area that is key to characterizing Bolshevik political culture during the NEP is the attitude towards dissent both within and outside the Communist Party. The concept that has attracted the most attention has been democratic centralism; this original Leninist precept evolved during the 1920s in such a way that it served to restrict the arena of acceptable debate over policy options to an ever narrower group of the Party's inner circle. Beginning with the restrictions and outlawing of noncommunist parties during the Civil War, proceeding to the ban on factionalism at the Tenth Party Congress, then to the measures taken to discipline Trotsky and the Left Opposition, and culminating in the defeat of both Left and Right oppositions at the end of the 1920s, Soviet citizens had less and less input in the debates that most affected their lives.

For today's reformers Bukharin has become a symbol of the political pluralism and tolerance that valiantly went down at the hands of the Stalinist tyranny. But here too myth-making has supplanted what the historical record shows about politics in the 1920s. As early as 1923, Bukharin, perhaps unwittingly, played a crucial role in polarizing Party politics with his often vicious attacks on Trotsky and later the Left Opposition. Despite the fact that the Party probably was "a negotiated federation between groups, groupings, factions, and tendencies," few, including Bukharin, wanted it that way.[46] On the issue of involving the

---

[44] For more on the policy of indigenization, see Mace, *Communism and the Dilemmas of National Liberation*; and Massell, *The Surrogate Proletariat*, pp. 173-80.

[45] See Mace, *Communism and Dilemmas*, Chapter 5.

[46] Cohen, in his pathbreaking biography, misquotes Bukharin as approving of the Party's factional character. In fact Bukharin, in the name of Party unity, fought against all factional groups who surfaced to question the Central Committee's claims on political power. "Our party has never been

non-Party masses in political decision-making, Bukharin was equally authoritarian. He spoke in favor of collaboration between classes in the social, economic, and cultural spheres but was not prepared to grant most of the population, including the peasantry, the right to participate meaningfully in political affairs. His tendency to assign alien-class epithets to any and all who disagreed with him, especially when he was at the height of his influence from 1925 to 1927, contributed to a growing intolerance of dissent both in and outside the Party to which he himself eventually fell victim. Bukharin, for all his attractiveness as an alternative to Stalin, remained, in the words of his biographer Cohen, "trapped by Bolshevik assumptions," assumptions that were fatal for democracy and for himself.

THE RELEVANCE OF NEP FOR TODAY

How has Bolshevik political culture evolved since the late 1920s? If the Stalin period witnessed the progressive militarization of Soviet socialism, then one angle from which to view the current reforms is as a demilitarization of politics, economy, society, and culture. At least to judge by the public pronouncements of Gorbachev and his allies, the Party is far more willing to tolerate markets and dissent than ever before in its history. Gorbachev has committed himself to completing the retreat from the "proletarian Sparta"[47] that Khrushchev set in motion as part of his de-Stalinization of Soviet politics. He has introduced a demilitarized rhetoric of international relations, has proposed major cuts in the Soviet armed forces, and has legitimized an expansion of civil society that has been occurring since the 1950s. The critique of "the administrative-command system," the current euphemistic shorthand for the Stalin system, refers precisely to militarized socialism, according to which obedience, discipline, and conformism were favored over individual initiative and the private realm. Under Brezhnev, the Soviet state began to legitimize the private sphere and a consumerist ethos, even though official ideology failed to make the appropriate adjustments away from the conformism of collective self-sacrifice that had set the tone of public discussion since the Stalin years.

---

and—we hope—never will be a federation of groups, groupings, fractions, and tendencies negotiating among themselves." Nikolai Bukharin, *K voprosu o trotskizme*, Moscow/Leningrad, 1925, p. 11.

[47] A "proletarian Sparta" was the ideal of Nikolai Podvoisky, chairman of the Universal Military Administration during the Civil War and a fervent advocate of the socialist militia. In the mid-1920s, Mikhail Frunze and his allies in the Party and army, in their campaign to militarize the civilian populace, advanced many ideas similar to those of Podvoisky. See von Hagen, *Soldiers in the Proletarian Dictatorship*, the chapters on the Frunze reforms.

The state has retreated from the earlier utopianism and the faith in the utter plasticity of humanity that still colored much of Khrushchev's vision of communism.

Under Gorbachev the unofficial has become official, symbolized to a large degree by the legalization and taxation of much of the black market, or second economy, and the sanctioning of comparisons with the West. Simultaneously, and often with a synergistic impact, environmentalism, feminism, petty capitalism, and nationalism have emerged to challenge the old orthodoxies of social and political thought. Although all these isms had some analogues in the 1920s, their collective fates were sealed by the structural crises of the new regime and by a Bolshevik political culture that tolerated no space for such "counterrevolutionary" trends. The outstanding question, then, remains, whether the Party has changed to the degree that it can now tolerate such challenges to its recently indisputable hegemony.

Certainly, the conditions of the late 1980s are drastically different from those of the 1920s. Most of today's political and economic problems are very different from those that dominated the 1920s. The nation is no longer a primarily agrarian economy with a weak army in a threateningly hostile international environment. True, the political and military elites clearly are not satisfied either with the poor performance of the economy or the low level of Soviet influence in international affairs, but the USSR today is an industrial-urban nation with a remarkable degree of national security and with a developed or, at the very least, emerging civil society.[48] The search for solutions to today's dilemmas in the makeshift compromises of the 1920s is a futile and ahistorical exercise. New, imaginative solutions are needed to problems of industrial stagnation, environmental pollution, arms proliferation, and national irredentism.

Finally, it can only be hoped that the new electoral politics in the Soviet Union will act to legitimize the leaders and institutions with some version of popular sovereignty. If the system thereby gains legitimacy in the nation's eyes, the elites will no longer be forced to cull the past for some mythical analogues to current political agendas. As a consequence, history can be depoliticized, in the sense that historians have lacked any meaningful autonomy from the formal ideological apparatus, and politics can be considerably dehistoricized. Soviet historians and leaders must abandon the unimaginative adherence to too strict an understanding of the stages of historical development. Today they often speak of recapturing the momentum of the NEP that Stalin thwarted for so many decades. The USSR cannot return to 1927 and

---

[48] For more on the changes that the Soviet system has undergone since the 1920s, see Moshe Lewin's *The Gorbachev Phenomenon: A Historical Interpretation,* Berkeley and Los Angeles, University of California Press, 1988.

resume its development as if nothing had intervened. Instead, politicians, historians, and social scientists in general should turn their attention to the enduring taproots of militarized socialism and work towards creating an environment more conducive to reformism. The narrow dogmatism of Stalinist Marxism might then be abandoned for a more dynamic and creative socialism; historians would be freed from the tasks of legitimating the political program of the moment.

4

Ownership Issues in *Perestroika*

Philip Hanson

In the Soviet Union and Eastern Europe private enterprise is being rehabilitated. Tentative and limited though this rehabilitation is, it has already, in Poland and Hungary, provided exceptions to Aslund's Law—i.e., the proposition that the contribution of the private sector in socialist economies is doomed to fluctuate around a necessarily low share of national income.[1] In the 1980s the nonstate sector in these two countries has grown considerably. Nonstate production in each of them may now account—measurement is problematic—for around a quarter of gross domestic product. In the USSR public discussion and legislation since 1987 have suggested that a similar evolution may occur in the socialist heartland itself. This essay will seek to establish, as far as possible, the reasons for such a trend in Soviet economic development and to assess both the influences now fostering it and those working against it.

Von Mises's Revenge: Some Intellectual Prehistory

The sustained growth of an officially permitted private sector in any communist country is hard to square with Marxist teaching. It is also curiously hard to fit into the Western tradition of neoclassical economic analysis. In mainstream Western economic theory the relationship of resource ownership to economic performance, both in static efficiency and in long-term productivity growth, remains unclear. If neoclassical economists are capitalist lackeys, they have been lax in their lackeying.

---

[1] See Anders Aslund, *Private Enterprise in Eastern Europe: The Non-Agricultural Private Sector in Poland and the GDR, 1945-83*, London, Macmillan, 1985. In his recent book, *Gorbachev's Struggle for Economic Reform*, London,

In the first half of this century the economics of socialism was an evidence-free subject, hospitable to pure theorizing. After 1917, it is true, there was one country in which socialism of a sort was being tried, but the evidence about Soviet economic performance was suppressed, and so were the economists. Western economists were free to conduct the debate on what became known as "the economics of socialism," unencumbered by practical experience.[2]

That debate used the language of neoclassical, not Marxian, economics. The neoclassical economics of the period had little to say about imperfect information, transaction costs, agent-principal relations, and the like, and the debate revolved around the question of static efficiency: whether resources could be efficiently allocated in a country where private ownership of land and capital had been abolished. Of those who contended they could not, it was Ludwig von Mises who made ownership the key issue.[3] Others, such as Friedrich von Hayek, dwelt mainly on the issue of planning versus the market, which is not— or at least not self-evidently—the same thing.

The chief argument of Mises was that only if there were markets in capital and land could fixed assets be valued in a way that reflected their productivity in their various possible uses. If land and capital were owned by the state, there could be no markets in them and no meaningful valuation of them; there could therefore be no basis for the scarcity pricing of products and no guide to the efficient allocation of resources.

Those who contended that social ownership and efficient allocation were compatible argued as follows. Decision-makers in a centrally planned economy—in Oskar Lange's version of the socialist blueprint, a central planning board, industry managers, and enterprise manag-

---

Pinter Publishers, 1989, Aslund notes in Chapter 6 the boldness of the new Soviet attempt to create a nonstate sector of some size and legitimacy but remains cautious about the prospects of its success. He suggests that the current state of reforms with respect to property rights in the USSR is comparable with that in Poland in 1957. For another excellent discussion, focusing on the recent developments in Poland, see Jacek Rostowski, "The Decay of Socialism and the Growth of Private Enterprise in Poland," *Soviet Studies*, April, 1989, pp. 194-215.

[2] For a good retrospective on the debate in the light of current reforms, see Gertrude Schroeder, "Property Rights Issues in Economic Reforms in Socialist Countries," *Studies in Comparative Communism*, Summer, 1988, pp. 175-88. One of the most accessible sources for the key original papers of the 1930s and 1940s on socialist theory is Morris Bornstein (ed.), *Comparative Economic Systems: Models and Cases*, Homewood, Illinois, Irwin (in most if not all of the successive editions of this book of readings).

[3] Ludwig von Mises, *Socialism: An Economic and Sociological Analysis*, New Haven, Connecticut, Yale University Press, 1951.

ers—could be given operating rules that would lead them to replicate the resource-allocation decisions of a perfectly competitive economy. That already put them ahead of any real-world capitalist market economy, in which competition will always be imperfect. In addition, these rules could accommodate the deployment of "a social dividend" to adjust for externalities, or divergences between private and social cost, and make income distribution more equitable. Real-world markets are not only imperfect and therefore normally not efficient; their workings do not guarantee an income distribution that appeals to people's sense of fairness, and they have no built-in mechanisms for handling externalities. Lange could thus argue that his socialist blueprint was more efficient and more equitable than any capitalist economy could be.

This conclusion was reached, in the best neoclassical manner of the 1930s, by assuming away two basic difficulties—that economic information is necessarily incomplete in any economic system and that the rewards and penalties that make people observe the rules of any game are at least as important as the logical status of the rules themselves. Hayek and, later, Abram Bergson pointed out these weaknesses. Hayek, who has never argued within the confines of a neoclassical approach, made a powerful case for real-world markets as mechanisms for handling incomplete information. He gave some persuasive arguments for expecting markets to be better at this than anything central planners could do, simulated markets included. Yet in contemporary Western textbooks on comparative economic systems—though not in contemporary theory—Lange's "refutation" of Mises has survived, battered but not demolished. Western economists trying to account for differences in efficiency between different economic systems still dwell on the issue of planning versus markets and neglect the role of ownership in the working of markets.

In any judgment of the comparative performance of different kinds of economies, static efficiency is not the only criterion. At the time of the Mises-Lange-Hayek debate in the interwar period, however, it came close to being so considered—hence, what now seems the narrow focus of that debate. Among those economists who operated outside the conventional neoclassical approach of the period, there were, nonetheless, some who had other concerns. Joseph Schumpeter, in lectures delivered in the late 1930s, addressed a subject that now seems equally important: innovation and long-term economic development.[4] Marxian economic thought had kept growth and technical change on its agenda, while most Western liberal economists had decided they were someone else's business. Schumpeter, an authority on both the theory of economic development and the history of economic thought, put

---

[4] Joseph Schumpeter, *Capitalism, Socialism and Democracy*, New York, Harper and Row, 1950.

forward his own, non-Marxian, vision of the processes that governed capitalist economic growth. Mises had made a case for the inherent inefficiency of socialist ownership; Schumpeter provided arguments that can account for the other chronic problem of socialist economies— their lack of technological dynamism.

Schumpeter thought that capitalism would eventually be replaced by socialism. Unlike Marx, he was not sure that this would be a happy ending. In Schumpeter's scheme of things, capitalism had a built-in growth mechanism, and socialism did not. Capitalist entrepreneurship, according to Schumpeter, was propelled by the search for the temporary monopoly profits that accrue to successful innovators, whose successful innovations spread like epidemics because businesses that failed to keep up with the profitable new products and processes were wiped out. Schumpeter argued that this "gale of creative destruction" was the essence of capitalist competition in the long run. It was through this competitive process that average levels of productivity and material prosperity were raised. There was no equivalent mechanism under socialism, so far as Schumpeter was concerned. He saw socialism as necessarily centralized, bureaucratic, and nonentrepreneurial. It would therefore lack technological dynamism. It would, nonetheless, probably replace capitalism because very high levels of prosperity would bring a dwindling demand for new products and processes. There would be less call for entrepreneurship and less readiness to put up with the economic turmoil and insecurity that accompany material progress. Routine bureaucratic management of production was all that would be needed, and socialism could provide that. The process would be hastened by capitalism's cultural contradictions, including its tendency to alienate its own intellectuals.

Schumpeter's writings, like those of Hayek and Mises, do not fit into the neoclassical approach to economics and remain outside the main tradition. Even so, they have influenced much later research on the innovation process in the West.[5] They have also seemed, to several students of the socialist economies, to provide a good explanation of those economies' inability, once industrialized, to match Western levels and growth rates of productivity.[6] The apparent failure of market-socialist reforms and the drift of Soviet and East European reforms towards changes in property rights suggest that both Schumpeter and Mises were on to something.

---

[5] For example, R. R. Nelson and S. G. Winter, *An Evolutionary Theory of Economic Change*, Cambridge, Massachusetts, Belknap Press, 1982.

[6] Philip Hanson and Keith Pavitt, *The Comparative Economics of Research, Development and Innovation in East and West: A Survey*, Chur, Harwood Academic Publishers, 1987; S. Gomulka, *Growth, Innovation and Reform in Eastern Europe*, Brighton, Wheatsheaf Books, 1986.

REFORM OF THE REFORM IN THE USSR AND EASTERN EUROPE

Soviet and East European economic reformers mostly lack a clear idea of the organization of the new system they are seeking. When the picture of a reformed system has been clear, it has turned out to be unrealistic—a vision of an economy that somehow combines the stability and central control of the plan with the efficiency and dynamism of the market. That has proved to be an overoptimistic notion that one could eat one's cake and have it too. By the time Soviet leader Mikhail Gorbachev began to launch *perestroika*, such ideas had, in Eastern Europe, come to seem naïve.[7] Despite the uncertainty that now exists about the exact nature of a desirable reform, one fundamental requirement of a reformed economic system is present either explicitly or implicitly in the writings of most Soviet and East European reformers. By itself, it is not enough to prescribe the shape of the reformed system, but it is the crucial feature by which alternative institutions and operating rules can be judged. This requirement might be described as follows: the reformers want to establish an economy in which most producers are most of the time more worried about their customers and their competitors than they are about the central authorities.

Both the traditional system and the partially reformed Hungarian system lack this characteristic, except perhaps in the Hungarian farm sector. The chronic problems of wasteful use of resources, hidden reserves, shortages, poor quality of products, and technical backwardness are all the result of this lack. The same lack is at the root of the low levels of productivity and prosperity that prompt reform in the centrally administered economies in the first place. The question is what reforms are needed to push an economy across the dividing line between a regime dominated by the authorities and a regime dominated by competition. Do the reforms have to amount to the restoration of capitalism? Or is there an alternative? Can socialism be made competitive? The Party leaders insist that there is an alternative. So does a certain percentage of the population—varying, to venture an estimate, from perhaps close to zero in Poland to perhaps a majority in the USSR.

Where reforms have made progress towards the threshold of a competitive order, inflation and other sorts of instability have threatened social upheaval (China, Yugoslavia, Hungary). In all these cases, reformist leaders have adopted a flexible approach, extending to changes in property rights. It has so far served them well only in the Hungarian and Chinese farm sectors. The dictum of Deng Xiaoping that "it doesn't matter what color the cat is so long as it catches mice" was

---

[7]   Janos Kornai, "The Hungarian Economic Reform Process: Visions, Hopes and Reality," *Journal of Economic Literature* , No. 24, 1986, pp. 1687-1744.

key to a remarkable improvement in food supplies in China after 1978, effected by reestablishing peasant farming.[8] In April, 1989, however, student protesters were carrying banners saying "the cat is dead." Those successes in Hungary and China that can be attributed to reform seem to have come from a shift from state to mixed, partially private, ownership. The questions that will be addressed in what follows here are: Why is this? Is it likely to be true for the USSR? What moves has the USSR been making in this direction? What have been the successes and setbacks so far in Soviet attempts to modify ownership arrangements?

OWNERSHIP AND ECONOMIC PERFORMANCE

Most of the Western literature on comparative economic systems, Mises and Schumpeter notwithstanding, treats the resource-allocation mechanism (market or plan) as crucial and the resource-ownership system as secondary. The relationship between these two dimensions of an economic system is usually treated as flexible. It is pointed out that ownership arrangements in various national economies range from predominantly public to predominantly private and that resource-allocation methods range from predominantly market to predominantly hierarchical (i.e., by central administration, operating through a single national economic hierarchy). It is usually said, or implied, that these two characteristics are independent. True, most socialist economies are run as single hierarchies, and most developed capitalist economies are market economies; but there are some apparent exceptions. Hungary and Yugoslavia can be presented as examples of market socialist economies, and Britain in World War II and Germany in the late 1930s as examples of private enterprise combined with central administration.

The most recent studies of the East European reforms, however, many of them by Polish and Hungarian economists, conclude that "market socialist" reforms (devolving decision-making within the state sector) have failed to create market economies. All they have achieved, the argument goes, is a form of indirect central control. Moreover, the usual assessment in Eastern Europe is that these limited reforms have not, by and large, cured the chronic ailments of the traditional system. Insofar as there has been some success, it has been confined to farming and has been based on the reinvention of a nonstate sector.

What the reformers in Poland and Hungary now stress is the need to extend the market back from products to factors. They have in mind especially land and capital markets, at present virtually nonexistent.

---

[8]   See Wolfgang Quaisser, "The New Agricultural Reform in China: From the People's Communes to Peasant Agriculture," in Peter Gey, Jiri Kosta, and Wolfgang Quaisser (eds.), *Crisis and Reform in Socialist Economies*, Boulder, Colorado, Westview Press, 1987, pp. 173-97.

Their general argument could extend to markets in rights of various kinds—e.g., land-use rights on leased land, inventions, etc. Only if market reforms extend to the creation of a capital market, it is argued, will they improve economic performance.[9] That implies, for many East European economists, a significant amount of privatization. As David Granick, exaggerating slightly, observes, American neoclassical economics still favors Lange, while East European economists are coming to favor Mises.[10]

The arguments that are put forward for creating capital markets are as follows:

- The existence of markets for land and capital enables prices to be put on them that relate to their potential earnings in various alternative uses. That certainly helps—and may be essential—in the setting of prices of products that reflect the opportunity cost of the resources used in making them. This is Mises' main argument.

- The ability of the center to make the right decisions on the allocation of investment—i.e., on long-run changes in economic structure—has come to be doubted. Central control over the allocation of investment is still a standard ingredient in Soviet reform proposals. The notion that the center, by allocating a large part of investment, can make the economy grow faster than it would under mainly market allocation of investment has, however, lost credibility in most of the developed world. It is disputed by many East European reformers as well as by many Western economists disillusioned with government industrial policies. In Poland and Hungary many economists now argue that more or less competitive markets in land and capital will do better in determining the uses of fixed assets, for most of the economy, than centralized investment allocation.

---

[9] D. Mario Nuti, "Financial Innovation under Market Socialism," European University Institute, Working Paper 87/285, 1987; Philip Hanson, "Ownership and Economic Reform," *Radio Liberty Research Bulletin*, RL 154/88, April 6, 1988, citing Brus and others at a conference in Gyoer, Hungary, in March, 1988.

[10] David Granick, "Property Rights vs. Transactions Costs in Comparative Economic Systems Analysis," *Journal of Institutional and Theoretical Economics*, No. 144, 1988, pp. 871-77.

- If the central authorities control most investment, that gives them leverage over enterprises' current output decisions as well, since they can offer investment finance as a reward for good behavior and threaten to withhold it as a penalty for nonconformity. Central control over investment and current output decisions is, even in the Soviet Union, widely believed to be disastrous.

- To motivate producers to make the best use of their fixed assets, it seems to be necessary to link their rewards to the earning power of the assets they manage. In a capital market, the expected future earning power of a firm's assets, strongly influenced by that firm's recent performance, determines their value. If that value falls below what other potential users of the firm's property believe they can achieve by more effective use of the firm's capital, the firm is in danger of being bought up. Even if the firm's managers are not its owners, that will generally be bad news for them. The need to keep shareholders happy and to be able to repel corporate raiders is a powerful incentive to manage assets efficiently. Whatever the shortcomings of competitive capital markets, no other arrangement so far seems to provide this incentive so effectively. It is an ever-present threat, spurring management to cut costs, introduce new products and processes, and explore new markets. As capital markets in the Western world have become more international, this pressure has, if anything, increased.

- Markets in factors provide flexibility in dealing with both successes and failures in the management of production. In other words, problems of market entry and market exit seem to be better managed than they are, in practice, by central decision-making. Capital markets are never perfect, but there is generally scope for a successful entrepreneur or management team to expand an existing business or move into a new market. Conversely, the liquidation or takeover of a poorly managed company, or one that has simply been overwhelmed by some unexpected change in its environment, takes resources out of activities in which they are not effectively used and does so, however ruthlessly, without the delays and economic waste that often

attend a more political method. In other words, it facili-
tates the flow of resources between branches, known to
Soviet Marxists as *pereliv kapitala.*

These are powerful arguments for markets in capital and natural
resources. Perhaps arrangements could be devised that would make
such markets socialist: the buyers and sellers on them might, for
example, be restricted to state holding companies. There would, though,
have to be enough of these market operators to generate competition,
and they would themselves have to be strongly motivated to maximize
their own asset values. Another consideration is that much of the
effectiveness of modern capital markets comes from the fact that they
are international. If the Soviet Union and Eastern Europe were eventually to be integrated into world markets, not only for products but also
for capital, they would be joining a game in which most of the players
were private. The assimilation process would be hard to resist, as
Eastern bloc tennis players such as Nastase, Fibak, Chesnokov, and
Zvereva have shown. Some sort of private ownership is likely, but there
might be some residual socialist restrictions that could be retained, such
as a rule that no fit person of working age could live on a purely rentier
income, without working, and high rates of tax on capital gains and
inheritance. (The notion that shares should be purchased only by the
employees of the enterprises issuing the shares would probably be too
restrictive. It would prevent the development of a secondary market in
shares and, hence, a competitive valuation of assets, and it would
drastically limit interbranch capital flows.)

The extension of markets to land and capital would mean, according to these arguments, that the economy would become a real market economy with competitive pressures of a kind that purely
market-socialist reforms seem unable to generate. That should be
the basis for faster growth in productivity and prosperity in the course
of time. In the short run, the adjustment costs would be high as
enterprises were liquidated, pruned, or merged. In the long run, the
costs would be less tangible—higher levels of personal economic insecurity (even with a state safety net) and higher average levels of work
effort and stress.

OWNERSHIP ISSUES IN THE SOVIET ECONOMIC REFORM DEBATE

In the Soviet economic reform debate the case for privatization has not
(yet?) been addressed. This is not because there are no Friedmanite true
believers in capitalism. The Soviet population has always contained
some antisocialist liberal thinkers, though perhaps not many. Before
Gorbachev changed the rules of the game, they could be encountered

only in conversation or in *samizdat*.[11] Now they are allowed out. Doubts about state ownership are routinely expressed in the media. Doubts about socialist ownership in general, more or less obliquely expressed, surface from time to time. The doubts about state ownership are sanctioned in speeches made by Soviet leaders. In leaders' statements these doubts are usually linked with one of two concerns. The first is that state ownership has not ended the alienation of workers from production. The second is that state ownership has provided weaker incentives to efficiency and technical progress than those that operate in the West.

In an article for a Western business readership, Politburo member Aleksandr Yakovlev expressed these concerns in strong terms.[12] Some of his phrases contained echoes, perhaps by chance, of the nineteenth-century liberal philosopher Herbert Spencer. On alienation Yakovlev said: "Without such a change [from state ownership to cooperatives and other forms of ownership] socialism is destined to be an illusory utopia. The end result would then be man totally alienated from property and social power, insignificant against the backdrop of the state." On efficiency he said: "The state is not a suitable leader of trade, since it is itself financed by society. The state can, however, supervise commerce well, regulate the money flow and maintain order in salaries. Nevertheless the state is unable itself to institute a system of output-based remuneration."

Gorbachev himself is more cautious when addressing Westerners. This is not only because his translators are less inclined to use Victorian turns of phrase. He too criticizes state ownership in strong terms and avoids saying just what set of property rights should replace it; but he also insists that the alternatives must be found within something called socialism. In his most systematic exposition of his views to the outside world—his book *Perestroika*—he says: "We are looking within social-ism, rather than outside it, for the answers to all the questions that arise." He then goes on to say that more socialism means "a more dynamic pace and more creative endeavor, more organization, law and order, more scientific methods and initiative in economic management, efficiency in administration, and a better and materially richer life for the people." He also says that more socialism means "more democracy, openness and collectivism in everyday life, more culture and human-ism in production . . . more patriotism . . . more active civic concern." In short, more socialism means something bland enough to be sung about in the Eurovision Song Contest. Apart from that one word, "col-

---

[11]   On liberal economic writings in *samizdat*, see Philip Hanson, "On the Limitations of the Soviet Economic Reform Debate," CREES Discussion Paper, General Series 2, July, 1985.

[12]   "As Strong as the Weakest Link," *Moscow Business*, No. 1, 1989, p. 5.

lectivism," more socialism seems to mean more of everything except socialism; the list contains no reference whatever to social ownership of the means of production. Later on, Gorbachev describes the deterioration of Soviet society under Brezhnev. One of the symptoms was that "Public property was gradually fenced off from its true owner—the working man." Property was "deprived of a real owner," and Soviet man was alienated "from the property of the whole people." There was a lack of harmony between public and personal interests.[13]

The connection between what the leaders say and what the intellectuals say in the Gorbachevian reform debate seems to be reciprocal. Often the economists pick up a phrase from one of Gorbachev's speeches and elaborate on it, as though it were a kind of permission to address the subject matter involved. In other instances, an argument appears first from an economist, economic journalist, or manager and later enters the discourse of the leaders' speeches. The former seems to be more often the sequence than it is in Western public discourse on economic policy, but the latter is not uncommon now. In addition, intellectuals sometimes go on public record with ideas that the leaders show no sign of endorsing at all—for instance, Nikolai Shmelev in 1987 on a necessary margin of unemployment and on collectivization as, simply, a disaster; Larisa Piyasheva (Popkova) on the incompatibility of markets and socialism and the unplannability of technical change; and Anatolii Strelyanyi on the need for a return to peasant farming.[14]

Over changes in property rights, Gorbachev gave a lead quite early on. In February, 1986, at the Party Congress, he said that intracollective farm contracts with families should be encouraged and that cooperatives providing consumer goods and services should be reestablished.[15] In July, 1986, visiting Khabarovsk, he elaborated on the point about cooperatives and criticized (in a conversation shown on Soviet television) farm managers who were against peasants selling their own produce on the local markets.[16] In that year legislation on the private

---

[13] Mikhail Gorbachev, *Perestroika: New Thinking for Our Country and the World*, 2d ed., London, Fontana, 1988, pp. 36-37 and 47.

[14] Nikolai Shmelev, "Avansy i dolgi," *Novyi mir*, No. 6, 1987, pp. 142-58; and an unpublished talk summarized by Paul Quinn-Judge, *Christian Science Monitor*, June 16, 1987; Larisa Popkova, "Gde pyshnee pirogi?" (letter) *Novyi mir*, No. 5, 1987, pp. 239-41, and Larisa Piyasheva (Popkova's married name), "Sotsial'nye tseli i ekonomicheskie rezul'taty," *Tekhnika i nauka*, No. 11, 1988, pp. 8-11; Anatolii Strelyanyi, "Raionnye budni," *Novyi mir*, No. 12, 1986, pp. 231-41; and a dialogue with Viktor Lishchenko, "Mesyats v derevne," *Literaturnaya gazeta*, December 3, 1986.

[15] *Pravda*, February 26, 1986.

[16] *Izvestia*, August 3, 1986; and BBC *Summary of World Broadcasts* (SWB) SU/8328/C, pp. 1-7.

sector appeared. First, there were decrees directed against it—the measures of May, 1986, against so-called "nonlabor income"; then, towards the end of the year, a law intended to help it—the Law on Individual Labor Activity. The latter provided, for the first time, a legal framework for private enterprise, but the framework was restrictive (see below).[17] Legislation on cooperatives was slower in coming; the Law on Cooperatives (see below) was passed only in mid-1988.

The academics seemed at this stage to be following Gorbachev's lead rather than generating ideas for him (the offstage relationship may have been different, but the public debate showed little sign of independence). Academician Leonid Abalkin, it is true, predicted in November, 1986, that a revived and expanded cooperative sector would produce 10-12 percent of national output by 1996.[18] Gorbachev's public statements had, however, already indicated that he wanted to see something like that. Some decrees making limited provision for cooperatives were issued beginning in October, 1986. Gorbachev meanwhile developed in public his ideas about private initiative in agriculture. He talked of renting land and equipment out to small teams and families.[19] This quickly developed into a campaign, so that in 1988 the press was full of happy families renting land from their farms, together with cautionary stories about farm managers and local Party officials who were hampering the leasing of land to families.

Policies on ownership turned radical only in 1988, with the Law on Cooperatives and the development of family leasehold farming. The published reform debate of the previous year foreshadowed these developments, but the censors and editors, and perhaps the authors too, seemed to be taking their cue from Gorbachev. One possible interpretation of the course of events is as follows. The defects of traditional state ownership were being reflected on by many people. People of independent and unorthodox views, from journalists like Strelyanyi and Aleksandr Levikov[20] to Gorbachev himself, were considering alternatives. Among them were several academic economists and philosophers, some obscure and some well known. The ideology of ownership relations was being reconsidered by small, probably informal, groups in the more independently-minded institutes like Academician Oleg Bogomolov's Institute of the Economics of the World Socialist System (IEMSS). Relaxation of the censorship unleashed writers like Strelyanyi, Levikov, and Popkova. The same relaxation, plus signs that

[17] *Izvestia*, May 28 and November 21, 1986, respectively.

[18] *Boston Globe*, November 28, 1986.

[19] At a meeting in the countryside outside Moscow, (see *Izvestia*, August 7, 1987).

[20] See Levikov's hymn of praise to the private sector in the GDR, "Remeslo," *Novyi mir*, No. 4, 1986, pp. 180-99.

Gorbachev himself was tackling the issue, encouraged well-known senior economists like Bogomolov and Abalkin to address ownership matters in public. It was also possible for books and papers revising the standard ideology in more scholastic ways to appear. An example of the latter is a collection of papers published in 1987 in a print run of only 200 copies by IEMSS with the title *Problems of Ownership in the Countries of Real Socialism.*[21]

For a brief summary of the debate, it is best to start with the heavyweight reformers, Academicians Abalkin and Bogomolov. Both have written at some length on ownership, and both are of considerable eminence in Soviet society. It is true that until Abalkin's recent elevation to a deputy premiership, neither of them had a post with any responsibility for policy. On the other hand, they have both been consulted from time to time by the government, and Abalkin now heads a new State Commission on Economic Reform.[22] They both have the rank of academician in a society highly conscious of rank, they have "their" institutes and journals to deploy, and they are public figures in a way that few of their less highly-placed colleagues are (Gavriil Popov and Shmelev are among those few). Both Abalkin and Bogomolov have been elected to the Congress of People's Deputies.

Abalkin and Bogomolov have published articles in which they aim to alter official Soviet doctrine about property. In October, 1988, Abalkin gave the opening address at an All-Union Research Conference on "Problems of Socialist Ownership: Structure and Restructuring of the Forms of [Its] Realization."[23] He suggested two criteria for judging the "socialisticity" (*sotsialistichnost'*) of any set of property rights. First, it must allow the economy to be as productive and innovative as possible. (He did not use a word directly denoting "innovation" but referred to the property of creating savings of [labor]-time, i.e., raising productivity.) The USSR must not, he said, build backwardness (*otstalost'*) into its definition of socialism. Abalkin's

---

21   *Problemy sobstvennosti v stranakh real'nogo sotsializma*, Moscow, IEMSS, 1987.

22   *Izvestia*, June 11, 1989, p. 2.

23   L. I. Abalkin, "Obnovlenie sotsialisticheskoi sobstvennosti," *Ekonomicheskaya gazeta*, No. 45, 1988, p. 10. This is based on a report prepared by a group at the Institute of Economics, headed by L. V. Nikiforov. For a fuller version, see *Voprosy ekonomiki*, No. 4, 1989, pp. 82-92. The text there is followed by a summary of discussion and some recommendations. In a number of interviews over the period from September, 1986, to May, 1988, Leonid Abalkin expressed a strongly favorable view of cooperatives and other novel ownership arrangements in the USSR. See L. I. Abalkin, *Perestroika: puti i problemy, Interv'yu s akademikom*, Moscow, Ekonomika, 1988, which is a collection of interviews with both Soviet and foreign journalists.

78

Philip Hanson

second criterion of socialisticity was that the economic institutions must be such as to resolve the problem of unemployment, provide a system of social guarantees, and exclude alienation, so that the labor collective at a place of work must feel itself to be, in the familiar Soviet phrase, the real boss (*khozyain*).

In other words, any system of property rights that cannot match the productivity and adaptability of capitalism (and therefore its high average levels of prosperity) cannot be counted as properly socialist. At the same time, however, to be socialist it must be compatible with the maintenance of full employment, provide "social protectiveness" (*zashchishchennost'*), which seems to mean a minimum income, health care, and housing safety net, and something like workers' councils. Abalkin went on to say it was not clear that such a system could be found. At present, he said, socialism (meaning the current Soviet variety) cannot meet these criteria, while capitalism meets only the first. (It might be added that it is, of course, capitalism that creates the first criterion; if the West did not exist, socialism could have its present levels of efficiency and prosperity without anyone knowing that anything better was possible.)

Elsewhere Abalkin has elaborated on the notion of social guarantees.[24] They do not include job security. He distinguishes between full employment, where there are always jobs available for redundant workers, and job security, where every occupant of every existing post has security of tenure. Like almost all Soviet reformers, he sees the need for plant closures and redundancies. Otherwise, what he has in mind is an income safety net. When he refers, in his paper of 1988, to "capitalism" not providing these things, it is tempting to interpret him as having a special definition of capitalism that excludes some of the present mixed economies-cum-welfare states, such as Sweden. Along with several other reformers, he has taken recently both to visiting Sweden and to praising it. He does say in the same paper that there are at present just two systems in the world, so presumably what he is calling for is a search for that elusive third way that somehow combines the best of all possible worlds. He does not (yet? in public?) agree with the Hungarian Free Democrat quoted by Timothy Garton-Ash who says that one simply has to choose between socialism as it now exists and capitalism.[25]

Bogomolov has written more extensively about the question of what makes an ownership system more conducive to efficiency. In the autumn of 1987, he published in the Party's theoretical journal

[24] Interview with Abalkin published in *Sovetskaya Rossiya*, July 19, 1987, as included in Abalkin, *Perestroika: Puti i problemy*, pp. 53-66.

[25] Timothy Garton-Ash, "The End of Communism in Poland and Hungary," *New York Review of Books*, June 15, 1989, pp. 3-10.

Kommunist, an article that summarized the process of change under way in the socialist countries—politically, economically, and in relations with the outside world.[26] He listed seven changes in the economy. These included a shift from imperative to indicative planning and from supplier to customer domination of production decisions. One of these changes was from almost exclusive state ownership to a mixed system of ownership in which individual, family, and small-group ownership of capital coexisted with "social" ownership.

In an interview earlier in 1987, Bogomolov had made the distinction between two different kinds of property rights.[27] On the one hand, he spoke of the *sobstvennik*, the person (i.e., juridical person) who has the right to derive income from the asset and to dispose of it. On the other hand, he mentioned the *vladelets*, the person who is in control of the use of the asset. This is the familiar distinction between ownership and control that may be applied to shareholders and managers in a joint-stock company. Bogomolov noted that the *sobstvennik* may, but need not, be the same person as the *vladelets*. In the article in *Kommunist* he made the point that, if assets are to be efficiently managed, there should be a link between that control (*obladanie*) and the incomes of the controllers. Both the leasing of state assets to individuals and small groups and the creation of cooperatives allow production units to benefit from the incentive effects of such a link.

What heavyweight reformers like Abalkin and Bogomolov do not seem to have done is to take the public debate a step further and address the question of incentives related not to current income from assets but to changes in the value of assets. The issue is far from academic. Suppose that a family, cooperative, or work collective leases assets—e.g., land—from the state. The lessees pay a rent that is predetermined for some fixed period. The point being made by many of the reformers, including Abalkin and Bogomolov, is that in this case the lessees are better motivated to use the land productively than the usual state enterprise or kolkhoz collective. The latter have a contractually fixed income that is independent of the performance of the enterprise; the former—the individual, cooperative, or work-collective lessees—will, on the contrary, derive the residual net income from their activities after payment of rent and taxes. Instead of the state clawing back any gains from improved productivity, the workers or managers will themselves feel the benefit of their efforts. This is not the full story, though. If the assets are not theirs to sell, the lessees lack the incentive of capital gains. They could in the short- and medium-term raise their income by running down the value of the assets—by, for example, not maintaining

---

[26]   Oleg Bogomolov, "Mir sotsializma na puti perestroika," *Kommunist*, No. 16, 1987, pp. 92-103.

[27]   *Izvestia*, May 14, 1987.

the fertility of the land—over the term of the lease. It is no doubt for this reason that Soviet rules on leasing (see below) were quite rapidly extended, in the case of agriculture, to "fifty years or more." The argument leads back to the notion of a capital market. It has been debated by Hungarian economists[28] but is just beginning to attract attention in the Soviet Union.

The issuing of shares, it is true, has been not merely discussed but, in a number of cases, put into practice (see below). So far, however, there is great caution about this. The general view expressed by Soviet reformers in public is that shares should only be issued to other enterprises and to workers of the enterprise issuing the shares. The creation of a capital market on this basis would be difficult, if not impossible. With, in addition, low ceilings on the proportion of an enterprise's capital that can be represented by shares, the incentive effect of capital gains is considerably weakened even if a secondary share market is allowed. Such ceilings are at present considered appropriate, at least for state (though not cooperative) enterprises.[29] There are some writers who have stuck their heads above this particular parapet. Shmelev, for instance, has advocated the sale of shares to private individuals without adding the rider that they must be employees of the firm in question. A Soviet history professor has argued for a capital market through which capital could flow between branches of the economy. That would be incompatible with the restriction of share ownership to employees only and hard to implement through state holding companies.[30]

Only Popkova has put the political question squarely, asking whether socialism is compatible with the market. The idea that one could combine plan and market, she wrote in 1987, is like the idea that one could be "a little bit pregnant." Free enterprise is not in decline in the West, she said; on the contrary, it has a bright future. The less developed countries that have adopted the market system are catching up with the socialist world. Where there is more market, "the pies are bigger and better." In her famous article in *Novyi mir* (printed, in fact, as a very long letter, no doubt to reduce the editors' risks) she gave no reasons for her assertions. Elsewhere, however, she has argued that only incentives tied to the success of individuals will be powerful enough to raise the prosperity of all; also that technical innovation has by definition to do with the unexpected and is therefore unplannable. In other words, she judges that egalitarianism and planning are both inimical to the raising of average productivity levels.[31]

---

[28] E.g., Marton Tardos, "Ownership," in English, mimeographed, 1988.
[29] See the discussion in *Vorprosy ekonomiki*, No. 4, 1989, pp. 82-100.
[30] Shmelev, "Avansy i dolgi"; A. Volkov, "Nuzhny li den'gam nogi?" (letter), *Izvestia*, July 28, 1988.
[31] See the works by her cited in Note 14.

No wonder she was criticized. The establishment reformers seem to have considered that she was rocking the boat: better to redefine socialism than to denounce it. The conservative reprimand—in *Pravda*, naturally—accused her of advocating a free-enterprise society under the disguise of a new kind of socialism.[32] That was not in fact what she had done, but it was what a conservative must consider that Abalkin and Bogomolov are doing. The *Pravda* critic wound up with a suitably sinister and obscure conclusion: "The desire to go beyond the bounds of socialism could lead to 'bigger and better' pies with an inedible filling."

Others who want to reform ownership are either more circumspect or have different beliefs about what is possible. Two arguments have been widely used. The first is that, in the search for enterprise independence, the 1987 Law on the State Enterprise has proved inadequate; the only way an enterprise can break free from state supervision is for its work force to rent their assets from the state or to create a cooperative. Thus ownership changes are presented simply as a matter of pursuing the logic of enterprise autonomy.[33] The second argument has to do with the socialist content of such new arrangements; they are to be justified to the extent that they bring about "real worker-ownership."[34] It is not hard to imagine that the argument about incentives will sooner or later collide with the argument about participation.

In general, the Soviet debate has steered around some tricky issues. Can you create a capital market without allowing extensive secondary sales of shares and the sale of complete businesses? If not, how are you going to avoid creating three unmistakably capitalist phenomena: the coupon-clipping rentier; the small businessman who succeeds, sells up and becomes filthy rich; and the worker made redundant by the competitive process? Rather than answer these questions, the contributors to the Soviet debate have mostly chosen to sidle past them, making polite remarks about the economic systems of the cozier neutral states— Sweden, Austria, and Switzerland.

Recently, the writer Chingiz Aitmatov has extended the list beyond the neutrals, to include Canada and Spain; in effect, he defines socialism as democratic capitalist countries with good welfare provision. Abalkin, Bogomolov, and other ownership-reformers have nonetheless avoided putting limits on the "acceptable" varieties of ownership arrangements. In this they differ from a number of writers who appear super-

---

[32] V. Lipitsky, "Vot kakie pirogi," *Pravda*, June 7, 1987.

[33] For an example, see M. Krushinsky, "Khozraschet: davlenie snizu," *Izvestia*, July 25, 1988.

[34] E.g., the pre-Party Conference appeal by the Party group at the Central Economics-Mathematical Institute (TsEMI) of the USSR Academy of Sciences, *Literaturnaya gazeta*, June 22, 1988.

ficially reformist on this issue, wanting limits to be prescribed. A whole series of such articles appeared in the weekly *Ekonomicheskaya gazeta* in early 1989.[35] They all stress the need to move away from the traditional form of state ownership. Some of the authors (e.g., Yurii Sukhotin of TsEMI) are chiefly concerned that leasing and similar arrangements should be managed democratically, but the idea that is common to all of them is that there is something inherently good about "all-people's ownership" and something inherently dangerous about "the group egoism" of ownership by work collectives. This leads them to favor the renting of assets by work collectives from the state, with the lessor representing "the social interest." Either directly or indirectly, these writers convey the message that cooperatives are not quite socialist. This is a reasonable point of view. The problem is that cooperatives have been endorsed by the Party leadership, so the argument often proceeds towards the downgrading of cooperatives and then, inconsistently, concludes that they are all right within limits.

"Group property" and "group egoism" are phrases well adapted to conservative use. They suggest a need to retain a center that will somehow represent the whole of society. The Leningrad Oblast Party boss, Yurii Solov'ev, complained in a key speech precisely of "group production egoism." The speech was his contribution to the conservative counterattack at the Central Committee plenum in April this year.[36] Conservatism of this kind, resentful of any change in the old order, is one of the obstacles to the implementation of new ownership arrangements in practice. Despite the conservatives—or perhaps because they were not invited—the open-minded approach of Abalkin seems to have characterized the research conference on ownership in Vladimir in October, 1988. In the reports published in *Voprosy ekonomiki* the impression is of general support for an eclectic combination of ownership forms, with no tendency to favor leasing over cooperatives or to prescribe limits for the latter.[37] V. V. Kulikov, for example, called for a "de-state-ization" of the economy, with only one of four categories of enterprise to be unequivocally "state" enterprises, and the category of

   [35] Yu. Sukhotin, "Sobstvennost': perestroika otnoshenii," *Ekonomicheskaya gazeta*, No. 1, 1989, p. 17; K. Khubiev, "Kooperativy, arenda, sobstvennost'," *Ekonomicheskaya gazeta*, No. 2, 1989, p. 8; V. Cherkovets, "Sobstvennost' i protivorechiya raspredelitel'nykh otnoshenii," *Ekonomicheskaya gazeta*, No. 3, 1989, p. 11; A. Seleznev, "Sobstvennost': gosudarstvennaya i kooperativnaya," *Ekonomicheskaya gazeta*, No. 5, 1989, p. 14; R. Malakhinova, "Sobstvennost': ekonomicheskaya i pravovaya," *Ekonomicheskaya gazeta*, No. 10, 1989, p. 20; and P. Osipenkov, "Sobstvennost': kak preodolet' otchuzhdenie," *Ekonomicheskaya gazeta*, No. 14, 1989, p. 10.

   [36] *Pravda*, April 27, 1989.

   [37] *Voprosy ekonomiki*, No. 4, 1989, pp. 92-100.

rental enterprises and cooperatives to be greatly expanded. The recommendations at the end of the conference included the prescription of two criteria of socialisticity that would set some limits to possible changes. One is the usual requirement of social guarantees. The other is that there should not be any exploitative relations or classes without rights of ownership over (productive) wealth. These are vague and adjustable limits. The limitations of what has so far been implemented are, on the other hand, considerable.

IMPLEMENTATION

The developments in Soviet ownership arrangements in practice can be summarized—leaving the most interesting till last—under five headings: individual labor activity, shares, leasing, intellectual property, and cooperatives. Joint ventures with foreign firms are omitted.

Individual labor activity was encouraged by a law published in November, 1986.[38] The law permits the licensing of individuals to operate small-scale businesses, primarily in the service sector, using family labor only, and with the further restriction that no fit person of normal working age can be engaged full-time in such a venture. A list of activities in which these small family businesses may operate is provided, but there is scope for local authorities to license individual labor activity in additional areas. The licensing is normally to be for up to five years, though local authorities can at their discretion allow some unlicensed individual business. There are fees to be paid for the licenses, and the level of fees is set by the republics.

Many black-market entrepreneurs must have chosen not to register. The advantage of registration is that one has official approval for one's activities. There should be less chance of getting into trouble and less need to pay bribes for protection. The disadvantage is that one will be taxed, will have to pay for the license, and cannot be sure of being picked on by the local authorities at some future date. It is hard to conduct a small family business in the Soviet Union without breaking the law in order to acquire materials, premises, etc. The local authorities (often hostile) and the centralized supply system, between them, make it difficult to avoid this. There also cannot be much confidence that the present encouragement from on high will continue and be transmitted down the hierarchy to the local Party. Therefore registration does not necessarily do away in practice with the requirement to pay bribes.

---

[38] *Izvestia*, November 21, 1986, and commentary by I. I. Gladkii, the chairman of the State Committee for Labor and Social Problems, *Pravda*, November 20, 1986. The law came into effect on May 1, 1987. The data on numbers engaged, given below, are from *Ekonomicheskaya gazeta*, No. 47, 1988, p. 6, and *Pravda*, April 27, 1989.

Family leasehold farming raises some different issues (see below under "Leasing"). In the nonfarm sector individual family businesses, at least as a registered activity, have been swallowed up by the cooperatives since the Law on Cooperatives came into effect in mid-1988. By October, 1988, there were already more people officially recorded as engaged in cooperatives than in individual labor activity: 770,000 against 628,000. By April, 1989, there were, officially, 2.7 million people engaged in the two sectors together (of whom 1.6 million had more than one job); of the 2.7 million, the great majority must be cooperative members and cooperative employees.[39]

Shares. In his concluding speech that he gave at the conference held in Vladimir, Abalkin referred to the issue of shares as one of the ways in which the alienation of workers might be overcome. It appeared what that he had in mind was the issue of shares only to employees of the organization issuing the shares. His argument was that a worker with shares in his enterprise had more control over the use of "his" assets than he would have over the use of funds he had paid in tax or put into the State Savings Bank. Shares (*aktsii*) have indeed been issued by both cooperatives and state enterprises. It is not yet clear, however, what the limits are to the spread of this device.

The Law on Cooperatives envisages the issue of shares by cooperatives, and state enterprises can also issue shares. Shares can be issued by cooperatives to their members, to their nonmember contract employees, to state enterprises and probably to other cooperatives.[39] The "shares" envisaged in the Law on Cooperatives are debentures: they are to have a fixed nominal value, a fixed term, and a yield set by the cooperative. The intention appears to be that the return can vary according to performance. The value of the shares probably cannot, since they can only be sold back to the cooperative, presumably at their nominal value. The Supreme Soviet decree on the introduction of the law said that detailed regulations on shares would be provided by the Council of Ministers. The law itself specifies that local financial authorities must vet cooperatives' share schemes.

For cooperatives, the principle is recognized that the income of cooperative members is governed by the size of their capital contribution, as well as by their labor. Formal share schemes, however, have not got very far—or at least had not done so in the early stages of the cooperatives' development.[40]

---

[39] Professor Leonid Bazil'evich of the Leningrad Financial-Economics Institute has developed a business game that shows, among other things, why cooperatives tend to absorb individual labor arrangements.

[40] L. Nikiforov, "Obshchee i lichnoe: novye formy svyazei," *Ekonomicheskaya gazeta*, No. 8, 1988, p. 17.

The issue of shares to workers in state enterprises had been discussed in 1987 and, occasionally, in earlier years. As long ago as 1980 Popov had even advocated the issue of shares to the general public.[41] There have been several experiments with share issues by state enterprises to their workers in the past two years or so and some preliminary regulations on share issues in general. The usual idea is that payments of dividends on worker shares in state enterprises should come from the enterprise bonus fund (which is one segment of the enterprise's post-tax profits). This has been criticized on the grounds that it is merely a relabeling of the standard bonus arrangement (presumably, though, with the difference that what each individual gets will depend in part on the size of his shareholding). Some have argued that such schemes are too narrow and that personal savings can best be tapped by the issue of shares to all comers.[42] That is not yet legal, however—or at least, not yet clearly legal.

Usually, the size of share issues is regulated so that it is not large in relation to enterprise capital. In the cooperative law it is laid down that share issues should not "usually" exceed the value of annual sales. Practice with respect to state enterprises seems to be to set lower limits than this. Over time, a state enterprise or an enterprise leased by its work force from the state could nonetheless come to replace state-owned assets by employee-owned assets. If new equipment is treated as being purchased by share issues while older equipment written off is treated as the state's, the enterprise could come to be seen by its work force as their own property. (See under "Leasing" below.) This prospect, like the growth of cooperatives, worries those who oppose "group property" and "group egoism."

Like many other ownership issues, the question of limits to share-issuing awaits legal clarification. The Soviet Union will probably have to follow Poland and Hungary in reinstating company law and creating a legal framework for joint-stock companies. Meanwhile, employee share schemes seem to be of limited importance.

Valerii Rutgaizer, the most active promoter of leasing schemes, nonetheless links worker shares with leasing (see below). He wants to see workers holding equal shares in their enterprises, the value of which can be paid to them on retirement. "Dividend" income would be allo-

---

41 Gavril Popov in *Pravda*, May 24, 1980.

42 F. Klugman, "Aktsionernyi trest: pochemu by i net!" *Ekonomicheskaya gazeta*, No. 48, 1987, p. 16; review of readers' comments, "Lichnye sredstva—v kopilke predpriyatiya," *Ekonomicheskaya gazeta*, No. 7, 1988, p. 7; Leonid Grigorev, "Becoming Shareholders," *Moscow News*, No. 34, 1988, p. 11; E. Babek, "Chimkentskie dividendy," *Ekonomicheskaya gazeta*, No. 5, 1989, pp. 18-19. The preliminary guidelines on the issue of shares were published in *Ekonomicheskaya gazeta*, No. 45, 1988, p. 23.

cated in proportion to labor income. It is possible for enterprises to set up joint ventures on a share basis—for example, the Leningrad Innovation Bank, which is jointly owned by several state enterprises and open to participation by cooperatives and universities.[43] Again the legal framework is not clear. New banking laws are among the many legislative requirements. Banking expertise is also needed. The only people with such skills, by and large, are the Soviet international bankers who have worked abroad—for instance, in the Moscow Narodnyi Bank.

Leasing. The Soviet word *arenda,* usually translated as "rent" or "lease," has been one of the most fashionable new words in the Soviet reform debate. Like other overworked words, it has many meanings, all of them foggy. The word is used in two different sectoral contexts, agriculture and the rest of the economy, and at two different institutional levels. In the farm sector it is used for a variety of schemes in which the lessor (*arendodatel'*) is usually the state or collective farm and the lessee (*arendator*) is variously a family or some other group of employees of the farm in question. A law on leasing is supposed to be presented to the USSR Supreme Soviet by July 1, 1990. A recent Supreme Soviet decree provides the framework for leasing in the meanwhile. It seems to be mainly concerned with arrangements in the farm sector.[44]

According to that decree, lessees can be state, cooperative, or individual labor concerns or groups of citizens. The duration of the lease can be "from five to fifty years and for a longer period of time." This marvelous legislative fudge is still further fudged by an additional stipulation that in some circumstances the lease could be for less than five years. If the lessee dies within the term of the lease, it passes to one of the group (e.g., a household) working with him at the time of his death. On the expiration of a lease, the lessee and family members working with him have first claim on a renewed lease on the property in question. (Estonian legislation provides specifically for land to be leased to a farming family in perpetuity. That is clearer but may be in conflict with the USSR legislation.)

For the farm sector, Gorbachev himself and many of the reformers came during 1987-88 to put increased emphasis on the leasing of land to families. In his speech to the Collective-Farm Workers' Congress in March, 1988, Gorbachev said that leases for up to fifty years were desirable. He referred to the rapid growth in food production in China

---

[43]   "Risk—bankovskoe delo," *Ekonomicheskaya gazeta,* No. 34, 1988, p. 5.

[44]   "Ob arende i arendnykh otnosheniyakh v SSSR," *Ekonomicheskaya gazeta,* No. 16, 1989, p. 4. For comments, see John Tedstrom and Philip Hanson, "Supreme Soviet Issues Decree on Leasing," *Report on the USSR,* No. 17, 1989, p. 17.

that followed when "they gave the land to the families" (*oni dali sem'yam zemlyu*)—a remarkable formulation, not reproduced in the *Pravda* text of the speech.[45]

Controversy among the chattering classes has focused on the extent to which this policy should be pursued. Should state and collective farms in general be disbanded, or should leasing be encouraged within them, with perhaps limited and selective abolition of state and collective farms in a few areas where they work particularly badly? The argument of the radical reformers is that only a few Party bureaucrats responsible for rural areas have a real interest in the preservation of a structure of over-large state and collective farms. These giant farms have been a disaster, the reformers argue. As long as they remain, any leasing agreements that they make with groups of their workers will not be freely negotiated between equal partners; instead they will dictate terms to the lessees. These terms will include prices, supply of inputs, and probably delivery of output. The pessimists go on to argue that peasant skills and peasant culture have been destroyed, at least in the Russian Republic, and that even under better conditions, there would be no takers for the new leasehold peasant farms.

A more constructive reform view is that the way forward is to liberate the state and collective farms by giving them the independent status of the new cooperatives. This is envisaged in the Law on Cooperatives but is not happening. It would mean that they would decide independently what and how much to produce in the light of state purchase prices. Along with this, the proposal is to convert existing state and collective farms into loose associations of smaller cooperatives and family farms.[46] Policy so far has stopped short of this.

The issue is of enormous political importance because of food shortages. Many people think, reasonably enough, that the Soviet people should not need both to import about one-tenth of their calorie intake while subsidizing their own food production to the extent of about one-tenth of GNP and to have food queues and food rationing on top of that. It is true that Western Europe and the United States have large and wasteful food subsidies, but in the first place they are nowhere near as large as the Soviet subsidies, and in the second place

---

45 *Radio Moscow*, in Russian, 1130 GMT, March 23, 1988.

46 See, for example, Vladimir Tikhonov, "Time for Land Reform," *Moscow News*, No. 32, 1988, p. 10; roundtable (including Tikhonov), "Budet li u zemli khozyain?" *Izvestia*, December 20, 1988; V. Efimov and T. Kadyrov, "Kolkhoz—assotsiatsiya kooperatorov," *Izvestia*, April 5, 1988; Vasilii Belov, "Vozrodit' v krest'yanstve krest'yanskoe," *Pravda*, October 22, 1988; and writings by Strelyanyi cited earlier. For an excellent analysis of the limitations on the present *arenda* schemes, see Karl-Eugen Wädekin, "Agriculture," in M. McCauley (ed.), *The Soviet Union under Gorbachev*, London, Macmillan, forthcoming.

they have at least stimulated overproduction. When Boris El'tsin, at the Congress of People's Deputies, revives the slogan of 1917, "Land to the peasants!" he probably knows what he is doing so far as political resonance is concerned.[47]

The paradox is that in the Russian countryside there is strong resistance to the land being handed back to the peasants. This is partly a matter of obstruction by the local authorities. For example, in Vologda Oblast the state and collective farms and the local authorities assigned only the poorest land, and broken-down animals, to the local *arendatory*, charged them exorbitant rents, and starved them of supplies into the bargain. What is more, their reports of the number of leases granted (probably at the end of 1988) showed 37,284, while their internal records showed 1,023.[48] Similar stories are so widely reported the suspicion arises that reports of exaggerations are themselves exaggerated. Still, the pattern is predictable and basically convincing: top-down imposition of unfavorable terms, followed by malign neglect.[49]

What should be equally worrying for the reformers is the evidence of hostility from many Slavs to those of their number who take on (or worse, are told by the farm boss to take on) a family leasehold contract. There is, to cite but one example, the pathetic story of the Yakushik family, on a Belorussian farm. They reluctantly bowed to pressure from above to take on a family leasehold dairy farm. Having done so, they started making more money and producing milk at a lower cost than the rest of the farm. They were boycotted by their neighbors, who "created a vacuum around them" and made them miserable.[50]

The reformers argue, probably correctly, that five peasant families will produce more than 1,000 workers on a giant state farm. One snag is that any change towards peasant farming makes rural officials look as though they have been taking money under false pretenses for years. Another snag is that this is also true for literally millions of state farm and kolkhoz workers. That would not matter if most of them were keen to take risks on becoming their own bosses; but that does not seem to be the case, at least in the Soviet heartland.

Outside agriculture, leasing has been at two levels. First, there is the leasing of some equipment by a small group of employees from their enterprise, with contractual arrangements to deliver output to (usually) the lessor. Second, there is the leasing of a complete enterprise by its

[47]   *Izvestia*, June 2, 1989.

[48]   V. Filippov, "Arendnye mify," *Izvestia*, February 5, 1989.

[49]   E.g., E. Rostrukhov, "Kot v meshke dlya arendatorov," *Izvestia*, August 30, 1988; V. Konovalov, "Arendu zashchitit zakon," *Izvestia*, May 15, 1989.

[50]   N. Matukovsky, "Zavist' i len'," *Izvestia*, August 8, 1988.

work force, usually from the superior ministry. (Several Soviet writers have pointed out that ministries are not the legal owners of all-people's property and should not figure as the *arendodateli* in these arrangements. Nevertheless the arrangements reflect the realities of the traditional system.) The first of these two arrangements seems to be little more than a variant on group piece-rate schemes. The second is more interesting.

The guidelines for leasing enterprises were published in August, 1988.[51] The practice started earlier. Valerii Rutgaizer, now a deputy director of Zaslavskaya's All-Union Center for Public Opinion Research, began to develop the idea in the early 1980s.[52] Initially, Rutgaizer worked with Estonian officials. In 1987 the idea was applied to some Moscow state catering establishments.[53] At the end of 1987 it was extended to industry, and specifically to a number of building-materials works in the Moscow region. By the spring of 1988 there were about 100 rental enterprises in the Moscow area.[54]

In many cases it has been chronic loss-making enterprises that have been leased by their work forces. This was the case with one of the most widely quoted examples: the Butovsky building-materials *kombinat*. It is also the case that the pioneer enterprises were under local authorities rather than branch ministries. Part of the appeal of the idea, probably, was that the financial burden might be unloaded on the workers themselves; but it is also clear that these arrangements are seen as involving less independence, less risk, and less effort than turning a state enterprise into an independent cooperative. The relationship of the lessee to the lessor is such that the latter can guarantee supplies of materials in a way that nobody could to a free-standing cooperative outside the state planning system.[55] During 1988 the pattern altered. More successful enterprises chose to go for leasing from their ministry. They included the Orsk-Khalilovsk Metallurgical *kombinat* near Orenburg, with a work force of 25,000; the *Soyuzelektroset'-izolyatsiya* association with a work force of 16,000; the Frunze Science-Production Association at Sumi, with a work force of 22,000; and the Research Institute of Microsurgery of the Eye, with a

51   "Arenda gosudarstvennogo predpriyatiya trudovym kollektivom," *Ekonomicheskaya gazeta*, No. 36, 1988, p. 17.

52   V. Rutgaizer, "Voz'mi zavod v arendu," *Izvestia*, May 17, 1988, and *idem, Arenda predpriyatiya*, Moscow, Znanie, 1989.

53   V. Tolstov, "Chudesa arendnogo podryada," *Izvestia*, April 30, 1988.

54   E. Figurnov, "Novyi tip khozraschetnykh otnoshenii," *Ekonomicheskaya gazeta*, No. 22, 1988, p. 5.

55   M. Bocharev, Yu. Gradzion, "Arendnyi podryad beret kombinat," *Ekonomicheskaya gazeta*, No. 25, 1988, p. 16; M. Krushinsky, "Ob arende, riske i sotsial'nykh garantiyakh," *Izvestia*, August 17, 1988.

staff of 1,250.[56] These are individual cases with different features. Yet, a new category of enterprises leased by their staff can be detected—namely, privileged concerns.

The entrepreneurial and well-connected Svyatoslav Fedorov, director of the Institute for Microsurgery of the Eye, earns (and keeps) a good deal of hard currency. He presents his rental arrangement as real worker-ownership, voted unanimously by the members of the collective. His scheme has a share element in it: all the staff pay an equal share (442 rubles, or about two months' national-average wages) towards the first half-year's rental of the institute from the Ministry of Health. Those who leave will be repaid their shares, and all, he argues, stand to benefit in future years. At Sumi, the deal is one in which the association continues to receive targets from above. In fact, some 90 percent of its capacity usage continues to be specified in some detail by state targets.

The advantage of these rental schemes seems to be that they limit (in principle) the amounts the superior authority can take from the enterprise's net earnings. The enterprise typically gains only a little more freedom about what it does; but it should have more confidence in its ability to retain a predictable net income—a net income, moreover, that is positively related to its overall performance. These arrangements, in other words, are a way of securing against the arbitrary depredations of the superior ministry. To that extent they encourage more efficient use of resources to make a given product-mix, because they increase confidence that increased earnings will be retained. That is precisely what "the long-term stable normatives" of the 1987 Law on State Enterprise (and similar arrangements introduced in 1971) were supposed to achieve and did not.

Advocates of leasing such as Rutgaizer, Popov, and Pavel Bunich envisage a greater degree of independence than this. They fear that the law on leasing to be prepared for 1990 will be a compromise. In other words, it will leave the *arendator* fundamentally subordinate to its higher authority. They want arrangements that will promote allocative as well as x-efficiency. They see this coming from a market environment in which the negotiation of leases will be more like a negotiation between equals. They want the *arendatory* to be free to make their own decisions on the allocation of net income between investment and labor bonuses. They also want work collectives that lease state enterprises to

[56]   M. Krushinsky, "Ob arende"; P. Bunich, "Bez polumer!" *Ekonomicheskaya gazeta*, No. 20, 1989, p. 14-15; V. Moskalenko et al., "Sumsky NPO: novyi eksperiment," *Ekonomicheskaya gazeta*, No. 47, 1988, pp. 12-13; "Rubl' silen oborotom," interview with Moskalenko, *Izvestia*, March 22, 1989; S. Fedorov, "'My pochuvstvuem sebya nastoyashchimi khozyainami!'" *Izvestia*, June 14, 1988; and author's conversation with Fedorov in Birmingham, October 5, 1988.

be able to create their own "collective property" in the enterprise, building it up through worker shares and bank loans until they own the enterprise.[57] The problem at present is that all market-like innovations are hard to develop within a system that is still hierarchical and that still has centrally controlled prices, output targets, and centralized supply allocation.

Intellectual property. Efforts are under way to change fundamentally the Soviet patent law. "Efforts" is the right word, because several drafts were prepared and then stifled in recent years before a draft law "On Inventive Activity in the USSR" was published in January.[58] The published draft immediately stirred up more public controversy. The crucial change envisaged is as follows. Previously, the inventor's certificate gave the person to whom it was awarded some guarantee of reward for his invention. This was set at 2 percent of "the estimated economic effect"—a value that was hard enough to calculate in an administrative economy for cost-reducing process innovations and impossible for product innovations. Regardless of controversies over the amount due to an inventor, the existing system gives the inventor no control over the use of his invention. Once certificated, it is public property within the USSR and can be used by anyone. The new draft law would turn the inventor's certificate into a Western-style patent, giving the patentee the right to control the use of his invention.

That should mean that the inventor will be able to negotiate with alternative would-be users of his invention and charge what the traffic will bear for its use. Controversy in the Soviet Union centers on two points. First, the arrangements prescribe joint patenting between the individual inventor and his enterprise or research institute with respect to inventions made on company time; second, the fact that the economy is not yet a market economy means that marketing an invention is not yet an activity that fits in with the way the economy works.[59] Still, however flawed the details of the draft may be, the key idea of the new draft law is, from the point of view of ownership reform, a striking

---

57 V. Rutgaizer, "K razrabotke zakona ob arende," draft, June, 1989. I am grateful to Valerii Rutgaizer for permission to cite this unpublished draft. Rutgaizer's concerns about the legislation are summarized in his article "Kollektivnaya sobstvennost'," *Ekonomicheskaya gazeta*, No. 27, 1989, pp. 4, 6.

58 "Ob izobretatel'noi deyatel'nosti v SSSR," *Ekonomicheskaya gazeta*, No. 1, 1989, pp. 18-22.

59 See, "V Sovete ministrov SSSR," *Izvestia*, June 20, 1988; N. Yakovchuk, "Sovmin sovetuetsya s izobretatelyami," *Ekonomicheskaya gazeta*, No. 26, 1988, p. 4; S. Leskov, "Izobreli zakon ne dlya izobretatelei," *Izvestia*, February 21, 1989; and Yu. Boshitsky and V. Lalo, "Klyuchevoi vopros: sobstvennost' na izobretenie," *Ekonomicheskaya gazeta*, No. 5, 1989, p. 15.

one—the creation of intellectual or industrial property in the Western
sense of private property. Even where the patentee or co-patentee is a
state enterprise, this characterization of the draft still stands: the patent
would be the private property of that enterprise, and not of the state as
such.

Cooperatives are the subject of a separate contribution to this volume, so remarks about them here will be confined to placing their
development in the context of the whole array of ownership changes
being attempted in the Soviet Union. They are the only new ownership
forms so far established in the USSR that are both legal and outside the
centralized system of economic administration. More precisely, freestanding cooperatives are outside the administrative system; cooperatives attached to (*pri*) a state entity are not. Partly for this reason and
partly because they are widely seen as scandalous rip-off merchants,
the freestanding cooperatives are the most controversial of all the new
ownership forms.

The Law on Cooperatives of June, 1988, is better drafted than other
Soviet reform legislation. It is also strikingly radical. It puts no ceiling
on the size of cooperatives. It does leave room for some restrictions on
their sphere of activity, and this is a loophole that was soon exploited by
government decrees proscribing several activities and imposing some
price controls[60] even though the spirit of the original law was that only
activities criminal in themselves, such as unlicensed production of
firearms and narcotics, would be proscribed. The decree of December,
1988, proscribing cooperative production of most cultural artifacts and
most medical services, was a piece of counterlegislation from whose
drafting the cooperative members themselves and the radical reformers were excluded; it was the work of the executive and represented, in
the view of the reformers, the interests of the censorship and of a
Ministry of Health frightened of competition.[61] The law allows fit
people of normal working age to work full-time as members of cooperatives, something that had not been allowed for individual labor activity.
It also allows members of cooperatives to employ nonmembers as contract employees. The ratio of members to employees is usually stipulated in the cooperative's statute and is presumably subject to some sort
of monitoring by local authorities. Unofficially, it is said that ratios of
1:2 or 1:3 are common, but one Moscow café is known to have four
members and thirty employees. The law seems to favor part-time
contract employees without clearly proscribing full-time employees.
Statistical reporting does not distinguish between contract employees
(*dogovorniki*) and members, so the extent to which cooperatives are in

---

[60]   *Izvestia*, December 31, 1988, and February 3, 1989.

[61]   "Chto govoryat spetsialisty o novom postanovlenii po kooperatsii,"
(roundtable), *Izvestia*, January 19, 1989.

effect private partnerships employing full-time contract staff is unknown. It is believed that at the start of 1989 about 60 percent of all those engaged in cooperatives were employees (both full- and part-time).[62] In short, a cooperative can be a private employer.

The law proclaims cooperatives' equality in law and prestige with state enterprises. The reformers argue that the subsequent counter-legislation restricting cooperatives' activities is contrary to this provision. In a political system with a separation of powers, this point could be pursued in the legislature or the courts or both; so far, the reformers have had to rely on media campaigns on the issue. The law also protects cooperatives against interference by state agencies and allows them to issue shares and to engage in foreign trade. All of this is a remarkable departure from past Soviet doctrine and practice.

The rapid growth in numbers of people engaged in cooperatives has been mentioned. Apparently, at the end of the first quarter of this year, on a full-time-equivalent basis, just under two million people were engaged in cooperatives and individual labor activity, the great majority in the former. The collective farms, which are legally producer cooperatives, remain a separate category, under de facto state control. The legislation, could, however facilitate their assimilation to the same conditions as the new cooperatives. That would mean their liberation from the system of compulsory procurements. It would be a historic change.

The cooperatives that are most visible are the cafés. For this reason they are also the most vulnerable to popular resentment for their high prices. The development of cooperatives in recent months has been away (relatively) from services to the population and towards business services, including research and development, management consultancy, and software. There are some (probably only a few) medium-sized manufacturing cooperatives, such as the "Shtamp" engineering cooperative in Moscow, reportedly with a work force of 1,000, and an electrical equipment works with a work force of 1,500—450 members and 1,050 *dogovorniki*.[63]

The advantage of cooperatives is that they are outside the administrative system. That is also their main disadvantage. On the one hand, they can hire and fire as they choose, enter and leave markets as conditions indicate, and (with some restrictions) set their own prices. Given the extreme disequilibrium of all Soviet markets, it is not surprising that they can pick on the shortages, charge high prices, and make

---

[62] A. Glushetsky, "Kooperativ: trudovye otnosheniya," *Ekonomicheskaya gazeta*, No. 17, 1989, p. 9.

[63] V. Loshak, "Two Thousand and One Laws," *Moscow News*, No. 31, 1988, p. 12; and Romanyuk, "Kooperativ vykupaet zavod . . . ," *Izvestia*, February 27, 1989.

high incomes. In mid-1988 average earnings in cooperatives were said to be 50-100 percent higher than earnings for comparable work in state enterprises.[64] On the other hand, the cooperatives are usually starved of material inputs, have trouble finding premises, and are liable to be charged exorbitant prices by state suppliers. They therefore often break the law in getting supplies and are vulnerable to harassment by the authorities. They often have to spend a lot on bribes, and this means that their costs can be high.

Typically, a freestanding cooperative is vulnerable to supply problems, hostility from local officials, customers' resentment of its high prices (if it is selling to the population), and the pressure of bribe-seekers and criminals running protection rackets. (Presumably, the racketeers do not expect state enterprises to be such soft targets.) Perhaps most fundamentally, nobody can be sure that the Party line will not shift back against such nonstate entities. The temptation to make a quick profit in one market and move on to another must be great, and the inducement to make long-term investments must be correspondingly weak.

Despite these drawbacks and despite the lack of entrepreneurship commonly attributed to Russians, the numbers of cooperatives and the range of their activities have grown fast. One reason for this must be the obvious one—that they offer the prospect of high earnings. A less obvious reason is the freedom they offer from petty intervention in one's life by Party and other officials in a workplace in state employment. Pressure, for example, to accept a security clearance when his work did not require it encouraged one researcher to move to a cooperative research outfit "where there is no government and no government secrets."[65] A less encouraging reason, for those who favor market reform, is that many cooperatives are not freestanding but are attached to state enterprises; in this capacity they are close to being another variety of group piece-rate arrangement; by hiving off one of its activities into an attached cooperative, a state enterprise can get around controls on its wage bill and find ways of paying some of its staff more. The February decree strengthening price controls attempts among other things to stop the practice of paying cooperatives from the social-cultural and other non-wage-bill funds of state enterprises. A final reason that has been suggested for the rapid growth of cooperatives is more reassuring: the desire to do a job well without being impeded by officious idiots.[66]

---

[64] L. Kunel'sky, "Kooperatsii—dinamizm razvitiya," *Ekonomicheskaya gazeta*, No. 34, 1988, p. 12.

[65] D. Frenkel', "Pochemu ya vstal v kooperativ," *Vek XX i mir*, No. 10, 1988, pp. 6-7.

[66] Romanyuk, *op. cit.*

CONCLUSIONS

What are the circumstances that favor a further evolution of the Soviet Union towards a mixed economy? One is clear: there is a strong logic that leads from market-socialist reforms to reforms of ownership or, to put it another way, from creating a product market to creating factor markets. Like the Hungarian and Polish reforms, the Soviet reform process shows that the search for enterprise independence and competitive product markets leads away from traditional state ownership. In the Soviet case, it has led to both leasing and cooperatives, and the latter are often private firms employing contract labor.

A subsidiary influence working in the same direction is the eclecticism and open-mindedness with which Gorbachev himself and heavyweight reformers like Abalkin and Bogomolov approach the question of ownership. They are obviously reluctant to close off any options. They may not represent, in this matter, a majority of the Soviet population, but they do seem to represent a larger part of the socially active citizenry than many had thought. The traditional system is a deader duck for more Soviet citizens than most outside observers used to suppose. The strength of the pressure for reform is indicated by the experimental introduction of cooperatives in the defense sector.[67] The open-mindedness is closely connected with knowledge of the outside world. For many reformers a "normal" society seems to mean, not to put too fine a point on it, a Western one.

The obstacles to the growth of the nonstate sector are simply the obverse of these favorable factors. To begin with, the economic weaknesses that prompted the desire for reform in the first place have become more pronounced since the reforms started; they provide powerful reasons for pulling back on reform in general and ownership reform in particular. The greater part of the economy remains state-owned and centrally administered. Independent nonstate enterprises have shown some capacity to grow in this hostile environment, but as they grow they are associated with faster inflation, increased economic crime, and reduced control over resources for the central planners. Jacek Rostowski observes of Hungary and Poland that, in at least a long early stage, the growth of a legitimate nonstate sector is not at the expense of the black economy; rather, the two tend to grow together. This seems to be true for the USSR as well.

Decontrolling prices and supply allocation would help the nonstate sector, but worsening inflationary pressure is tending to delay any such decontrol. In this situation, it is not surprising that the government

---

[67] A. Isaev, "Reform i oboronnye otrasli," *Kommunist*, No. 5, 1989, pp. 24-31.

imposes additional restrictions on the nonstate sector. The fixed hostility of many officials is an additional obstacle, regardless of whether decontrol threatens economic destabilization.

The lack of both the expertise and the infrastructure to support a modern mixed economy is itself an obstacle. Mundane things like income tax returns, decent economic statistics, a modern telephone network, and electronic bank transfers are needed. So are slightly less mundane things like company law, management accounting, and ordinary banking skills. The recently announced intention of replacing the state enterprise and cooperative laws (and possibly the Law on Individual Labor Activity) with a single law on the socialist enterprise, and also of introducing a law on joint-stock companies, is promising.[68]

Walter Laqueur wrote several years ago about the curious durability of modern social systems. History has no examples of modern industrial states whose social orders have been radically transformed in a short space of time, except through war. One reason for this, presumably, is that social upheaval is unpleasant. Indeed, it seems that the fundamental obstacle in the way of the Soviet Union becoming a mixed economy is that a very large number of people believe they would lose from the change. A few of those people would be powerful conservative leaders who do not want to lose their power and who see, probably correctly, that it is linked to state ownership. A larger number are middle-level officials whose functions would disappear in a market economy. The majority are, though, probably ordinary people who fear change. The creation of a real market economy would entail many people being forced to move from one job to another, quite likely with a spell of unemployment in between. In a competitive environment most people would in the long run be better off, but they would on average have to work harder and worry more about their work. To people who are used to it, the price of prosperity may seem worth paying. To many people who are not, socialism may well seem the better choice.

---

[68] Final resolution of the Congress of People's Deputies on economic policy, *Ekonomicheskaya gazeta*, No. 23, 1989, pp. 1-6; speech by Ryzhkov to the Supreme Soviet, *Izvestia*, June 27, 1989.

5

Lessons from Eastern Europe

Vladimir Sobell

No SURVEY of *perestroika* in the USSR would be quite complete without giving some special attention to the experience of Eastern Europe with reform and without making some attempt to view that experience synoptically and provide a frame of reference for comparisons with it. Towards that end, two propositions will be presented and briefly discussed here.

The first is that the East European experience is transferable to the USSR mainly in an indirect and negative way. If that experience is useful at all, then it is so primarily as a guide to what should not, rather than what should, be done. The second is that half-hearted market-oriented reform or "market socialism" is a proven dead end and that the USSR would therefore be well advised to avoid halfway-house compromises and continue to supplement economic reforms with political reforms, which East European reformers avoided until very recently.

An overview of the East European reformist experience should perhaps begin with some idea of just what is being reformed. It is customary to depict the traditional Soviet-type economic system either in terms of institutional characteristics—that is, as a bureaucratic structure with a national planning agency at the top and individual enterprises at the bottom—or in terms of operational chartacteristics—that is, as an administrative process in which the center attempts to regulate the behavior of enterprises. It is then assumed that a reform of the system aims at minimizing the irrational and wasteful aspects of enterprises' performance and at promoting economically rational responses; the more market-oriented the system becomes, it is thought, the more likely that economically rational responses will predominate.

There is no reason to quarrel with this approach, but it may be more illuminating to place the emphasis not so much on the system, its institutions, and behavioral patterns as on its legacy. The Soviet, Hungarian, and Polish reforms have, after all, come at a time when the task is not simply one of changing or abolishing the traditional system but of somehow overcoming the disastrous legacy that system has bequeathed.

THE LEGACY OF THE SOVIET-TYPE SYSTEM

Taking the position espoused by the Polish economist Jan Winiecki to its logical conclusion,[1] it might be argued that some hundred years from now (maybe sooner) the Soviet-type system will be remembered mostly as an arrangement that brought economic mismanagement and distortion and disequilibria of all kinds rather than beneficial industrialization, economic growth, and the provision of welfare. To be sure, the system generated impressive growth in the early stage of its history, but it is now accepted in both the East and the West that this was growth of the wrong kind—today the CMEA countries are stuck with industries that drag them down economically and that consume rather than produce welfare.

In this view, the traditional Soviet-type system signifies, above all, the displacement of the market by the Party and its ideology; hence it fosters distortion of prices and ultimately lopsided industrial development. In comparison with the economies of other industrial countries, all CMEA economies display a common (and specific to them) tendency to generate overdevelopment of the industrial sector (and within that sector, of heavy industry) and underdevelopment of the consumption (consumer industries) and tertiary sectors. These economies have virtually no competitive high-technology industries and lack adequate infrastructure with respect to communications. A realist might go so far as to say that the system can be called "economic" only because it manages national resources but that, strictly speaking, it should be called "diseconomic" because national resources are systematically mismanaged rather than managed.[2]

---

[1]   Jan Winiecki, *The Distorted World of Soviet-Type Economies*, Pittsburgh and London, University of Pittsburgh Press and Croom Helm, respectively, 1988.

[2]   Those who consider this judgment too harsh should reflect on the following. Apart from the well-known disparities in the standard of living between the East and the West, it is known that the CMEA countries consume about twice as much energy and raw materials per unit of gross domestic product (GDP) as do the Western nations; that their productivity is about 40 to 50 percent of the Western levels and their exports hopelessly uncompetitive; and that they generate several times more pollution per unit of GDP than do Western countries (as *The Economist* is fond of saying, the CMEA industries are distinguished only by the amount of pollution they manage to churn out).

Distortion and lopsidedness in the structure of the economic sphere have led to corresponding imbalances in the structures of the political and social spheres. These structures have been reinforced over time, and there are enormous vested interests in maintaining them. Even if the command system that created them were to be destroyed, they would persist and continue to follow an economic illogic of their own. Inflationary overhangs resulting from the years of forced savings (or, as in Poland, a flight from the domestic currency) and widespread addiction to subsidization stand in the way of a smooth transition to market equilibrium and thus undermine the prospects for market-oriented reforms.

If this admittedly broad interpretation of the situation in the CMEA countries is accepted, it can be understood why it is so difficult to abandon the Soviet-type system once it is put in place. It also becomes obvious that the East European and Soviet establishments must contend not so much with systemic economic reforms as with potentially explosive political issues.

THE REFORM-RESTORATION CYCLE

East European reformism has a history dating to the mid-1950s, when the malfunctioning of the centrally planned system first became manifestly intolerable. As is known, all East European countries embarked at various points on reforms of varying degrees but eventually returned to a slightly altered *ancien régime*; in the case of Hungary and, to a lesser extent, Poland the restoration was less complete than in the remaining CMEA countries. It is possible to see the situation as a cycle consisting of three steps. First, the ruling elite became increasingly conscious of the dysfunction of the system and decided to do something about it. Because a decentralizing reform (and a partial revival of the market) was the only alternative, it ventured on "a market reform." Second, the reforms soon generated unwelcome side effects such as open inflation (or imminent prospects of inflation), "excessive " income in the private and cooperative sector, and a lack of control over the economy (for example, unrestrained investment by enterprises). Moreover, they began to threaten the bureaucratic and worker interests vested in the old system. Third, a retreat to the orthodox system followed.

As already indicated, the retreat was not always total and the old regime not always fully restored; however, any changes that were carried over tended to be superficial or attenuated and, in any event, failed to break the back of the centrally planned system—operational distortions (artificial prices) continued to exist, and structural distortions (loss-making industries) remained intact. The reformist pioneer Hungary replaced its command mechanism by a system relying on indirect and informal bureaucratic controls but with heavily regulated markets.

Nevertheless, the lessons of half-hearted reform have not been altogether lost: the reformers have realized that it is necessary to move from markets in limited spheres such as agricultural produce to markets in capital and labor. In the 1980s Hungary has proceeded to experiment with fiscal and monetary controls in place of normative arrangements, and has attempted to break up the traditional "monobank" financial system. An embryonic stock market is now operating in Hungary. In contrast with other member-countries of the CMEA, Hungary has the semblance of a genuinely entrepreneurial culture. (The same is true of Poland, but Polish entrepreneurship is channeled mainly into black markets.)

It is worth noting that in the past the inevitability of the reform-restoration cycle was ensured by rigid Soviet hegemony over Eastern Europe and the circumstance that this hegemonic power was in the hands of Leonid Brezhnev, the overseer of what is now in the USSR called "the period of stagnation." Whenever reforms in Eastern Europe approached a juncture at which their logic pointed towards radicalization and spillover into the political sphere, the Soviet leadership under Brezhnev moved to prevent such a development. The reforms were never permitted to reach a "critical mass," when the country in question would break through the cycle and propel its economy irrevocably towards a market-based model. It is only since Gorbachev that this external constraint seems to have been removed.

In a nutshell, this is the reformist experience of the East European countries. By examining in greater detail the cases of each East European country[3] (and China), significant variations as well as specific lessons might be discovered that would have some applicability to the Soviet Union, and very likely that is what Oleg Bogomolov and his colleagues at the Institute of Economics of the World Socialist System are busy trying to do. It is doubtful, though, that such variations or specific lessons would be more important than the primary lesson—that is, the inefficacy of the reform-restoration cycle. The impression is that so far Gorbachev has backed off from this lesson—witness the clampdown on the cooperatives. The question is whether he can afford to back off. Here the East European experience is instructive.

Reforms or Post-Communist Liquidation

The reform-restoration cycle in Eastern Europe has been accompanied by a progressive decline in rates of economic growth. The CMEA economies exhausted most of the factors of "extensive" growth in the 1960s. Because their Soviet-type systems remained essentially unmodi-

---

[3] For a recent survey, see Jan Adam, *The Economic Reforms in the Soviet Union and Eastern Europe since the 1960s*, New York, St. Martin's Press, 1989.

fied (and hence failed to switch to an "intensive" model of growth), these economies eventually stagnated in the 1980s. Their technological backwardness became increasingly glaring as the developed Western nations accelerated the communications revolution and as Western economies became uncoupled from their energy and raw-materials bases.[4] The solution of last resort—i.e., massive imports of Western technology on credit—was tried in the 1970s but failed to reverse the decline, instead sowing the seeds of the present-day crisis.

The moral of this story is rather tragic: it seems as if the cycle can only be broken when the economies in question are close to complete collapse, when the ruling *nomenklatura* really has no other way out, and when the vested interests (workers as well as bureaucrats) can no longer collect their "rent" from the existing system because the economies are de facto bankrupt. In an article entitled "Prosperity Undercuts *Perestroika*"[5] the Czechoslovak economist Karel Dyba was quoted as saying, clearly with Poland and Hungary in mind, that "it is easier to reform in a situation of near-total collapse than in a situation of mere stagnation."

Thus, what is now going on in the so-called reforming countries of the CMEA—Poland and Hungary (but also Yugoslavia)—is not so much a reform but a desperate attempt to engineer economic recovery, or what optimists might call "postcommunist reconstruction." Heavy indebtedness, open inflation or hyperinflation (in Poland and in Yugoslavia), chronic shortages of virtually everything (in Poland), and a lesser-developed-like backwardness after forty years of pseudo-industrialization, are the dominant concerns of the authorities.

Under these conditions, it is not quite accurate to speak of reforming the economic mechanism because there is so little left to be reformed. The old mechanism and the old industrial structures are immobilized and, given the need to service foreign debts, resolute liquidation of these structures ought not to be delayed. What is called for is an immediate termination of subsidies to the most inefficient enterprises and entire industries, closures of enterprises that cannot be modernized, privatization of viable enterprises, and promotion of the private and cooperative sector. Western assistance by means of debt-relief, relaxation of barriers to East European exports to the West, and direct injection of Western capital through joint or fully foreign-owned ventures are required for economic regeneration.

Radical proposals for a rapid transition to capitalism and reintegration with the Western economies along these lines emerged in the summer of 1989. One such plan, reportedly adopted at that time by the trade union Solidarity and the communist-ruled government of

    4   Peter F. Drucker, "The Changed World Economy," *Foreign Affairs*, Spring, 1986.
    5   *Christian Science Monitor*, June 20, 1989.

Poland envisaged the following measures. The government would hand all Poland's state-owned assets to a liquidating agency: this agency would reorganize the assets into joint stock companies and proceed by looking for buyers of capital. About a third of these assets would be put into trusts for debt service; the trusts would be managed by Poland's creditors, who would have the right to hold or sell the shares. The plan also foresaw the immediate termination of subsidies, the setting of a realistic exchange rate for the zloty, and the tying of the currency to the ECU. Most prices would be allowed to find their own level, and wages and social benefits would be fixed for between six to twelve months. After that, wages would be subjected to collective bargaining, and social benefits would be indexed to the cost of living. The entire scheme would, of course, have to be assisted by the the International Monetary Fund (IMF) and backed by Western governments. Six billion dollars in the form of new credits from the IMF and the International Bank for Reconstruction and Development and a reduction of interest payments would be required over a period of three years from the start of the plan.

Solidarity's takeover of power in August, 1989, signaled that a radical break with the communist past in the spirit of these proposals was in the cards. Indeed, the new government wasted no time in starting to negotiate an agreement with the IMF aiming at nothing less than a historically unparalleled Western-assisted transition from a (collapsed) Soviet-type economy to capitalism.

Hungary was heading in the same direction. A committee set up by the Central Committee of the Hungarian Socialist Workers' Party and headed by Ivan Berend released a report in May, 1989, entitled "Proposal for a Three-Year Transformation and Stabilization Program." Apart from expansion of private enterprise and the opening of the economy to the West, the report called for a change from state ownership to "common ownership forms" and the sale of state enterprises to organizations such as banks and insurance companies, other enterprises, and private individuals, including foreigners. State enterprises whose stocks could not be sold would be transferred to a newly established agency—the State Stock Fund (SSF). The SSF would be state-financed so the enterprises concerned would continue to be owned by the state. According to the plan, however, they would receive no preferential treatment, and the SSF would expect to receive some dividends on its stocks. The proposal also called for decreasing subsidies to enterprises from the present 200 billion forint to at least 120 billion by 1992, which would mean a reduction of 70 percent in real terms. It was estimated that Western investment of 1 billion to 1.5 billion dollars would be required over the next three years.

The "de-communization" of Hungary, most pointedly illustrated in the creation of a new Socialist Party from the ruins of the ruling Socialist Worker's Party in October, 1989, suggested that, as in Poland, a radical shift to a Western-style market economy and political pluralism was imminent. The Soviet reformers are bound to follow the outcome of these frightening but necessary experiments in Poland and Hungary with keen interest. It is unlikely that in the long run the USSR can avoid heading in the same direction.

6

The Reemergence of Soviet Cooperatives

John E. Tedstrom

As PART of Lenin's concessions to market economics during the early years of Bolshevik rule, cooperatives played a key role in revitalizing the war-torn Soviet economy. They remained a significant element in the economy up to and including 1960, even though their contribution to total output had decreased over time.[1] In recent years, Soviet leader Mikhail Gorbachev has taken a number of concrete steps to reestablish the cooperative as a legitimate component of the Soviet economic system, beginning with a Politburo statement in support of the cooperative movement in February, 1987.[2] Since that date, cooperatives have become one of the most controversial parts of the current Soviet program for economic restructuring. The hope is that cooperatives, through ownership incentives, will contribute to economic revitalization both by raising static efficiency of production and distribution and by encouraging technological development. Thus far, however, the revived Soviet cooperative movement has encountered strong (sometimes violent) resistance, and its future is far from secure.

Both support for, and resistance to, the cooperative movement can be found at all levels of Soviet society, making it a politically complex and sensitive issue. There is little agreement on whether, or to what extent, the cooperative movement is compatible with Soviet socialism. Traditional Soviet doctrine on prices, incomes, taxes, ownership, labor, and equality are all directly challenged by the existence of cooperatives. For these reasons, promotion of the cooperative movement has given rise to serious political, social, and economic tensions in the Soviet

---

[1]   While cooperatives contributed some 13 percent of total Soviet industrial production in 1928, by 1960 they were contributing about 5 percent. See Alec Nove, *The Soviet Economy*, New York, Frederick A. Praeger, 1961, p. 28.

[2]   "V Politburo KPSS," *Pravda*, February 6, 1987, p. 1.

Union that threaten the pace, if not the viability, of *perestroika*. At this juncture, the revived Soviet cooperative movement is still quite young. Data are sparse, and experience in monitoring the movement's development is limited. Still, it is possible to examine the way in which the Soviet cooperative movement has taken life, to draw some preliminary conclusions about its current status, and to take stock of its initial contribution to the Soviet economy.

FROM A TYPE OF MICROSOCIALISM TO A TYPE OF MICROCAPITALISM

Regardless of the political and economic environment in which cooperatives emerge, they almost invariably have a number of features in common. These are worth calling attention to as background for the particularized discussion of Soviet cooperatives that follows. Mario Nuti has helpfully grouped the generally shared characteristics of cooperatives into three categories:[3]

- *Self-management.* Members have exclusive participation in decision-making, with each member having an equal vote—either directly or indirectly through representative organs—on all medium- and long-term issues such as labor organization, employment (size of membership), income distribution, investment levels, and finance. Only day-to-day management is left to executives, who implement decisions based on the policies of the labor collective. A circular structure of authority (from members upwards, to representative organs and managers, and downwards again to members as employees) thus replaces the traditional hierarchical structures of the capitalist and socialist enterprises.

- *Income-sharing.* Members participate in the distribution of net income (net value added less capital rentals and interest on loans), also on equal terms except for the quantity and quality of labor services contributed by them and their relative contribution (if any) to enterprise capital. Thus, members draw an entrepreneurial income—i.e., a residual income after contractual fixed obligations have been met. Together, self-management and income-sharing give members the complete and exclusive role of entrepreneurs.

---

[3]   Mario Nuti, *On Traditional Cooperatives and James Meade's Labour-Capital Discriminating Partnerships*, Working Paper, No. 88/337, Florence, European University Institute, 1988, pp.1-3.

- *Social capital.* There are usually restrictions on the distribution of capital to members, at least for internally financed capital accumulation (which in Yugoslavia, Nuti points out, is called "members' past labor"); these restrictions are often accompanied by others on the payment of interest on members' capital contributions when they exist. Such restrictions originate in the historical roots of cooperatives as mutual societies.

Although these characteristics of cooperatives will differ in detail in every society, Nuti emphasizes their fundamental reliance on standard socialist premises such as democratic planning, egalitarianism, and he justifiably describes them as creating a type of "microsocialism."

During the period of the New Economic Policy in the 1920s, cooperatives occupied a place alongside the state sector and, indeed, were considered a "socialist" alternative to the true private sector, which Lenin revitalized but which always lacked the full confidence of the authorities and, in time, came to be increasingly vilified.[4] In the Soviet Union today, however, such features of cooperatives as non-state control over the means of production, decentralized prices, capitalist employer-employee relationships, and high incomes relative to the national average actually create a type of "microcapitalism." While distinguishing the revived Soviet cooperative movement from its antecedent, it is precisely this phenomenon that has succeeded in generating a good deal of hostility towards cooperatives and, by extension, *perestroika.*

A DIFFICULT START

A decree on the development of new forms of cooperative enterprise adopted by the USSR Council of Ministers early in 1987 set some basic guidelines for the formation and operation of cooperatives.[5] The decree was, however, not effective in preventing local authorities from impeding the development of the cooperative movement. The Soviet press was filled with letters and stories about the difficulties Soviet entrepreneurs faced when trying to establish cooperatives. Often, local officials would not allocate facilities for cooperatives; or, if facilities were allocated, they were often unsuitable for the kind of under-

---

[4] See, among others, Alec Nove, *An Economic History of the USSR,* London, Penguin Press, 1969, Chapters 4-6.

[5] *Sobranie postanovlenii SSSR,* No. 10, 1987, pp. 195-222. See Viktor Yasmann, "Obstacles in the Way of the Cooperative Movement," *Radio Liberty Research Bulletin,* RL 343/87, August 28, 1987.

taking proposed. Moreover, in places where local authorities were inclined to support the establishment of cooperatives, they were often at a loss how to go about it. Moscow apparently failed to pass on the necessary concrete instructions and rules and regulations. This created a good deal of confusion and frustration for everyone involved.[6]

As a result, the pace of development in the cooperative sector was not impressive. By January 1, 1988, some 23,000 cooperatives had been registered with the authorities in the entire country, but even that low figure somewhat overstates the true situation at the time. As of late April, 1988, only about 14,000 cooperatives, employing some 156,000 people, had actually begun to operate. The rest were waiting for facilities or refitting the facilities they had been allocated. The total spent on cooperative-produced goods and services in the Soviet Union during 1987 is estimated at 350 million rubles.[7] The output of cooperatives in the same year accounted for only 0.03 percent of total consumer-goods production in the Soviet Union. In the catering sector, the share was 0.3 percent; and in volume of marketed consumer services, only 0.5 percent. Speaking of the year 1987, Prime Minister Nikolai Ryzhkov has claimed: "On the average, across the country, consumer services worth 25 kopecks per person were rendered by cooperatives." This works out to about 70 million rubles for consumer services, meaning about 280 million rubles were spent by Soviet consumers on cooperative-produced goods. Ryzhkov went on to say: "In Azerbaijan, Kirgizia, and Turkmenistan the figure was under 10 kopecks. Only in Estonia did these services come to more than 3 rubles." The prime minister then contended that if the cooperatives were to make a significant contribution, these figures would have to increase by ten-fold or in some fields 100-fold.[8]

To help obviate the numerous obstacles the cooperative movement was facing, a draft law on cooperatives was published in March, 1988.[9] This law was intended to be much more comprehensive and resolute than the earlier decree. It was hoped that the draft law would create a

---

[6]   On this, see Prime Minister Nikolai Ryzhkov's speech to the USSR Supreme Soviet, *Sotsialisticheskaya industriya*, May 25, 1988, pp. 1-3.

[7]   According to an interview with Gelii Shmelev, section chief at the Institute of Economics of the World Socialist System, in *Trud*, April 24, 1988, p. 1. These figures were subsequently confirmed by Nikolai Ryzhkov in his opening address to the Supreme Soviet, *op. cit.*

[8]   Ryzhkov's speech to the USSR Supreme Soviet, *op. cit.*

[9]   *Izvestia*, March 6, 1988, pp. 2-5. *O kooperatsii v SSSR*. Literally, this translates as "On Cooperation in the USSR," not "On Cooperatives in the USSR." The title was no doubt chosen because Lenin addressed the issue in an article entitled "O kooperatsii."

more favorable environment for the cooperatives and that, in turn, their number would multiply and their contribution to the Soviet economy increase.[10]

IMPACT OF THE DRAFT LAW ON COOPERATIVES

While the draft law did go a long way towards improving the economic environment for cooperatives, a number of problems were not resolved either in theory or in practice. These difficulties were fully revealed in an open debate over the cooperative movement that took place both in the specialized economics literature and in the Soviet news media. Three broad, interrelated areas of difficulty can be identified from the debate: the lack of concrete legislation guaranteeing the rights of cooperatives, cooperative-state relations, and a mixed and skeptical public attitude towards cooperatives.

Lack of Concrete Legislation. Because the draft law was only a draft, it carried no legal weight. Local authorities who continued to impede the cooperative movement were therefore not subject to legal prosecution. A good deal of bureaucratic foot-dragging and (especially at the local levels) outright resistance to the movement tended to go unchecked as a result. Would-be Soviet entrepreneurs simply had no legal recourse. This question would be resolved with the formal adoption of the law by the Supreme Soviet. The other sets of problems—cooperative-state relations and public opinion—would not be so easily settled.

Cooperative-State Relations. There were three main issues with respect to cooperative-state relations. First, the intended relationship between cooperatives and official organizations such as local soviets was open to interpretation. While the draft law claimed that cooperatives had only to register with these local bodies, it was clear that in reality most cooperatives were having to gain either explicit or implicit *permission* to become established. Confusion also existed over how closely bound kolkhoz cooperatives would be to the central agricultural bureaucracy and to state orders (*goszakazy*). Second, there was great concern over the issue of prices. It was not clear to what extent cooperatives would be able to determine their own prices freely or to what extent the state would prevent them from charging "excessive prices" as mentioned in the draft law. Third, many cooperative managers complained that most of the Soviet supply network was still controlled by Gossnab (State Supply Committee), making it difficult for cooperatives (which operate outside the plan unless they are under contract or attached to a ministry or state enterprise) to get supplies.

---

[10] For an extensive analysis of the draft law, see Philip Hanson, "The Draft Law on Cooperatives: An Assessment," *Radio Liberty Research Bulletin*, RL 111/88, March 15, 1988.

Public Attitudes towards Cooperatives. Since the reemergence of cooperatives in the Soviet economy, the public attitude towards them has been quite mixed. On the one hand, reports in the Soviet press have, even at this early stage, indicated that many cooperatives were doing a brisk business and that cooperative markets were full and busy. On the other hand, there were (and are) many letters and editorials in the press opposing cooperatives on both economic and ideological grounds. The complaints made most often were (and are) that prices charged by cooperatives are excessive and that the high incomes usually earned by cooperative members contradict the socialist concept of equality.

Because public support for cooperatives was seen as important for their successful development, the authorities moved quickly, if not decisively, to address some of the public's concerns and to bolster support for the cooperative movement. On April 1, 1988, a new, progressive income tax scheme for cooperatives became effective. The marginal income tax rate was as high as 90 percent on income over fifteen hundred rubles per month. (See the discussion of taxes below.) Instead of increasing support for cooperatives, however, the new tax scheme only served to fuel the debate. Many officials, as well as economists, felt that the taxes were too steep and would lower entrepreneurial incentives. (Not incidentally, this was also the predominant view among Soviet entrepreneurs.) In an interview with *Trud*, Gelii Shmelev openly advocated revising the tax rates downward, and his opinion was subsequently supported by other well-known, reform-minded economists such as Abel Aganbegyan and Nikolai Shmelev.[11]

In sum, a good deal of controversy surrounded the draft law on cooperatives. The draft was scheduled to be ratified by the USSR Supreme Soviet at its session from May 24 to 27, 1988. Surprisingly, given the previous reputation of that body for rubber-stamping legislation, the bargaining and debating over a number of the draft's points continued up to the last minute, and some of the problems were resolved while others were not.

RATIFYING THE NEW LAW ON COOPERATIVES

The version of the draft that Prime Minister Ryzhkov presented to the Supreme Soviet indeed took into account many of the opinions and proposals advanced subsequent to the publication of the draft in March. Still, on a number of controversial issues, a consensus had not yet been reached. Ryzhkov reported that forty-two out of the law's fifty articles had been revised to one extent or another before the draft was finally

---

[11]   *AP*, May 27, 1988.

ratified.[12] The way in which many of these issues were finally resolved seems to have been a precursor of subsequent Soviet attempts to develop legislation democratically, so it seems important not only to examine the final complexion of the new Law on Cooperatives but also the process by which the law came into being, with particular attention to several provisions of the draft law that the deputies to the Supreme Soviet felt would serve to impede the development of the cooperative movement.

Cooperative Independence. One of the most contentious issues at the Supreme Soviet session was the guarantee of independence from the state for cooperatives. This was underlined by the heated debate over kolkhoz cooperatives' independence, which seems to have been resolved only the night before Ryzhkov's speech to the full Supreme Soviet on May 24. The debate took place in a joint session of the Commission for the Agroindustrial Complex and the Commission for Legislative Proposals of the USSR Supreme Soviet.[13] In the original version of the draft law, Article 31 made a reference to state orders for kolkhozes and other agricultural cooperatives. Members of these cooperatives feared the language was so vague that local authorities could use Article 31 to strip cooperatives of their independence from the state. A number of variants of the article, which included the words "state order (*goszakaz*)" but which also stressed the voluntary nature of cooperative-state relations, were proposed. Because many delegates were concerned that even a voluntary state order would ultimately become a mandatory state command, however, those proposals were defeated. The final version of Article 31 contained no mention of state orders whatsoever and thus was not an obstacle once the draft was presented to the Supreme Soviet.[14]

Prices. In addition to the change in Article 31, there were also changes in the original text on prices. Ryzhkov declared in his speech that violating the law of supply and demand aggravates "speculative and other negative phenomena in the market" and went on to assert that, through the formation of cooperatives on a broad scale, conditions of competition would be created in the socialist market that, in turn,

---

[12] See "Proekt odobren," *Izvestia*, May 24, 1988, p. 3. This article implies in its conclusion that some further action might be taken during the Supreme Soviet. See also Ryzhkov's speech to the USSR Supreme Soviet.

[13] See "Proekt odobren."

[14] See the chapter by Karl-Eugen Wädekin in this volume, "Is There a 'Privatization' of Soviet Agriculture?" Much of the credit for this victory in principle for the kolkhozes must go to Aleksei Ponomarev, chairman of the Commission for the Agroindustrial Complex, who led the successful campaign and was selected to make the final presentation of the full draft law to the Supreme Soviet for ratification.

would retard inflation. In principle, therefore, cooperative prices were to be essentially free-market prices. There were important exceptions, though. First, centrally determined prices were to apply when a cooperative sells output in fulfillment of a state order. Second, such prices were also to apply when a cooperative uses state-supplied natural resources to produce its output. Finally, centrally determined prices were to form the basis of retail prices when a cooperative sells products acquired through the central allocation system.

It is clear from Ryzhkov's language that there was in fact to be a mixture of free-market prices and centrally determined prices. What is important to understand here is that, through a varied application of the provisions for centrally determining prices, the state could either directly or indirectly create incentives or disincentives for cooperative production. For example, because of state subsidies on many inputs, cooperatives could be compelled to sell at lower-than-market prices. This would tend to make production less profitable. Through manipulation of prices, the state would still be able to influence the mix of goods and services offered by the cooperative sector. Moreover, many cooperatives have found it convenient to associate themselves with state enterprises (because of better access to space, machinery, and equipment and because of having a sure buyer of their products), with the result that they are not nearly as independent of the state sector as they might have hoped to be. Prices were thus only one of the aspects of their business operations that cooperative managers found were strongly influenced (if not outright controlled) by the traditional state economic bureaucracy.

Supplies. The revised draft law also tried to take account of the trouble cooperatives were encountering in acquiring supplies from the Soviet supply system. Stating that this was the cooperatives' most important problem at the moment, Ryzhkov claimed in his speech that 84 percent of the cooperatives in Moscow Oblast were having "considerable difficulties" in obtaining supplies. Ryzhkov's long-term solution was for the cooperatives to become involved in all phases of production including the mining and processing of raw materials. In the short term, he asserted, Gossnab must become a more effective supplier for the cooperatives. Both of these proposals were unrealistic. As for the first, although there is no legal limitation on the size of cooperatives, they are clearly intended to be small- and medium-sized affairs, primarily oriented towards supplying the Soviet retail market with goods and services.[15] Moreover, it is highly unlikely that any significant presence of cooperatives in the extractive industries can or will emerge soon. For one thing, cooperatives' influence over resource allocation, prices, and goods distribution in such key sectors of the economy is

---

15   See below, under "Role of Cooperatives and Areas of Activity."

probably not on the leadership's wish list for *perestroika*. It is also doubtful whether the cooperative sector could become strong enough to finance ventures in the capital-intensive primary industries in the near term. Even if it could, it is doubtful whether the cooperatives would be able to take advantage of the economies of scale necessary for profitable production in those and similar industries. As for Ryzhkov's suggested short-term solution, when Gossnab cannot satisfy centrally planned needs within the state sector, how can it be expected to supply cooperatives effectively? Supply problems are likely to be one of the chief complaints of cooperative managers for quite some time.

Taxes. Taxes were another issue that led to heated debate. In his speech to the Supreme Soviet, Ryzhkov implied that the question of taxes was still not fully resolved. That the goals of the tax policy had been clearly developed, though, was apparent from his statement that "flexible tax policy is a reliable tool for regulation in the hands of the state. It makes it possible to stimulate production of goods for which there is increased demand and to restrict production of other goods that are less necessary." Ryzhkov also asserted that progressive taxes help to keep prices low. Although he did not elaborate on how he reached that conclusion, what he probably had in mind were tax breaks for those cooperatives that sell their goods and services at state-sector prices. Finally, with respect to the scale of taxes, Ryzhkov indicated that "decisions will be made according to the interests of the cooperative movement and the principles of social justice in society."[16]

The tax scheme that raised so many objections was a fairly straight-forward, progressive one, with increasing marginal taxes assigned to income over 500 rubles per month. The average wage for blue- and white-collar workers in the Soviet state sector was 217 rubles per month in 1988. The average wage for cooperative employees was about 2–2.5 times that amount, and the marginal tax on incomes between 501 rubles per month and 700 rubles per month was to be 30 percent, for example (see Table 1).

Besides this, a tax was assigned to cooperatives' profits. The tax on profits was much lower than that on members' incomes in order to encourage profits to be reinvested into the cooperative instead of distributed as wages. Still, it could be stiff. The law stated that, in the first two years of its existence, a cooperative would pay between 2 percent and 5 percent of its profits in a flat tax. At the end of two years, that tax would be raised to 10 percent. Moreover, 12 percent of the profits were to go to social insurance and, on average, 10 percent towards the formation of a fund for "the industrial and social development of the cooperative."[17]

[16]   Ryzhkov's speech to the USSR Supreme Soviet.
[17]   *Argumenty i fakty*, No. 18, 1988, p. 8.

Table 1
INCOME TAX ON COOPERATIVE MEMBERS' INCOMES
(ORIGINAL VERSION, REJECTED BY USSR SUPREME SOVIET IN MAY, 1988)

MONTHLY INCOME RUBLES	TOTAL TAX
Up to 500	Same rate as that established for the income of blue- and white collar workers.
501-700	60 rubles, 20 kopecks + 30% of the amount over 500 rubles.
701-1,000	120 rubles, 20 kopecks + 50% of the amount over 700 rubles.
1,001-1,500	270 rubles, 20 kopecks + 70% of the amount over 1,000 rubles.
1,501 and above	620 rubles, 20 kopecks + 90% of the amount over 1,500 rubles.

SOURCE: *Argumenty i fakty*, No. 18, 1988, p. 8.

After Ryzhkov's speech on May 24, disagreements arose in both chambers of the Supreme Soviet over the issue of taxes, and it was announced on May 25 that the vote on the draft law would be postponed. It later became known that at a meeting of one of the commissions of the Supreme Soviet (the commission was not named) some twenty-three deputies had spoken against the draft law, primarily because of their objections to the tax policy.[18] The meeting went on late into the night of May 25, and Politburo members Viktor Nikonov and Georgii Razumovsky were present, as was Finance Minister Boris Gostev, the author of the tax decree.[19] Finally, on May 26, it was announced that a number of revisions had been made in the draft law, including important changes in the tax scheme. For the short term, local authorities were given the power to grant tax breaks and other, similar incentives to cooperatives, their members, and employees (subcontractors) on a case-by-case basis. For the longer term, it was announced that a new law on taxes would be drafted. The new law would take into account the debate during the Supreme Soviet session and would "concern a scale of tax rates that should reconcile the

---

[18]   Aleksei Ponomarev's speech to the USSR Supreme Soviet, *Izvestia*, May 27, 1988, p. 4.
[19]   *Reuters*, May 26, 1988.

interests of the cooperative movement with the principles of social justice in society."[20] Just how the local authorities were, in the meantime, to determine who gets what tax breaks was left unclear.

Despite the temporary delay caused by the debate over taxes, the Law on Cooperatives was unanimously passed on May 26. It is worth stressing that virtually all of the revisions in the new law were in the direction of further liberalization. While there were still a number of issues to be resolved and a number of obstacles to be overcome, this law took its place as one of the most significant elements of Gorbachev's economic reform program.[21]

KEY PROVISIONS OF THE NEW LAW ON COOPERATIVES

Role of Cooperatives and Areas of Activity. As was the case with the draft law, cooperatives were established as one of the fundamental elements of the Soviet socialist economy: "Cooperatives, together with state enterprises (associations) are the main component in the unified national economic complex. Work in cooperatives is honorable and prestigious and is encouraged in every possible way by the state" (Article 1, Point 4). The chief function of cooperatives is to meet the needs of the economy and population for food, consumer goods, housing, technical production, and "to boost the material prosperity" of cooperatives' members (Article 4, Point 1). On the one hand, the law gives cooperatives free reign to conduct any economic activity not proscribed by USSR or republican legislation (the reference to "republican legislation" was not included in the draft law). On the other hand, the law encourages cooperatives to engage in certain types of activities by listing those regarded by the law's drafters as particularly appropriate for cooperatives. This list is fairly long and, in general, involves those sectors of the economy that directly affect people's everyday lives and are thus highly visible.[22] In some cases, (such as cooperative cafés), this visibility would prove to be one of the cooperatives' most important weaknesses.

Types of Cooperatives. Two types of cooperatives are allowed by the law, producer cooperatives and consumer cooperatives. "Producer cooperatives produce goods, products, and jobs, and also provide paid services to enterprises, associations, institutions, and citizens." Con-

---

[20]   Ponomarev's speech to the USSR Supreme Soviet.

[21]   The final text of the law was published in *Ekonomicheskaya gazeta*, No. 24, 1988, pp. 3, 13-18.

[22]   The list includes such activities as everyday services, public catering, housing construction, retail trade, cultural-leisure activities, medicine, transportation services, etc. (see Article 3, Point 2).

sumer cooperatives engage in "trade and consumer services, and the requirements of cooperative members for housing, dachas, garden plots . . . and sociocultural and other services." Although the general distinction between producer and consumer cooperatives is that producer cooperatives engage more in industrial- or wholesale-type activities and consumer cooperatives operate more in the retail sphere, all cooperatives are essentially granted the right to engage in any activity. The law also recognizes what it refers to as "mixed cooperatives," or cooperatives that operate in both the industrial and the service sectors of the economy (Article 3, Point 2).

Legal Protection of Cooperatives' Property. One of the sharpest departures from traditional socialist practice is the guarantee of property rights assigned to cooperatives. The law states that "Cooperative ownership as a form of socialist ownership is inviolable and is protected by the state. It enjoys legal ownership on par with state ownership" (Article 8, Point 1). Essentially, cooperatives are free to do with their property (both material and financial) what they wish. They may sell it, lease it, or transfer or merge it with the property of any other enterprise, organization, or institution or with any citizen's property, as they see fit. An important point in this set of issues is that of cooperative members' claim to their capital contributions. The standard arrangement is such that when a cooperative member leaves the cooperative, his initial and any subsequent contributions are not returned to him. Even when members own shares, they have no claim to any increments in the value of the cooperatives' assets, unless the cooperative is liquidated.[23] This must contribute to higher dividends paid to shareholders in the cooperative than if shareholders had a claim on increments to the value of cooperative assets through the right to redeem their shares.[24]

Cooperative Independence. One of the most controversial issues in the debate over cooperatives was their independence. The law states: "Interference in the economic or other activity of a cooperative by state or cooperative organs is not permitted, save where envisaged by this law." As envisaged by the law, the state's involvement in cooperative

---

[23] See also the chapter by Philip Hanson in this volume, "Ownership Issues in *Perestroika.*"

[24] Nuti makes the point that it could also lead to more frequent "artificial liquidation" of cooperatives because in this case increments in the cooperative's assets *are* distributed based on the proportion of shareholdings. This is probably complicated by the fact that such a liquidation must be agreed upon by all members of the cooperative, not just the shareholders, and certainly those with little or no shares have an incentive to keep the cooperative going so that they can earn current income. See Mario Nuti, "The New Soviet Cooperatives: Advances and Limitations," *Economic and Industrial Democracy,* Vol. 10, 1989, pp. 311-27.

affairs does not extend to oversight of management or operational issues. Rather, the state coordinates plans, collects taxes, and ensures that the cooperative is not breaking any laws. If a cooperative incurs any losses as a result of the fulfillment of directives from the state violating the cooperative's rights, the cooperative shall be "reimbursed by these organs." Any disputes over reimbursement of losses are to be settled either in the courts or by state arbitration (Article 10, Point 2).

The issue of the role of the Party organization in the cooperative was raised in the draft law and also comes up in the law itself. Here again the changes in the text appear to favor the cooperative. The text of the draft reads:

> The cooperative's Party organization, as the political nucleus of the collective, operates within the framework of the USSR Constitution, directs (*napravlyaet*) the work of the entire collective and the trade union, Komsomol, and other public organizations, and monitors the activity of the cooperative's board (chairman) (*pravlenie* [*predsedatel'*]).[25]

When the law was passed, the role of the Party organization had been diminished somewhat. The text of the law reads:

> The cooperative's Party organization, as the political nucleus of the collective, operates within the framework of the USSR Constitution, facilitates (*sposobstvuet*) raising the productive initiatives and social activity (*sotsial'naya aktivnost'*) of the members of the labor collective, the growth of their political self-awareness, and the manager's (*khozyain*) sense of responsibility for the results of the activity of the cooperative.

It has been reasonably argued that this wording represents a "dilution" of the Party's power within the cooperative organization.[26] In traditional planning language, it might be called a shift from "directive" towards "indicative" involvement by the Party organization.[27] As far as known, no reports of troublesome interference by the Party organization in the daily management decisions of the cooperative have come to light, which suggests that in practice the average cooperatives' Party or-

---

[25] Article 5, Point 3.

[26] See Mario Nuti, "The New Soviet Cooperatives."

[27] A confusing aspect of the two different passages is the switch from the reference to "cooperative board (chairman)" to "manager." Board chairman is more specific than manager, but perhaps this is in recognition that it is the manager who is concerned with day-to-day operations, while board chairmen tend to focus on questions of policy and are therefore already more closely bound by the cooperative's charter.

ganization is quite weak relative to both the Party organizations of state enterprises and the labor collective and management councils of the cooperatives.

Creation of a Cooperative. Over the course of the life of the draft law, many cooperative managers and would-be entrepreneurs complained about the difficulties they had encountered when trying to set up cooperatives. Ryzhkov also touched on this point in his speech to the Supreme Soviet on May 24, 1988. As mentioned earlier, though the draft law only required cooperatives to register with local authorities, many in fact were having to secure *permission* to become established. Because cooperative managers had no legal recourse, local officials were able legally to impede the formation of cooperatives. The new law states flatly: "The creation of a cooperative is not contingent on any special permission from soviet, economic, or other organs" (Article 11, Point 1). Local authorities need only be satisfied with the legality of the work the cooperative proposes to undertake. If local authorities persist in delaying the establishment of a cooperative, the cooperative can (after waiting for one month) take its case to higher organs (Article 11, Point 4).

Termination of Cooperatives. This is a minor matter, but it underscores the degree of liberalism with which the law was drafted and passed. A cooperative may terminate its activities through merger, amalgamation, subdivision, separation, transformation, bankruptcy, or simple liquidation of its assets. Thus, a cooperative has virtually all of the alternative forms of action available to businesses in the West when they face intractable crises in their markets or in their financial position. The law also states that the local authorities may, if a cooperative is incurring losses on a continuing basis, liquidate the cooperative and dispose of the cooperative's assets in whatever way necessary to repay any bad debts (Article 15, Points 1, 2, and 3). Upon liquidation of a cooperative, any remaining assets (after settling all debts) are to be distributed to the members of the cooperative in proportion to each member's total capital contributions. It should be repeated here that this is the only way that cooperative members seem to be able to derive any "capital gains" on their investment in the cooperative.

Planning. The new law states that cooperatives must draw up their own five-year operating and financial-budgetary plans. These plans are then to be broken down into annual plans. This is to be done "independently," and the plans are to be ratified by a general meeting of cooperative members. The cooperatives are to take into account various kinds of information when formulating their plans. This includes economic information such as prices, perceived demand, supplies, etc. It also includes: "long-term economic norms set by the state, such as price and tariff levels of goods and services produced and sold under contracts for the execution of a state order; tax rates; the interest rate on bank loans; the norms for payment for natural resources; payments for discharging pollutants into the environment; and the norms for deductions paid into the state social insurance fund." The cooperatives' plans are then to be coordinated with relevant local organs. In theory, such coordination is supposed to be a meeting of two equal parties: "The management organ, together with the cooperatives . . . ensures comprehensive coordination of cooperatives' proposals and takes them into account in the plans for the economic . . . development of the region" (Article 18, Points 1, 2, 3, and 4).

Prices. Prices have been another quarrelsome topic in the debate on cooperatives. In his speech to the Supreme Soviet, Ryzhkov clearly outlined a plan for a mixture of market-determined and centrally determined prices.[28] As far as the law is concerned, "Prices and tariffs on production (goods and services) should reflect socially necessary costs for production, consider user characteristics, quality of goods (work, services), and consumer demand. They should be built taking account of the mutual interests of the cooperative, the consumer, and the national economy in general (Article 19, Point 1). Practice has shown that when goods and services are produced entirely with the means of the cooperative itself, prices tend to be set by the cooperative mostly on the basis of its perception of what the market will bear. The law also states that "Competition in the goods (work and services) market should help reduce the cost of goods (work and services) and cut prices (tariffs)" (Article 19, Point 2), which is not a typical construction in Soviet economic legislation. Practice has shown here, however, that a competitive environment, especially with regard to cooperative-state sector competition, has not developed. There are too many scarcities and too few cooperatives in the Soviet economy for that to happen.

On January 5, 1989, the Politburo took action to strengthen central control over all prices, expanding the use of state orders and instructing the State Committee on Prices (Goskomtsen) "to intensify price controls."[29] This action was foreshadowed by a Politburo decision of October 13, 1988, directing the government to draw up measures "to stop the unjustified raising of retail prices" and "to step up monitoring of prices and incomes."[30] If there were any doubts about these pronouncements being largely targeted at the cooperative movement, they were dispelled by the Council of Ministers resolution on prices and price formation of February, 1989.[31] In general, the resolution is a major step backwards on the path of *perestroika,* but it devotes significant attention to the issue of cooperatives' prices in particular, with the aim of

---

[28]   Ryzhkov's speech to the USSR Supreme Soviet, *op. cit.*

[29]   *Pravda,* January 5, 1989. See the foregoing discussion, under "Cooperative Independence."

[30]   *Pravda,* October 14, 1988.

[31]   *Izvestia,* February 3, 1989.

bringing them and state-sector prices closer together. For example, it is "recommended" that enterprises negotiating contracts with cooperatives use prices prevailing in the state sector as their base. There are also stricter controls laid down for cooperatives that are drawing on inputs from the state sector. All the same, to judge by all the complaints in the press and the evidence of cooperatives' higher prices in systematic studies, it would appear that the cooperatives have been able to find ways around most of these obstacles.

Taxes. The most controversial aspect of the debate on cooperatives was the issue of taxes. Although the details of the tax policy are not a concern of this law, a few principles are outlined. Tax rates on cooperatives were to be differentiated on the basis of the type of cooperative and the aim of its activity. The tax rate for a cooperative was to be fixed for a period of five years "to boost its interest in increasing output." Income taxes for cooperative members and employees (subcontractors) would be on a progressive scale. When cooperatives sell their goods and services at state-established prices, their members and employees (subcontractors) would be taxed at the same rate as state enterprise employees. All cooperative tax revenues were to go to local soviets and other local organs that can grant tax breaks to stimulate the development and the production of cooperatives (Article 21, Points 1 and 2). A report carried by *Izvestia* quoted Gostev as saying that a new tax law for cooperatives and their members would be prepared by July 1, 1988, so that it could go into effect with the new Law on Cooperatives. He indicated that the marginal tax rates on members' incomes would be lowered but that the tax on cooperative profits might be raised.[32] Finally, on July 13 Gostev presented his final version of the revised tax law to the Presidium of the USSR Council of Ministers. What Gostev's final tax schedule looked like was never reported in either the East or the West. It was sharply criticized, though, and rejected by the Presidium, which ordered that a new draft be prepared with the participation of specialists, leading scholars, and cooperative members.[33]

It is clear from the debate that there was much pressure to revise the tax code downwards. By how much is not clear, but there have been calls in the Soviet press (by Academician Leonid Abalkin, and others) to abolish special tax rates for cooperatives and tax everyone equally.[34]

---

[32] "Progressivnyi nalog s kooperatorov bydet izmenen," *Izvestia*, May 31, 1988, p. 2.

[33] *Pravda*, July 14, 1988.

[34] See, e.g., "Pri otkrytykh dveryakh," *Sotsialisticheskaya industriya*, July 15, 1988, p. 2, which gives an account of a session of the Presidium of the USSR Supreme Soviet that heard presentations by representatives of cooperatives, academics, and government officials on the topic of cooperative taxes. The session was carried on Soviet television as well.

In fact, a new draft income tax scheme looking very much like the one floated in June, 1988,[35] and applying to all persons, not just cooperative members, has been published by the government. [36] The marginal tax rates are lower than those proposed in the original draft law on cooperatives, but the government surely had cooperative members in view when it was drawing up the new income tax rates. As far as the taxes on cooperative income is concerned, a decree was issued by the USSR Supreme Soviet stating that this question was thereby devolved to republican governments.[37] Subsequently, the Congress of People's Deputies took initiatives to recentralize the responsibility for taxes, but this must be reconciled with all-Union and republican legislation on economic autonomy before a clear tax policy can emerge.

Kolkhozes. The situation of kolkhozes is dealt with at length by Karl-Eugen Wädekin elsewhere in this volume. What needs to be pointed out here is that, essentially, kolkhozes are treated by the law just as any other cooperative with respect to planning, pricing, and property. As for the controversy over kolkhoz independence raised during the recent session of the USSR Supreme Soviet, the law states: "Kolkhozes . . . may on a voluntary basis conclude with enterprises and organizations engaged in the procurement . . . of agricultural output, contracts for the sale of such output, and may also sell it at their own discretion to any other consumers and on kolkhoz markets." The text of the law reads: "Kolkhozes . . . may conclude with enterprises and organizations engaged in the procurement and processing of agricultural output contracts for output supply based on the state order issued to agroindustrial associations . . . [and other] organizations." So it would appear that, in theory, kolkhozes have been freed from mandatory state orders. The prices for these sales are to be determined by market forces, unless the kolkhoz is selling to a state enterprise in fulfillment of a state order. Then the price is to be centrally determined. If the kolkhozes are in reality granted the independence the law indicates (the relevant provisions mentioned are to be found in Articles 33, 34, 35, and 36) and if state procurement orders are kept to a small share of kolkhoz output, this would be a historic turn of events for it would effectively

[35] See *Literaturnaya gazeta,* June 29, 1988, p. 11, and John Tedstrom, "The Tricky Business of Cooperative Taxes," *Radio Liberty Research Bulletin,* RL 329/88, July 15, 1988, for an assessment.

[36] *Ekonomicheskaya gazeta,* No. 17, 1989, p. 3. For an analysis, see John Tedstrom, "New Draft Law on Income Taxes," *Report on the USSR,* Vol. 1, No. 24, 1989, pp. 8-10.

[37] The decree was issued on February 23, 1989. For an example of how one republic approached the problem, see the draft decree of the Latvian Supreme Soviet in *Sovetskaya Latviya,* June 27, 1989, p. 3.

mean the end of procurement. Evidence presented by Wädekin in his contribution to this volume suggests that this has not been the case.

A STEP BACKWARDS?

During the summer of 1988, official action regarding the cooperative movement waned. For the most part, cooperatives were left on their own, suffering relatively less bureaucratic interference than previously. By the end of the year, the size of the cooperative movement had swelled considerably, as Tables 2 and 3 show. The high profile that the cooperative movement had been assigned in the Soviet press did not wane, however, and neither did the controversy over cooperatives' incomes, prices, and even areas of activity. By the late fall of 1988, the cooperatives were still facing considerable resistance from the grass-roots level and even from an increasingly strong organized opposition, referred to in the Soviet press as "a mafia." The reference came into use because of instances in which managers of cooperatives were being exhorted to pay "safe money" and cooperative members and their families threatened with physical harm. Pressure was mounting on the Soviet government to give some kind of official word on the cooperative movement's place and role in Soviet society.

As one of its last acts in 1988, the USSR Council of Ministers issued a decree that would seem to curtail the activities of cooperatives in the Soviet Union.[38] In the weeks following the publication of the decree, a number of Soviet and Western observers commented on it, and all of them characterized it as a severe setback. Soviet officials, however, maintained that the number of cooperatives affected by the the decree was small and that the new measures were meant only to protect the Soviet consumer. Because of the controversy over cooperatives and the mixed reviews they continued to receive in the Soviet press, the new decree raised some serious questions not only about the cooperative movement but also about the status of *perestroika*. In an appendix, the decree forbids cooperatives to engage in the following activities:

- the manufacture of guns and ammunition, dangerous substances, medicines, narcotics, liquor, jewelry, medals and stamps, and icons and other religious objects;

- the provision of medical treatment for patients suffering from—among other conditions—drug addiction, cancer, psychiatric disease, venereal or other infection; surgery, including abortions;

[38] *Izvestia*, December 31, 1988.

Table 2
DISTRIBUTION OF ACTIVE COOPERATIVES BY UNION REPUBLIC AND TYPE OF ACTIVITY
(AS OF JANUARY 1, 1989)

REPUBLIC	TOTAL NUMBER	EVERYDAY SERVICES	PUBLIC CATERING	PRODUCTION OF CONSUMER GOODS	BY-PRODUCT PROCESSING	OTHER
USSR	77,548	23,716	7,583	16,152	2,352	27,744
RSFSR	38,895	12,123	3,479	7,183	1,090	15,020
Ukraine	13,534	4,252	852	2,575	510	5,345
Belorussia	2,518	756	97	354	116	1,195
Uzbekistan	3,226	1,113	423	517	56	1,117
Georgia	2,089	378	403	1,051	35	222
Azerbaijan	1,291	421	255	309	40	266
Lithuania	1,569	379	143	528	70	449
Moldavia	1,644	566	85	324	40	629
Latvia	1,190	453	81	240	32	384
Kirgizia	1,265	413	205	245	40	362
Tajikistan	723	258	130	98	39	198
Armenia	3,616	682	658	1,611	22	643
Turkmenistan	447	200	95	112	26	14
Estonia	969	331	90	164	41	343

SOURCE: *Ekonomicheskaya gazeta*, No. 17, 1989, p. 9.

• the running of lotteries, games of chance, pawn shops, or any enterprise that involves dealing in foreign currency or precious metals;

• publication of scholarly, artistic, or literary material; making, showing, or distributing films or videos; service of the national communications and broadcast networks; running of a school;

• preparation or sale of food products under unsanitary conditions.

A second appendix lists activities in which a cooperative may engage provided it has a contract with a state enterprise, organization, or institution primarily involved in that activity. This list includes:

Table 3
BASIC INDICATORS OF COOPERATIVE ACTIVITY
BY REPUBLIC
(As of January 1, 1989)

REPUBLIC	TOTAL NUMBER	NUMBER OF WORKERS (THOUSANDS)	VOLUME OF PRODUCTION (MILLIONS OF RUBLES)	OUTPUT PER EMPLOYEE	OUTPUT PER COOP
USSR	77,548	1396.5	6060.6	4.3	78.1
RSFSR	38,895	708.2	3325.5	4.7	85.5
Ukraine	13,534	248.8	900.9	3.6	66.6
Belorussia	2,518	43.5	143.1	3.3	56.8
Uzbekistan	3,226	71.6	229.3	3.2	71.1
Kazakhstan	4,572	72.6	275.4	3.8	60.2
Georgia	2,089	32.3	204.0	6.3	97.7
Azerbaijan	1,291	15.8	69.0	4.4	53.4
Lithuania	1,569	25.5	118.2	4.6	75.3
Moldavia	1,644	38.5	158.1	4.1	96.2
Latvia	1,190	28.7	190.5	6.6	160.1
Kirgizia	1,265	15.8	63.5	4.0	50.2
Tajikistan	723	12.5	35.3	2.8	48.8
Armenia	3,616	56.4	223.3	4.0	61.7
Turkmenistan	447	4.8	22.9	4.8	51.2
Estonia	969	21.5	101.6	4.7	104.8

SOURCE: *Goskomstat, SSSR*, Release No. 57, February 20, 1989.

- the manufacture or repair of jewelry made from semi-precious metals or gems; the treatment of secondary or waste materials that contain precious metals;

- the provision of medical treatment (except for those conditions listed above); the organization of health and other types of camps for children;

- the production of perfumes, cosmetics, and other chemicals in everyday use;

- the provision of editorial and publishing services to organizations that have the right to publish; the sale of print matter; the organization of concerts, discos, and other entertainment; the manufacture of reproduction

equipment; the production, circulation, or sale of record-
ings made using various media; lecture activities; and

- the provision of services to foreign tourists.

Does the decree represent a severe curtailment of cooperative activity? Soviet officials claimed that only about one percent of the cooperatives in the Soviet Union would be affected by the decree, so it would
not appear to be a serious reversal for the cooperative movement. It
should also be recognized that many of the activities forbidden in the
first appendix were already illegal in the Soviet Union—the production
of drugs and firearms, for instance. In some cases, the interest of the
public makes regulation perfectly reasonable; indeed similar controls
can be found in all Western countries—for example, with regard to lotteries, gambling, the manufacture of drugs, and sanitary conditions for
food preparation. Other cases reflect perennial concerns of the Soviet
state. One is the prohibition of the production of jewelry containing
precious materials; another is education—for ideological reasons. The
regulations on publishing; video production, sales, and shows; and
manufacture of religious items are noteworthy steps backward for the
Soviet Union insofar as becoming a more open society is concerned, and
this aspect of the legislation reflects the leadership's lingering obsession
with a controlling ideology. Still, it is likely that grass-roots pressure
against this rigidity will produce some type of easing of the regulations
on cooperatives in these fields. It would be fairly easy, for instance, to
regulate video production and shows within socially acceptable bounds
without banning this activity altogether. As for the ban on medical cooperatives, data published by FAKT, a Moscow-based cooperative specializing in business-consulting and market research for the cooperative movement, indicate that the types of services proscribed in the
regulations were not those frequently offered by medical cooperatives.[39]
Since the issuance of the decree, most indications are that the remaining
medical cooperatives are experiencing increasing demand. Whether
these cooperatives are providing illegal services on the side is unknown, but it would seem that the blow to the medical cooperatives,
while serious, was not fatal.[40]

There are good socioeconomic arguments for prohibiting or regulating certain types of business activity. The free market operates on the
principle that, if a customer receives bad service, he will take his business elsewhere, compelling the seller to improve his operation or close

[39]   *Komercheskaya khronika 1988*, Moscow, Mir, 1988.
[40]   See Margot Jacobs, "Are the Restrictions on Medical Cooperatives
Justified," *Report on the USSR*, No. 13, 1989, pp. 9-12, for a comprehensive review of this issue.

down. Sometimes, though, the customer is not able to bring the necessary pressure to bear, and government must intervene to force changes or shut a business down. At this early stage in the process of reform, the Soviet authorities say they are concerned about the rights of consumers.[41] To be sure, citizens have sent torrents of mail to the Soviet press to complain about bad service, high prices, and shoddy products at cooperatives. Soviet cooperatives are legal entities according to the Law on Cooperatives (Article 5, Point 3) and can therefore be sued by injured parties. There is, however, almost no tradition of private litigation in Soviet legal culture, and it may therefore make sense for the state to take upon itself the interest of the public in controlling cooperative activity by regulation.[42] A further consideration is that a number of activities are regarded as the exclusive province of the state in the USSR because they either concern social rights—such as health care and education—or because they have implications for security—such as foreign-trade operations. In short, the regulations do not seem to take away much of what the cooperatives had before and do not therefore seem all that radical.

This is not to deny the serious psychological impact of the regulations. Recent statements by members of the Soviet cooperative movement leave the impression that the new measures represent a big step backwards. Perhaps most telling are the remarks of Vladimir Yakovlev, the president of FAKT, who says that the decision was based on "emotions" and that the government will be forced by economic logic to repeal the legislation. He called the decision "a most unpleasant fact in the history of the cooperative movement."[43] Not to be overlooked, of course, is the possibility that instead of directly doing severe damage to the existing cooperative movement, this decree—and similar ones such as that on price formation and that on cooperative taxes—may tend to increase uncertainty in the market and thus heighten potential entrepreneurs' sense of risk. If additional regulations affecting cooperatives were to be forthcoming, the perceived risk might even increase to a level that would seriously impede further development of the cooperative sector.

Another potential problem lies in the application of the law. For the sake of equity, all cafés and restaurants, for example, should be subject to the same sanitary standards, whether they are cooperatives or state

---

[41] This was the view expressed by almost all official commentators on the new regulations. See *Trud*, January 4, 1989, and *Izvestia*, January 2, 1989, for two examples.

[42] It is worth noting that several cooperative doctors were held "accountable to their patients" even before the new regulations. (*Argumenty i fakty*, No. 48, 1988.) Also, several consumer protection groups have sprouted in the USSR in hopes of giving Soviet consumers more clout.

[43] *AP*, January 18, 1989.

enterprises. But if a cooperative café is unfairly singled out, what legal recourse will it have against administrative rule? Probably not much, though it is very difficult to predict the future course of legislation and legal reform in the Soviet Union and how it might affect business.

Plainly, it is still too early to assess the overall impact of the new regulations on cooperative activities, but the indications are not all negative. The Law on Cooperatives states that cooperatives may participate in any activity save those proscribed by law,[44] and in the changing climate of the Soviet Union today the new regulations may go just as easily as they came. In any case, many of the regulations do little more than formalize previously written or unwritten rules, as noted; and others are prudent measures to ensure the health and safety of the public. Lastly, this may be one more sign that the Soviet legal system is moving away from the maxim that "what is not allowed is forbidden" to "what is not forbidden is allowed." If such a policy were pursued, it would encourage entrepreneurs. For that to happen, however, Gorbachev will have to make it clear that the continued development of the cooperative sector is a top priority for Party and government.

THE STATUS OF SOVIET COOPERATIVES

Where does the cooperative movement stand one year after it was officially rehabilitated? It must be said that, despite many of the obstacles placed in its way, the continued growth of the Soviet cooperative movement has been impressive. As might be expected, the cooperatives have tended to fill in holes (i.e., increasing the supply of goods and services for which there is greatest excess demand) in the state-sector economy. Currently, about one-third of the cooperatives are in the service sector. One in five produces consumer goods, and one in ten is in public catering. This development, while having "positive" effects in the eyes of the Soviet consumer—essentially in easing the shortages of many goods and services—has also led to problems. Because cooperatives have tended to provide goods and services for which there is excess demand, they are generally in a position to charge above-state-sector prices, leading to a perception of increased inflation among Soviet consumers (never mind that people who frequent cooperatives pay less in nonmonetary expenditures because they spend less time queuing). This, coupled with high incomes of cooperative employees, the sometimes dubious quality of cooperative goods and services, and independence from the state tend to create an image of cooperatives as more or less negative phenomena in the eyes of many Soviet consumers. Indeed, because of opposition to the cooperative movement at all levels of Soviet society, its future development is far from certain.

---

[44] See above.

In 1988, cooperatives produced goods and services worth about 6 billion rubles, as compared with only 350 million rubles in 1987. Nearly half of the total in 1988 was earned in the production of consumer goods (1.5 billion rubles) and through the rendering of everyday services (1.3 billion). By the end of 1988, cooperatives contributed about 1.0 percent of total Soviet national income and 0.4 percent of consumer-goods output.[45] Part of the reason that cooperatives' share of total Soviet output has grown as quickly as it has is because many cooperatives are not really new enterprises but former state enterprises that have been taken over—either wholly or in part—on leasing or on other arrangements by a cooperative collective (often a group of employees of the former state enterprise). This practice became especially popular in the last quarter of 1988, and it was responsible for the creation of 37 percent of the total number of cooperatives that year, which produced a staggering 57 percent of total cooperative output for the entire year. The explanation for this lies partly in the fact that cooperatives that are attached to (pri) a state enterprise tend to be larger and have easier access to equipment and inputs through the "sponsoring" state enterprise or ministry than totally independent cooperatives. The overall growth rate for cooperatives looks even higher for 1989. By the end of the first quarter, the total number of cooperatives in the USSR was over one hundred thousand, and their total output was valued at slightly more than 4.3 billion rubles.[46]

The highest growth rates by type of cooperative were registered by those in the spheres of science, engineering, medicine, and other social services. Their share in the total number of cooperatives increased from 7 percent to 29 percent over the year; the share of their employees increased from 9 percent to 35 percent; and they produced 27 percent of total cooperative output. This is indicative of a general movement of cooperatives towards the business sector, where they are less visible and hence less vulnerable to public hostility, and where they can have privileged access to facilities and supplies.

Regionally, the most dynamic development of the cooperative movement has taken place in the Baltic. In Latvia, the value of all goods and services produced by cooperatives equaled about seventy-one rubles per person, and in Estonia, sixty-four rubles per person. Armenia and Georgia were next with about sixty-eight and thirty-seven rubles per person respectively.[47] (See Table 4.)

---

[45] That is an impressive jump from 1987, when they produced only 0.1 percent, and 0.03 percent respectively.

[46] *TASS*, as reported by *Radio Moscow*, June 30, 1989.

[47] *Ibid.*

Table 4
PER CAPITA PRODUCTION OF COOPERATIVES
(As of January 1, 1989)

Republic	Population ('000)	Coops per 1000 Population	Volume of Realized Production*	Output per Capita (rubles)
USSR	286,717	0.27	6,060.6	21.14
RSFSR	147,386	0.26	3,325.8	22.57
Ukraine	51,704	0.26	900.6	17.42
Belorussia	10,200	0.25	143.1	14.03
Uzbekistan	19,906	0.16	229.3	11.52
Kazakhstan	16,538	0.28	275.4	16.65
Georgia	5,449	0.38	204.0	37.44
Azerbaijan	7,029	0.18	69.0	9.82
Lithuania	3,690	0.43	118.2	32.03
Moldavia	4,341	0.38	158.1	36.42
Latvia	2,681	0.44	190.5	71.06
Kirgizia	4,291	0.29	63.5	14.80
Tajikistan	5,112	0.14	35.3	6.91
Armenia	3,283	1.10	223.3	68.02
Turkmenistan	3,534	0.13	22.9	6.48
Estonia	1,573	0.62	101.6	64.59

Source: *Pravda*, April 29, 1989; and *Gokomstat SSSR*, Release No. 57, February 20, 1989.

* In millions of rubles.

CONSUMER DEMAND AND COOPERATIVES

FAKT has produced a study of "demand" for various types of goods and services from cooperatives based on the number of telephone inquiries it receives during a given quarter.[48] At the beginning of 1988, cooperatives specializing in apartment exchanges were most in demand, claiming 25 percent of all calls in the first quarter of the year. Over the course of the year, calls of this nature dropped off, and by mid-year

[48]   The "demand" measured by FAKT here is the demand for information about cooperatives in a given field, and not the demand for a cooperative or its products. For example, it is likely that the most popular cooperatives are so well known that their "demand" as measured by FAKT would be low. Still, in the absence of more appropriate data, the FAKT data are useful as rough guides.

comprised only 8 percent of all calls. By the end of the year they had risen slightly, to 13 percent. Demand for cooperative cafés showed a similar trend, dropping from 8 percent in the first quarter to 3 percent by the end of the year, mostly because of higher prices and their high visibility in society.

Indeed, cooperative cafés got off to a quick start in late 1987, but, despite a doubling of their number during 1988, their share in the total number of cooperatives fell from 22 percent to 10 percent by the end of the year, and their share of total cooperative output from 25 to 6 percent. The explanation for this is that many cooperative cafés have higher operating costs than do state-sector cafés. A number of factors are involved here. First, cooperatives tend to take over already profitable state cafés. This tends to lead to high contract (*dogovornye*) wholesale prices of equipment and more expensive leases (otherwise, there is no incentive for the state enterprise to give up the café), and they are forced to pass on these costs to consumers. In addition, cooperative cafés must buy their food and supplies at more or less market clearing prices (at least they are usually not able to buy at state prices but, rather, must rely on the nonstate retail market or even the black market), which forces their costs up even more. These factors have generated price levels that are on average two to three times that in a state-sector café, creating an especially bad reputation for the cafés among Soviet consumers.[49]

The most dynamic growth was registered by trade-procurement (*torgovo-zakupochny*) cooperatives. Their number grew by fourteen times in 1988 to stand at 4,418, and their output exceeded that of the public catering, procurement, and by-product processing cooperatives combined, although at the beginning of the year trade-procurement cooperatives lagged behind each of these other categories. While no concrete data are available, this suggests that trade-procurement cooperatives are in a very profitable business. In mid-1989, the smallest number of moonlighters (*sovmestiteli*) were in trade-procurement cooperatives no doubt because of these businesses' high profitability. That profitability, though, makes them even more vulnerable to regulation.[50]

PROFITS AND PRODUCTIVITY

Rumors about the high profitability of Soviet cooperatives as compared with that of state-sector enterprises are in general true, but there are a few caveats. First, many cooperatives are able to procure equipment and space from a sponsoring enterprise at zero cost because

49 See *Argumenty i fakty*, No. 18, 1989, p. 6.
50 The least number of moonlighters overall are in public catering—27 percent. See A. Glushetsky, "Kooperativ: Trudovye otnosheniya," *Ekonomicheskaya gazeta*, No. 17, 1989, p. 9.

state enterprises often find it worthwhile to turn over idle or unproductive facilities to cooperatives. Second, the tax rates on cooperatives have been relatively advantageous compared with the taxes levied on state enterprises.[51] Third, despite their generally higher prices, cooperatives tend to sell everything they produce and thereby earn huge profits. Still, anecdotal evidence (including the fact that state enterprises are eager to "sponsor" a cooperative inside their operations) suggests that even after adjusting for these factors, cooperatives are likely to generate more final product per unit of input than do Soviet state enterprises.[52] The key factor here would seem to be the simple existence of a hard budget constraint, which consists essentially in the threat of bankruptcy and the loss of entrepreneurial investment.

The result of this relatively high degree of productivity is that for every ruble of wages paid by the cooperative, they earn 2.18 rubles. This is roughly twice the ratio of the average state enterprise. More specifically, for every ruble of labor remuneration a cooperative earns on average 2.63 rubles if it produces consumer goods, 4.23 rubles if it produces baked goods and confectioneries, 4.26 rubles if it is engaged in public catering, and 2.26 rubles if it is involved in a category of activities labeled "other," which must include a large share of everyday services.[53] The highest earnings are realized by retail-trade (*torgovye*) cooperatives, which generate 14.89 rubles per ruble of labor wage, and the wholesale cooperatives in the trade-procurement sector, which earn 10.45 rubles per ruble expended on labor.

WAGES AND LABOR

Cooperatives have, in the short time they have been fully covered by legislation, accrued huge profits. As mentioned earlier, the original tax schemes for cooperatives and their members and employees anticipated this and structured the taxes so as to encourage the cooperatives to plow their profits back into the firm instead of distributing them as wages. The rationale was not that cooperative members and employees should not be wealthy but that their incomes should not exceed the incomes in the state sector by a "socially unjustifiable" amount. This in large part did not happen, and cooperative members' incomes far and away surpass the average income in the state sector.

---

[51]   Taxes on cooperative members' and employees' wages have tended to be relatively high, though.

[52]   See, for example, A. Shelev, "Ekonomicheskie problemy kooperatsii v stroitel'stve," *Planovoe khozyaistvo*, No. 7, 1989, pp 99-105, for an assessment of the relatively high productivity of cooperatives in the construction industry.

[53]   M. V. Shpil'ko, "O nalogooblozhenii kooperativov," *Finansy SSSR*, No. 6, 1989, p. 44.

In the fourth quarter of 1988, the average salary of a cooperative worker was 700 rubles per month. (With the rate of inflation, it is likely that this has jumped a good deal already.) The highest wages were paid in cooperatives in the everyday services sector, about 1,000 rubles per month on an all-Union average. Next were cooperatives producing consumer goods, about 770 rubles per month, and finally those in catering, 720 rubles per month. Cooperative wages appear to be highest in the Georgian republic (over 1,300 rubles per month) and in Lithuania and Turkmenistan (1,100 rubles per month). Cooperative salaries in Estonia and Latvia tend to be higher than the all-Union average.

About one half of the workers in producer cooperatives have more than one job and earn only about 200–250 rubles per month in part-time cooperative work to supplement their state-sector incomes. This means that the average wage for full-time cooperative members is higher than the 700-ruble-per-month average cited above, in fact totaling about 1,200 rubles per month. One problem associated with this is that only cooperative members have a claim to cooperative profits through their shares. Some Soviet commentators are concerned that the cooperative-member collectives can become "exclusive" and keep their numbers small while employing large numbers of contract employees.[54] The remedy put forward is to regulate the ratio of cooperative members to employees. (In Hungary, for example, contract employees can only make up 20 percent of a cooperative's work force.)

More and more, people are moving to cooperatives to find full-time work.[55] While in January, 1988, some 65 percent of cooperative workers were moonlighters, by January, 1989, only 47 percent were. In much of the Soviet literature on cooperatives, this somewhat clouds the issue of the low wages paid to contract employees of cooperatives relative to the earnings of cooperative members, because roughly half of the contract employees are part-time and have other, primary incomes.

PUBLIC OPINION AND COOPERATIVES

Who patronizes cooperatives and why? As mentioned at the outset, attitudes towards cooperatives are quite varied. Although data are scanty, the FAKT cooperative has provided some. FAKT commissioned a telephone survey of six hundred people by a group of sociologists on the attitude of Soviet consumers to the cooperative movement.[56] Thirty-four percent of men surveyed considered the development of the

---

[54] Yu. A. Danilevsky and N. I. Pikunov, "Izderzhki kooperativnogo dvizheniya," *Finansy SSSR*, No. 6, 1989, pp. 46-50.

[55] *Argumenty i fakty*, No. 18, 1989, p. 6.

[56] It cannot be assumed that the sample interviewed by telephone is representative, even of Moscow. Among the many unknowns are the time

cooperative sector "extremely important," while only 14 percent of the women considered it so. A further 24 percent of the men and 14 percent of the women supported the movement on the whole, noting that not all of the problems had been resolved.

Among Moscow blue-collar workers, 58 percent of the men and 28 percent of the women supported the cooperative movement, while 10 percent of the men and 12 percent of women thought the advantages of cooperatives to be fully offset by the disadvantages. Twenty-two percent of the men and 31 percent of the women in the same group regarded the development of the cooperative sector as a mistake.[57]

It is probably safe to assume that those people who have access to goods because of their position or contacts are not those whose first inclination is to shop in a cooperative. Indeed, those in the bureaucracy are probably less inclined to support cooperatives, which challenge the position of the *apparat*, than those who are not. Because of the relatively high prices in cooperatives, it is also probably safe to speculate that those people in lower-income levels do not tend to frequent cooperatives. This is likely to include pensioners, students, and others with low fixed incomes, in addition to those whose regular jobs bring relatively low salaries. In Moscow, 70 percent of all cooperative patrons are women, and 40 percent of those are between twenty-six and thirty-five years old. This group also makes 35 percent of all purchases in the cooperatives.

When asked how often they visit cooperatives, 7 percent responded "often," 21 percent "sometimes," 59 percent "seldom," and 8 percent "a first time."[58] The share of visitors to cooperatives who actually make purchases is low relative to the share in state enterprises—only 7 percent of the visitors to cooperative markets make a purchase before they leave, while 11 percent of the visitors to cooperative stores make a purchase. In state organized-markets, the figure is 15-18 percent, and for state stores it is 15 percent (again, in Moscow). The explanations often given for not making a purchase were high prices and the desire to just shop and satisfy one's curiosity about cooperatives.[59]

WHO ARE THE KOOPERATORY?

The average *kooperator* is a thirty-five-year-old male who formerly held a leadership post in a state enterprise. He became involved in the

---

of day that the survey was made, whether households or businesses or both were called, the age and sex distributions of the sample polled, the distribution of telephones, etc.

[57]   *Kommercheskaya khronika 1988*, Moscow, Mir, 1988, p. 55.
[58]   *Ibid*.
[59]   *Ibid*.

cooperative movement because of "the greater opportunities" it offers and "to earn more money." About one of every six *kooperatory* in Moscow is a member of the CPSU, and one in thirteen is a member of the Komsomol (these figures are bound to be lower in other regions).[60] Ninety percent contribute directly to the rendering of services or production of goods. Forty percent see the major contribution of the cooperative as improving the quality of consumer goods and services. The most difficult problems they say they face are acquiring deficit equipment (40 percent of respondents) and transporting their goods (20 percent of respondents). Many also noted problems with financial organs, ranging from establishing credit to paying taxes.

FAKT also inquired about the attitudes of citizens towards *kooperatory*. Here, 23 percent of the men and 8 percent of the women considered them enterprising and businesslike people worthy of respect and support. Forty-seven percent of the men and 35 percent of the women were more restrained in their assessments but at the time of the survey (unknown, but probably late 1988) did not hold negative opinions about *kooperatory*. More than a fourth of the men and over a third (38 percent) of the women considered *kooperatory* opportunists who bettered their own lot "at the expense of honorable labor."

CONCLUSIONS

The cooperative movement in the Soviet Union is only just getting on its feet. It has aroused both enthusiasm and animosity among the Soviet populace like few issues that Gorbachev has proposed as part of his *perestroika* package. Despite resistance at grass-roots level, petty bureaucratic foot-dragging, and some all-Union legislation designed to thwart it, the cooperative movement is growing because people are able to free themselves from the traditional reins of the Soviet workplace, express their creativity and initiative, and earn a wage that is more commensurate with their marginal product. It appears that there is, among the *kooperatory*, a recognition of the importance of their movement and a determination to press on even in the face of obstacles. If that is indeed the case, perhaps there is hope that the movement will make a contribution not only through increased output of goods and services but also by promoting a more complete understanding and appreciation of economic and political freedom in the Soviet Union.

---

[60]   *Ibid.* These figures square with anecdotal evidence cited widely in the Soviet press. See, for example, "Portret kooperatora," *Moskovskie novosti*, No. 52, December, 1989, p. 12.

Supporting Data

Table 1
SELECTED INDICATORS OF COOPERATIVE ACTIVITY
(As of October 1, 1988)

Republic	Number of Registered Coops	Number of Active Coops	Number of Coop Employees	Millions of Rubles of Production I-III Quarter
RSFSR	40,000	24,100	379,100	388,900
(Moscow)	2,500	1,400	43,800	171,800
Ukraine	14,300	8,100	139,600	375,000
Belorussia	2,700	1,700	25,300	63,300
Uzbekistan	4,200	2,300	49,100	115,400
Kazakhstan	4,500	2,600	37,100	108,600
Georgia	3,200	1,600	25,700	114,600
Azerbaijan	2,000	1,000	10,100	34,500
Lithuania	1,500	1,200	17,900	62,500
Moldavia	2,200	1,000	22,500	69,200
Latvia	1,600	800	6,700	89,900
Kirgizia	1,300	700	9,700	27,600
Tajikistan	800	600	7,900	17,900
Armenia	7,100	1,800	28,400	96,700
Turkmenistan	400	300	3,500	11,200
Estonia	1,000	700	4,800	47,800

Source: *Argumenty i fakty*, No. 50, December 1988.

Table 2
SOVIET PUBLIC OPINION:
COOPERATIVE VERSUS STATE ENTERPRISE
(In Percent)

	Higher		Equal		Lower	
	WOMEN	MEN	WOMEN	MEN	WOMEN	MEN
Quality	12	44	20	9	17	6
Service efficiency	58	31	3	8	0	1
Prices	78	70	3	1	1	1

Source: *Kommercheskaya khronika 1988*, Moscow, Mir, 1988, p. 55.

7

Is There a "Privatization" of Soviet Agriculture?

Karl-Eugen Wädekin

Aware that at least for the foreseeable future the large public farms will not be able to increase food production to the extent required by the needs of the population, the Gorbachev leadership is looking to private interest, initiative, and labor to come to the rescue. Official benevolence towards the private sector is thus prompted by a desire to have "personal subsidiary" producers contribute more to the solution of the food problem, or at least not cause the situation to become worse by letting what they now contribute fall off. This benevolence is, however, accompanied by an unmistakable intention insofar as policy is concerned not to allow private food production to become a part of the economy that is independent of the public sector and its central planning authority. It is also accompanied by an effort to instill a greater element of private, or personal, motivation in socialized production by introducing an output-oriented system of labor organization and remuneration in subunits of the public farms. The hoped-for result would be the integration of private into socialized production and the reorienting of the latter towards a kind of individualization. Both would have to market their produce through state-controlled public channels.

With respect to traditional private plot and animal production, the difficulty of such an approach consists in the fact that the productive potential of this sector can be expanded only slowly, if at all, under prevailing conditions and constraints. This poses a dilemma for the leadership. To relax these conditions and constraints would lead to "the danger of private capitalist entrepreneurship," but measures and rules aimed at circumventing this danger would be likely to stifle the chances for increasing output. True, limits on the size of private plots are practically lifted or modifications in them left (under legislation of 1988 and 1989) for the Union republics to determine. (In fact, local administrations were always entitled to modify these limits, but within the framework of a restrictive general policy.) The potential additional private output of greater-sized plots, however, has few market outlets other than through the public sector.

Both the resolution of the Central Committee of the CPSU, as published with some delay after the plenum held in March, 1989, and the subsequent decree of the USSR Council of Ministers[1] spelled out more than once what "the diverse forms of socialist property and the kinds of economic activities" involved in so-called agroindustrial production today are. Included were "peasant farms and their cooperatives," "personal subsidiary plot farms," and "collective fruit and vegetable gardens." The latter two kinds of farming are known.[2] The "peasant farm" (*krest'yanskoe khozyaistvo*), is, however, a term that to the present writer's knowledge has not been used in official documents in recent decades except in a historical context—that is, with regard to farming at past stages of socioeconomic development.

Some Soviet reformers consider the establishment of true family farming, independent of collective and state farms, in at least part of Soviet agriculture as a way of achieving genuinely private farming within an overall socialist setting. It is, however, Politburo member and Central Committee Secretary Egor Ligachev, in particular, who seeks to limit "privatization" of production to controlled growth of traditional Soviet plot farming, and Soviet leader Mikhail Gorbachev has so far not spoken out publicly in favor of the more "radical" reformers' ideas.

By way of addressing the question of privatization in Soviet agriculture, recent developments in traditional Soviet private plot and livestock farming are discussed here first; then an attempt is made to assess the nature of family farming under a production commitment (*podryad*, or contract); and, finally, the phenomenon of more or less independent "peasant" farming is examined.

Role and Development of Private Plot Production

The positive interest that the Soviet leadership has been showing in "personal subsidiary farming" has, among other things, resulted in a considerable increase in public information on the private sector. In

---

[1]   *Sel'skaya zhizn'*, April 1 and 12, 1989.

[2]   For a description up to 1985-88, see Stefan Hedlund, *Private Agriculture in the Soviet Union*, London and New York, Routledge, 1989; this book is centered on an interesting interpretation in terms of social and political psychology. See also by the present author: *The Private Sector in Soviet Agriculture*, edited by Jerzy Karz and translated by Keith Bush, Berkeley, Los Angeles, London, University of California Press, 1973; and "The Private Agricultural Sector in the 1980s," *Radio Liberty Research Bulletin*, RL 251/85, August 2, 1985.

greater detail than ever before, the weight of the private sector's contribution to Soviet agriculture as a whole as well as its importance in the economy as a supplier of food for the population is revealed in official Soviet publications. These data provide a basis for assessing the success or failure of current agricultural policy as mirrored in the growth or decline of the private sector in the traditional meaning of the term.

Only a few pre-1980 figures will be reproduced here, as these have already been analyzed in detail elsewhere (see Note 2, above). Among the newer data, there are some that contain corrections of earlier data, and there are also some that create inconsistencies. To begin with, overall private plot area, given in the statistical annual for 1987 as 8.21 million hectares of agricultural land, of which 6.14 arable (as of November 1), is said in a more recent official source to be only 7.8 million hectares, of which 5.9 arable ("in 1988"). An actual reduction of the area in so short a time is unlikely in view of its slow but steady post-1980 expansion. In yet another official source, livestock numbers for the mid- and late-1980s have been corrected.[3]

The year 1980 marked a low for privately owned livestock herds (except for sheep and goats, where the lows were at the end of 1976 and 1978 respectively), but the subsequent recovery during 1981-82 was slow and came to a halt afterwards (see Table 1).

Table 1

LIVESTOCK IN PRIVATE OWNERSHIP
(MILLION HEAD AT END OF YEAR)

	1980	1982	1984	1986	1987	1988
Cows	13.2	13.4	13.4	12.9	12.9	13.0
Other cattle	9.8	10.7	10.6	10.8	10.5	10.8
Pigs	14.0	15.8	14.1	13.6	13.6	14.5
Sheep and goats	30.2	31.9	32.5	33.4	33.4	34.7

SOURCE: *Sel'skokhozyaistvennoe proizvodstvo v lichnykh podsobnykh khozyaistvakh naseleniya*, Moscow, 1989, p. 22.

---

3   For the different figures for overall private plot area, see *Narodnoe khozyaistvo SSSR v 1987 g.*, Moscow, 1988, p. 183; and *Razvitie agropromyshlennogo proizvodstva v SSSR*, Moscow, 1989, p. 126. For the corrections of livestock numbers, see *Sel'skokhozyaistvennoe proizvodstvo v lichnykh podsobnykh khozyaistvakh naseleniya*, Moscow, 1989, p. 22.

The "personal subsidiary farms" (by definition excluding the "collective gardens" and perhaps also individual gardens around urban houses) were said to have contributed 23.6 percent to total Soviet agricultural output in 1988.[4] One wonders, but so far can only guess, whether the same source, by a changed statistical categorization, reduced not only the plot area but also the percentage in the total output value (see Table 2).

Table 2
TOTAL OUTPUT VALUE OF "PERSONAL SUBSIDIARY PRODUCTION"
(BILLION RUBLES IN 1983 PRICES)

| | FIVE-YEAR AVERAGE | | | THREE-YEAR AVERAGE | | | |
	1971-75	1976-80	1981-85	1986-88	1986	1987	1988
Total	50.1	49.4	52.4	52.5	53.5	52.1	51.8
Of which:							
Value of crop production	17.6	17.6	18.4	17.4	18.8	17.3	16.3
Value of animal production	32.4	31.7	34.0	35.0	34.7	34.9	35.5
Percent of animal production	(65)	(64)	(65)	(67)	64.8	66.9	68.6

SOURCE: *Sel'skokhozyaistvennoe proizvodstvo v lichnykh podsobnykh khozyaistvakh naseleniya,* Moscow, 1989, p. 85-87.

NOTE: Soviet "total output" of agriculture contains some double-counting of feed, seed, etc. Percentages in parentheses are derived from the absolute ruble values.

SALES TO THE PUBLIC SECTOR

It is a widely held but erroneous belief that most of what private plot ("personal subsidiary") producers do not consume themselves is sold on free markets. Quite the contrary, they increasingly sell their "surplus" mainly to the state—directly or through the public farms. Considerable quantities are involved, and these increased after 1980 and had by 1987 amounted, to take but two examples, to one-fourth of milk output and one-sixth of vegetable output. The quantities sold on the free markets most probably declined.

---

[4] *Razvitie agropromyshlennogo proizvodstva,* 1989, p. 89.

Table 3 shows that most of the meat and milk purchases on behalf of the state have increasingly gone to the public farms, which since 1980 are entitled to have them counted towards their own plan fulfillment. (The statistics for "sales" and for "purchases" are obviously collected in different ways. The data for state procurement purchases of meat, milk, and wool in 1988 are derived as residuals.)

As for meat, roughly one-fourth or more of private output in recent years was sold to the state, directly or through the public farms. Moreover, while the figures in Table 3 for intra-farm sales and intra-farm purchases of other livestock products are consistent (taking into account rounding of data and the difference between greasy wool and its weight on a recalculated fiber basis), they are not so for meat. Thus, for 1985 and 1986 the numerical ratio of live-weight intra-farm purchases to slaughter-weight intra-farm sales shows an impossible near-identity of both measures. The ratio is inversely implausible at 100:28 in 1987. With somewhat different figures from another official Soviet source, the ratio looks more convincing, though a bit auspicious (for Soviet conditions) at 100:66 (see last note to Table 3). A possible explanation would be that the purchases by consumers' cooperatives, which are not explicitly included in the sales figures, increased by an astounding 800,000 tons during one year, 1987. According to unofficial information received in 1989, however, meat purchases by consumers' cooperatives, have, on their own (statistical) account, remained insignificant, and these cooperatives have continued to purchase mainly eggs, potatoes, other vegetables,[5] fruit, and berries. A more plausible explanation would be that the quantities of meat sold without preconcluded contracts apparently do not form part of the statistics.

What is not covered by the statistics is the production of animals, which are tended and fattened privately but remain the property of the farm.

OUTPUT OF THE PRIVATE SECTOR

Formerly, official Soviet statistics considered intra-farm sales (on these, see the preceding section) to be part of socialist output. Such sales were already taking place before 1981, if semilegally and on a smaller scale. But since 1988 (in Latvia and Lithuania, since 1984), the statistical publications frequently credit intra-farm sales to "personal subsidiary" production. Spontaneous sales without a contract, however, still seem to be counted as part of socialist production without any indication of

---

[5]   Some 3.5 and 1.5 million tons of potatoes and other vegetables, respectively, in 1980, according to *Lichnoe podsobnoe khozyaistvo*, edited by A. F. Kalinkin, Moscow, 1981, p. 110. See also G. I. Shmelev, *Lichnoe podsobnoe khozyaistvo*, Moscow, 1985, pp. 21-22.

Table 3

OFFICIAL DATA ON PURCHASES FROM, OR SALES BY, "PERSONAL SUBSIDIARY" PRODUCERS THROUGH PUBLIC CHANNELS

(Thousands of Tons)

I. Purchases	1970	1980	1985	1986	1987	1988
Livestock and poultry, live weight						
State procurement system	1,300	900	600	600	500	460
Intra-farm and consumer cooperatives*	—	198 (1981)	798	1,046	1,794	1,881
Total	—	—	1,389	1,666	2,350	2,341
Milk						
State procurement system	1,500	3,200	700	400	200	140
Intra-farm and consumer cooperatives*	—	1,366 (1981)	5,611	6,052	6,748	7,414
Total	—	—	6,256	6,461	6,942	7,557
Eggs, million pieces						
State procurement system	2,000	1,400	1,000	800	800	—
Total	—	—	999	863	784	773
Wool, pure fiber, recalculated						
State procurement system	31	46	57	58	58	57
Intra-farm and consumer cooperatives*	—	—	7.2	6.9	7.4	10.6
Total	—	—	63.9	64.9	65.1	67.9
Potatoes, state procurement system	1,802	3,522	3,903	3,963	3,858	2,165
Other vegetables, state procurement system	647	1,362	1,374	1,395	1,356	1,399
Fruits and berries, state procurement system	563	1,268	1,039	975	806	931

140

II. INTRA-FARM AND COMPARABLE SALES**	1970	1980	1985	1986	1987	1988
Meat, slaughter weight, thousand tons	—	300 (1981)	800	800	500	500
Deviating source***	—	—	900	900	1,200	—
Milk, million tons	—	1,400 (1981)	5,500	6,000	6,500	7,100
Deviating source***	—	—	5,400	6,000	6,400	—
Wool, physical weight, thousand tons	—	—	—	—	18	22
Deviating source***	—	—	—	—	15	—

SOURCE: Sel'skoe khozyaistvo SSSR, Moscow, 1988, p. 337; Sel'skokhozyaistvennoe proizvodstvo v lichnykh podsobnykh khozyaistvakh naseleniya, Moscow, 1989, pp. 30, 38, and 39.

* That is, purchases by kolkhozes, sovkhozes, and other agricultural production enterprises "on the basis of contracts" and also by consumers' cooperative societies.

** Sales to kolkhozes, sovkhozes, and inter-farm and other agricultural production enterprises "in accordance with concluded contracts." ("Consumers' cooperative societies are not explicitly mentioned.)

*** These data are the earlier ones of the official statistical handbook SSSR v tsifrakh v 1987 godu, Moscow, 1988, p. 122. They apparently include, without explicitly saying so, sales to agricultural enterprises other than kolkhozes and sovkhozes. In 1983, 1,088 thousand tons of meat and 4,307 thousand tons of milk were sold to such enterprises according to V. Sidorenko, Sel'skaya zhizn', January 4, 1985, p. 3. The deviations most likely are due to a changed definition of "contract" sales in the statistics released after May, 1988.

their origin in the private sector. Purchases by the state procurement system are obviously credited towards private production, but the situation is less clear with respect to purchases by some other public agents. Of these, consumers' cooperative societies are the most important; their meat, milk, and wool purchases on kolkhozes and sovkhozes seem to have declined or else to have been included in the plan fulfillment of these public farms. At any rate, reported intra-farm sales have considerably changed the former output statistics.

The figures in Table 4 for potatoes, vegetables, fruit, and berries (excluding wine grapes and citrus fruit) are likely not to include the output of "collective garden plots" (cf. below). The percentages show that the share of the private sector in Soviet food production has decreased as total Soviet production has increased. Yet the important point to make is that, as distinct from earlier published statistics with their disregard for intra-farm sales,[6] the physical output of main products has on the whole remained relatively stable at a level above that of 1970. It is true, potato production has declined sharply, but fruit, meat, and wool resumed the rising trend of the late 1960s and early 1970s after a low in the late 1970s.

DEMOGRAPHY AND REGIONAL DIVERGENCIES

For the volume of private plot and livestock production to have been maintained and even to have achieved some slow growth is quite remarkable in view of the decline in the size of the rural and agricultural population. Apparently, some of the growth is due to expanded plot production among the urban population in small- and medium-sized towns and on the outskirts of large cities. In their gardens, whether individual or collective, these urban farmers mainly produce vegetables and fruit and, presumably, only hold limited numbers of animals. In the years from 1981–1987 kolkhoz households, which are essentially rural, produced only 41 to 43 percent of total private-sector output of vegetables, while for meat, milk, and potatoes their share of the total output was almost 50 percent.[7] The percentages for 1988 in Table 5 suggest that sizeable numbers of animals are raised by sovkhoz workers' households, and their share of total private livestock production seems to range from 30 to 40 percent. Thus, the agricultural population obviously still accounts for the bulk of private animal production.

---

⁶ The present writer pointed out the misleading character of Soviet statistics of the time already in 1985 (see *Osteuropa*, No. 1, 1986, p. 60).

⁷ *Kolkhozy SSSR*, Moscow, 1988, pp. 166-67 and 171-72, as compared with the sector totals. Data by urban and rural components for fruit and small animals such as rabbits are not available.

Table 4

OUTPUT OF PRIVATE SECTOR MAIN PRODUCTS, 1970-88
(MILLIONS OF TONS AND PERCENTAGES OF SOVIET PRODUCTION)

	1970	1980	1981	1985	1986	1987	1988	PERCENTAGE OF TOTAL SOVIET PRODUCTION			
								1980	1986	1987	1988
Meat, slaughter weight											
Excluding intra-farm sales	4.3	4.3	4.6	4.8	4.8	4.9	5.0	31	27	26	26
Including intra-farm sales	—	—	4.9	5.5	5.6*	5.4*	5.5	—	30	29	28
Milk											
Excluding intra-farm sales	29.8	27.1	25.5	22.6	22.0	21.6	—	30	22	21	—
Including intra-farm sales	—	—	26.9	28.1	28.0*	28.2*	28.3	—	27	27	27
Wool, physical weight, thousand tons											
Excluding intra-farm sales	79	96	102	116	120	102	—	22	26	26	—
Including intra-farm sales	—	—	103	116	120*	120*	122	—	26	26	26
Eggs, billion units	21.7	21.8	22.1	21.7	21.7	21.5	21.6	32	27	28	26
Potatoes	62.8	42.9	44.4	43.6	48.2	44.2	37.1	65	55	58	59
Other vegetables	8.1	9.0	9.4	8.0	8.3	8.4	9.4	38	28	29	31
Fruits and berries	3.9	4.5	—	6.0	6.1	4.4	4.7	58	—	54	54

SOURCES *Sel'skoe khozyaistvo SSSR*, Moscow, 1988, pp. 279, 290, 304, 474, for animal product quantities and their percentages in 1986-87; *SSSR v tsifrakh v 1988 godu*, Moscow, 1989, p. 242, for all products 1980, 1985, 1988 and their percentages in 1988; *Sel'skokhozyaistvennoe proizvodstvo v lichnykh podsobnykh*

Table 4 (CONTINUED)

OUTPUT OF PRIVATE SECTOR MAIN PRODUCTS, 1970-88

(MILLIONS OF TONS AND PERCENTAGES OF SOVIET PRODUCTION)

khozyaistvakh naseleniya, Moscow, 1989, for all products in 1970 and 1980 and, beginning in 1981, also meat, milk, and wool, including intra-sector sales; *Razvitie agropromyshlennogo proizvodstva v SSSR*, Moscow, 1989, pp. 62-63, 127, 132-133, for potatoes and vegetables, quantities and percentages excluding intra-farm sales of meat, milk,* and eggs in 1986-88.

* The statistical handbook *SSSR v tsifrakh v 1987 godu*, Moscow, 1988, p. 122, gave higher sales figures (see the last note to Table 3), which imply higher output figures—for meat by 0.1 million tons in 1985 and 1986 and by 0.7 million tons in 1987. For milk and wool, the deviations are small. The difference for meat is even greater if it is taken into account that not all sales are on the basis of contracts and to that extent are not reported in the sources. A small table in *Sem'ya beret podryad* by G. I. Shmelev, Moscow, 1987, p. 17, leads to the conclusion that the total output of the private sector amounted to at least 6.5 million tons. This fits in with the statement by a high-placed Soviet official quoted in the last note to Table 3, above.

Table 5
PERCENTAGES OF RURAL HOUSEHOLDS OWNING
COWS, PIGS, AND SHEEP
(AT END OF YEAR)

		COWS	PIGS	SHEEP
1970	Rural households	56	42	31
	Kolkhoz households only	58	44	29
1980	Rural households	48	33	24
	Kolkhoz households only	50	36	21
1985	Rural households	47	32	24
	Kolkhoz households only	48	35	21
1987	Kolkhoz and sovkhoz households	45	30	23
1988	On October 1			
	Kolkhoz households	57	63	25*
	Sovkhoz households	43	46	19*
At end of 1988, rural households		46	32	24

*　Including goats

SOURCES: *Sel'skoe khozyaistvo SSSR*, Moscow, 1988, p. 469 (for kolkhozes and sovkhozes together); *Kolkhozy SSSR*, Moscow 1988, p. 171 (for kolkhozes only, 1970-1985); Annual statistical report for 1988, *Sel'skaya zhizn'*, January 22, 1989 (for October 1, 1988); *Sel'skokhozyaistvennoe proizvodstvo v lichnykh podsobnykh khozyaistvakh naseleniya*, Moscow, 1989, p. 23 (at end of 1988).

The published statistics show that by far not all rural households raise livestock and that the share of such households without livestock is increasing. Policy statements have repeatedly made the same points in the nature of a complaint. Table 5 shows the percentages of those households that do raise animals. It should be kept in mind that part of the big public farms, sovkhozes in particular, may be located on the territory of settlements classified as urban, so that kolkhoz and, in particular, sovkhoz households could be both urban and agricultural.

The construction of Table 5 has in part been conditioned by the availability of data and is selective insofar as total numbers of cattle and goats have been omitted because of their lesser significance. The data not only show the low and slowly declining percentages of livestock-owning rural and agricultural households but also document what was otherwise more or less known—i.e., that the data regularly issued for the end of the year understate the annual average numbers. This can be seen by looking at the percentages on October 1, 1988, and the lower ones for the end of 1987 and end of 1988. The explanation is, of course, that the slaughter or sale of animals (intra-farm sales) by many private owners at the beginning of the winter season has an effect on the figures.

The percentage of kolkhoz and sovkhoz households holding live-stock varies in the different Union republics. It is far above the all-Union and Russian Republic averages in Lithuania, Belorussia, Georgia, and Kazakhstan and far below them in Moldavia. Not surprisingly, almost no pigs are privately held by the rural population of Islamic Central Asia and Azerbaijan, but the numbers of horned cattle and sheep are far above average.[8]

The numerical correlation between growth of rural population and sizes of herds held privately not only serves as a significant indicator of the private sector's development but also points to diverging regional trends that are of particular interest. Some Union-republican data have recently been made available in the form of Soviet livestock units, which essentially are cattle units but are in a consistent form only for 1980, 1985, and 1987. Moreover, the underlying meaning of them is not known.[9] For these reasons, the calculations in Table 6 assume cattle units where one cow is 1.0, one of another kind of cattle 0.5, one pig 0.25, and one sheep or goat 0.1. Poultry and horses are disregarded for lack of data. The results reveal great regional differences in absolute growth trends as well as in cattle units per hundred of the rural population. As always, the Russian Republic, by its sheer size, determines the all-Union totals and would require a regional breakdown, which is not possible for lack of data.

As there are also urban, if mainly by livelihood agricultural, owners of livestock, the figures per head of rural population overstate the correlation somewhat, but clear regional differences emerge all the same. They are corroborated by growth differentials in livestock production in terms of values at 1983 prices. In these terms, the 1986–88

---

[8]   *Kolkhozy SSSR*, Moscow, 1988, p. 171.

[9]   Are horses and poultry included? Are they calculated according to one of the two methods outlined in *Sel'skokhozyaistvennaya entsiklopediya*, Vol. 5, Moscow, 1975, p. 398, and if so, on the basis of value/cost or of feed requirements? In both cases, the ratio of one horse = 40 units of poultry, or else one cow = 50 poultry is unusual by Western standards.

Table 6

LIVESTOCK IN PRIVATE OWNERSHIP BY UNION REPUBLICS, 1970-1987
(CATTLE UNITS AT END OF YEAR)

I. THOUSAND HEAD	1970	1980	1982	1984	1985	1986	1987
USSR	27,695	24,620	25,110	25,390	25,360	25,043	24,892
Of which:							
Russian SFSR	12,853	10,425	10,885	10,375	10,240	10,037	9,804
Ukraine	5,317	4,218	4,532	4,368	4,268	4,081	4,024
Belorussia	1,716	1,419	—	1,359	1,334	1,253	1,196
Baltic republics*	1,239	945	1,012	981	—	936	912
Moldavia	275	269	308	301	—	263	242
Georgia	806	867	934	—	—	952	965
Armenia	244**	333**	—	—	—	303	293
Azerbaijan	807	906	—	993	—	1,031	1,039
Kazakhstan	1,898	2,185	2,301	2,307	2,412	2,565	2,646
Kirgizia	344	317	381	407	451	470	524
Uzbekistan	1,440	1,719	1,854	1,977	—	2,013	2,030
Tajikistan	480	606	658	—	—	707	732
Turkmenistan	274	338	—	388	410	434	435

Table 6 (Continued)

LIVESTOCK IN PRIVATE OWNERSHIP BY UNION REPUBLICS, 1970-1987
(Cattle Units at End of Year)

II. Per 100 of rural population	1970	1980	1982	1984	1985	1986	1987
USSR	26.4	25.2	26.0	26.4	26.4	26.2	—
Of which:							
Russian SFSR	26.6	25.4	27.3	26.4	26.4	26.1	—
Ukraine	25.0	22.9	24.9	24.8	24.7	23.9	—
Belorussia	34.1	34.4	—	36.0	36.2	33.1	—
Baltic republics*	42.8	37.9	41.2	40.4	—	38.8	—
Moldavia	11.2	11.4	13.2	13.2	—	10.8	—
Georgia	32.9	35.4	38.8	—	—	39.8	—
Armenia	24.3***	31.7**	—	—	—	28.0	—
Azerbaijan	31.1	31.4	—	32.4	—	32.9	—
Kazakhstan	29.1	32.2	33.9	33.9	35.4	37.7	—
Kirgizia	18.4	14.2	16.5	17.0	18.4	18.8	—
Uzbekistan	18.7	18.2	18.8	18.9	—	18.2	—
Tajikistan	25.7	23.0	23.5	—	—	22.9	—
Turkmenistan	23.6	22.4	—	23.2	23.9	24.7	—

SOURCES Livestock data for 1986 and 1987: *Sel'skoe khozyaistvo SSSR*, Moscow, 1988, pp. 470-471; for pre-1986: various statistical annuals and annual statistical press reports, as far as available. Rural population (only up to the beginning of 1987: *Naselenie SSSR 1987*, Moscow, 1988, pp. 16ff.

* Estonia, Latvia, and Lithuania
** For Armenia in 1970 and 1980, cattle unit numbers have been derived as residuals of all other Union republics and are therefore not reliable.

average exceeds that of 1976-80 by between 30 and 80 percent for Armenia, Azerbaijan, Kazakhstan, Uzbekistan, Kirgizia, and Turkmenistan ("only" 21 percent in Tajikistan). The Baltic republics and Belorussia register a decline, and there is only a moderate growth of 8 to 11 percent in Ukraine and Moldavia.[10] In these European republics, privately owned livestock herds decreased between 1970 and 1980 and again after 1982.

Table 6 demonstrates that the all-Union decline in private livestock raising towards 1980 and the ephemeral recovery in 1981–82 resulted from diverging regional trends that exhibit a striking parallel with demographic developments. From 1970 to 1980, the tendency was for numbers of livestock to decline faster than the size of the rural population, with the exceptions of Moldavia (where private livestock ownership has been very small anyway), Belorussia, and Transcaucasia; in most of Central Asia, excluding Kazakhstan, growth took place in both categories during that period but was slower with respect to numbers of livestock. This was so because a negative attitude towards private livestock husbandry prevailed among Party and state authorities for most of the decade or up to 1978 or so. It was not an officially declared and generalized line, though, and therefore it is conceivable that in those Union republics that represent exceptions statistically, administrative practice deviated under the impact of socioeconomic and demographic conditions—in particular, rural population growth in Central Asia and Transcaucasia. Georgia and Armenia have long been known for their special local policies.

It is Kazakhstan where deviant statistical development is especially interesting. Except for an interruption after the severe drought of 1975, private livestock holdings have steadily increased in this republic,[11] while the rural population has stayed at a level only 4 percent above that of 1970. For Kazakhstan's southern mountain and near-mountain areas, an increase in rural population similar to that in neighboring Kirgizia and Uzbekistan may be assumed. It has probably been counterbalanced by an economically undesirable outflow of population from the rural areas in the north, mostly Slavs who settled there during the Virgin Lands campaign of the 1950s. Both phenomena seem to have worked in favor of a tolerant policy towards private plots.

After 1977, and with greater insistence after 1980, Moscow's officially announced more benevolent attitude towards private livestock husbandry favored a renewed growth of herds. Evidently, in most Union republics it was this changed policy that in due course led to the restoration of the previous numerical correlation between private

---

10   *Sel'skokhozyaistvennoe proizvodstvo*, 1989, p. 7.

11   *Narodnoe khozyaistvo Kazakhstana v 1980 g.*, Alma-Ata, 1981, pp. 101-104.

livestock holdings and size of rural population. In Transcaucasia and Central Asia and in Kazakhstan, however, numbers of livestock grew appreciably faster than the rural population. The exceptions were Tajikistan and Uzbekistan with their Union-wide highest birth rates. There the growth of the rural population outran or at least equaled that of the livestock numbers. The increasing numbers of sheep per household (see Table 5) are a result of this general trend in Soviet Central Asia. With the shrinking rural population, the European Union republics had declining livestock herds in absolute terms but less so per household.

LITTLE EFFECT OF THE POLICY CHANGE

The restoration of the all-Union correlation between growth of rural population and privately owned livestock herds was achieved by the end of 1984. Subsequently, the absolute numbers of herds began to decline again, and in the years from 1985 to 1987 so did the correlation, despite appeals and incentives under Gorbachev's leadership aimed at encouraging the raising of more animals in the private sector. Apart from Azerbaijan, Georgia, Kazakhstan, Kirgizia, and Turkmenistan, the rest of the country largely underwent a process of returning to the previous population/livestock correlation. In absolute terms, this was at a level below that of 1970, because the size of the rural population had declined in the meantime. It has to be remembered that a decline in the size of a population implies that it is aging. Old people are less likely to expand their livestock holdings.

Obviously, the Soviet leadership had expected more. They seem to have underestimated the impact of demographic development, and to have overestimated the effect of their policy of encouraging private animal husbandry. The population/livestock correlation underwent ups and downs during the 1960s and the 1970s but remained more or less stable throughout the period. What changed was livestock productivity, which has slowly increased, as evidenced by growing absolute output, even though numbers of animals seem to have been stagnating or decreasing since 1983, an impression that may in part be an effect of a growing difference between the end-of-year herd numbers shown in Soviet statistics and the acutal annual average numbers.

Shortage of feed for privately owned animals is an ever-recurring complaint and in the European and northern parts of the country is often given as a reason for not keeping livestock. In the Asian regions, though, this problem has not prevented a growing population from increasing their herds, which is surprising because it would be reasonable to expect the shortage of feed in these regions to be particularly severe. There is, of course, the possibility that under pressure of rapid population growth and latent rural (less so urban) malnutrition, local authorities and managers give increasing quantities of animal feed to private holders or tolerate its theft. In Uzbekistan in 1987, almost two-thirds (1,693,000 tons) of milk output (including milk products, recalculated) originated in the private sector, compared with 957,000 tons from the public sector, while 1,138,000 tons had to be brought in from other republics. With meat, the private sector contributed almost half (197,000 tons) of the total output (404,000 tons), while 195,000 tons had to be imported.[12] No more than 29 kilograms of meat were available per inhabitant of Uzbekistan as late as 1987 (31 kilograms in Tajikistan), and only 17 kilograms per Uzbek kolkhoz member.[13] Some losses on the way to the consumer must be deducted from this official "consumption fund," and by definition it includes bones, fats, and edible offals. Under such circumstances, improving their own consumption must form a strong incentive for private producers to increase meat output.

By contrast, it may be deduced that in other parts of the USSR people will not be much interested in increasing their private livestock output beyond their own consumption unless there is good access to free urban markets or an efficient public purchasing organization. Such lack of interest might also be expected in such areas as Orel with its 115 kilograms total output of meat per head and a "consumption fund" of 71 kilograms, Krasnodar and Stavropol Krais (130/75 and 112/73 kilograms), Lithuania (145/85), or Latvia and Estonia (figures similar to those of Lithuania).[14] A comparable situation may prevail in the outlying areas of heavily industrialized provinces, which are relatively well supplied with meat because of large imports from other provinces—e.g., Moscow, Gorky, Kirov, Kuibyshev, the Donetsk Basin, southern Siberia, and the Far East.[15]

With the low purchasing power of the ruble, only selling on accessible free markets at high prices seems really attractive to private producers, as this would enable them to pay the high black-market prices for other coveted goods. There is not much incentive to raise private production in areas far away from urban free markets and with poor transport connections. Yet it is just these areas where idle pasture and haying resources would provide a basis and the potential for stepping up private animal production.

These are most likely some of the reasons why "personal subsidiary" producers are reluctant to expand private livestock holdings. There is too the effort of Soviet planners and leaders to prevent private producers from selling additional output on free markets and have them channel it instead through public marketing outlets at regulated

---

12   *Narodnoe khozyaistvo Uzbekskoi SSR v 1987 g.*, Tashkent, 1987, p. 129.

13   *Razvitie agropromyshlennogo proizvodstvo*, 1989, p. 169; and *Sel'skaya zhizn'*, August 18, 1988, p. 2.

14   *Razvitie agropromyshlennogo proizvodstvo*, 1989, pp. 165-168.

15   *Ibid.*

prices. Kolkhozes and sovkhozes are not entitled to pay more than the official procurement prices—without the legal premiums for overplan output and the markups for unfavorable conditions in a given location.[16] True, the agencies of the system of consumers' cooperatives in theory pay "prices according to contractual agreement," but in practice they are advised to pay substantially less than the free market price, sometimes even less than the state procurement price. Besides, they are ill equipped with storage and transport facilities, and their purchasing network is inflexible, inefficient, and does not exist in all villages.

Still, the state procurement price for meat and milk would seem high enough to stimulate private production and sales even without some of the premiums and subsidies paid to public farms. It is said often enough that private producers sell at high state procurement prices and then go to the public stores to buy for their own consumption at lower retail prices. But how many of them are near enough or have convenient transportation to the cities to do so? In the countryside such shops just do not exist, and in nearby medium- and small-sized urban locations the shelves of the official shops are empty most of the time. So output for one's own consumption enjoys priority over money income from product sales.

The above considerations, the overall quantitative performance, and the regional divergencies permit drawing two conclusions about the effects of policy on private animal farming:

- A repressive policy towards the sector (1970–77) can be successful to a limited extent, depending on other circumstances—in particular, demographic developments; and

- Measures and appeals encouraging private livestock husbandry since 1980 have so far had only limited effects beyond a rather stable correlation between livestock and rural population numbers and cannot do otherwise as long as the Soviet social and political environment does not change more deeply than it has hitherto. Demography and marketing conditions put a limit on output growth, even though livestock productivity has risen.

Crop production on private plots was previously limited by, above all, legal restrictions on plot sizes. It remains to be seen whether the total plot area will expand as a result of the new Model Charter for Kolkhozes and the Law on Cooperatives of May–June, 1988. The decline of private potato output from 1970 to 1980 seems to have been largely caused by

---

16   See *Literaturnaya gazeta*, March 15, 1989, p. 11.

an exodus from those rural regions where much of this crop is grown—
central and northern Russia and Belorussia. But there was a certain
recovery, not through higher hectare yields but through expansion of
sown area, during the 1980s (output in 1987 was atypical for meteoro-
logical reasons). Private production of other vegetables stagnated
during the 1970s as well as the 1980s.

What did expand greatly is the area of so-called collective gardens
in urban and suburban areas. It grew from 0.5 million hectares in
1970 to 0.6 million hectares in 1980 and reached 0.95 million hectares
by 1987.[17] It surely exceeds one million hectares by now. According to
Ligachev, the number of families with such garden plots has already
risen to 18 million as compared with 14.1 million in 1987.[18]

The way in which Soviet statistics present figures on collective gardens makes the observer assume that their output is not (or no longer?)
included in the data on "personal subsidiary" farming. Otherwise it
would be hard to explain why the latter category's fruit and berry
area declined from 1.54 million hectares in 1988 to 1.26 million hectares
in 1984[19]—that is, at the same time that the area of collective fruit
and berry gardens was slowly but steadily expanding. A Soviet survey indicates that in 1986 the collective fruit and berry gardens produced, together with the collective vegetable gardens, 3.9 million
tons of potatoes; 0.9 million tons of other vegetables, including cucur-
bitaceous plants; and 0.9 million tons of fruit and berries,[20] which
may have to be added to the total of Table 4 (above). The corresponding quantities for 1980 and earlier years were smaller, and this recent additional output would increase the overall growth of what
should be considered private output in spite of its formally "collective"
character.

The prospects for private crop production, specifically with regard
to potatoes, other vegetables, and fruit, are influenced by contradictory
factors:

- An enlarged overall plot area and official policy encourage
  an increase in output of these crops at the same time that
  urban "collective" production of them is expanding;

- Regional decreases in the size of the rural population are
  stemming potato output and production of some other
  vegetables;

---

[17]   *SSSR v tsifrakh v 1988 godu*, Moscow, 1989, p. 233.
[18]   *Sel'skaya zhizn'*, April 2, 1989, p. 2.
[19]   *Sel'skokhozyaistvennoe proizvodstvo*, 1989, p. 16.
[20]   *Narodnoe khozyaistvo SSSR za 70 let*, Moscow, 1987, p. 238, in combination with p. 237.

- Efforts are being made by the state to limit sales on free markets.

These factors, viewed together with similarly contradictory factors that are, as pointed out above, at work in private animal production, urge the conclusion that the private sector in the form of traditional plot and livestock production is likely to increase its output only slowly, if at all.

INTEGRATION OF PRIVATE AND SOCIALIZED PRODUCTION OR INDIVIDUALIZATION OF LABOR WITHIN THE BIG COLLECTIVE

If "individual" production is understood as including private production but encompassing other arrangements as well, such a sector would be an enhancement, but the dividing line with the socialized sector would be blurred, difficult to define socioeconomically, and impossible to delimit statistically. The ambiguity would emerge, for example, if the "individual," or "private," or "personal" productive activity were no longer restricted to rights of use on plot land plus precarious rights of grazing and haymaking on small strips of public, often idle, land, and to private property of strictly limited numbers of animals. The addition in land and livestock numbers might then be juridically based on a contract with the public farm for working the additional plots and for raising additional livestock on its behalf, no matter whether the animals were juridically private property or the property of a kolkhoz, sovkhoz, or other public enterprise or organization. Under such contracts, the individual producer would deliver or sell a stipulated main share of the output to the public farm and be free to dispose of what he produces beyond that amount.

At least as far as livestock production is concerned, the combination of plot and contract farming has existed to an unknown, though not negligible, degree and in semilegal forms for a long time.[21] It has involved labor remuneration in kind and open as well as hidden sales and purchases on both sides—e.g., sales of young animals, supply of fodder to plot-owning farm members, and sales of milk or slaughter animals to the public farm. It was officially propagated and made fully legal beginning in 1981.[22]

The point to be made here is that such arrangements now refer to individual production both on the private plot in the strict sense of the term and on land and with animals that are supplied additionally on the basis of advance contracts. There the arrangement becomes similar to

---

21   Wädekin, *The Private Sector*, pp. 232-246.
22   The decree was dated January 7, 1981.

156   *Karl-Eugen Wädekin*

the production commitment contract, or *podryad*,[23] which initially and
on principle referred only to organization and remuneration of social
production according to productive performance. It is not the basic idea
of *podryad* that is new[24] but its intensified propagation since March, 1983,
and its current predominance. By the end of 1987, it was in use by 70
percent of the agricultural labor force and applied to 85 percent of the
total arable land (193 million hectares, disregarding nonarable agricultural land).[25]

Usually, these subunits of public farms are big production units in
themselves with twenty-two permanent (plus seasonal) workers on
four hundred hectares (plus nonarable)—certainly a collectivist type of
agriculture. It has been said that a *podryad* brigade should not exceed
fifty workers.[26] This average, of course, hides unknown numbers of still
bigger units (brigades), of smaller groups of workers (e.g., a brigade or
zveno that may have six to ten workers), and genuine family or kinship
units. It is possible to imagine an individualization of labor organization
becoming effective in the links (unlikely in the big brigades) but hardly
an individualization or even a privatization of production.

It is different with the family, which as a farm subunit has been
officially propagated since early 1986 (see the interview with Gosagro-
prom chairman V. S. Murakhovsky in *Literaturnaya gazeta* of January 22,
1986). A family *podryad* can take very different forms, depending on the
nature of the product in which it specializes; family *podryad* units
without product specialization seem to be rare, if they exist at all.

In crop farming, it is mainly the labor-intensive, small-scale mecha-
nized kinds of production that are subcontracted (by *podryad*) to families (fruit, vegetables, cotton, tobacco, etc.) on an assigned parcel of a big
field. Frequently, some of the production processes such as plowing,
sowing, application of fertilizer and pesticide are performed by the
large farm with its machines and its technical personnel. Thus, only part
of the work is individualized, and the final productive performance
depends also on the other part and, last but not least, on input supplies.
Of course, there are instances in which a family or kinship group of
machinery operators take over grain or root crops on a rather large scale
and rent the necessary machinery from the overhead farm. But these do
not seem to be very frequent.

---

[23]   See Elizabeth Clayton, "Economics of Small-Scale in Soviet Agriculture: The Contract Collective," in *Communist Agriculture: Farming in the
Soviet Union and Eastern Europe*, edited by Karl-Eugen Wädekin, forthcoming,
pp. 202-14.
[24]   See, by the present writer, "The Re-emergence of the Kolkhoz Principle,"
Soviet Studies, No. 1, 1989, pp. 29-37.
[25]   *Sel'skoe khozyaistvo SSSR*, Moscow, 1988, pp. 50 and 428.
[26]   Leading article in *APK: ekonomika i upravlenie*, No. 12, 1988, p. 8.

Things look different in livestock farming. A family accepting twenty to thirty cows for milk production or sixty to eighty steers for fattening, getting twenty to thirty hectares of land for producing most of the green and dry fodder, and receiving a share of concentrate feed from the public farm seems a rather typical case; another is pig fattening with a greater part of the feed supplied by the overhead farm. In such cases, the animals are kept on premises near the family home, often in an outlying part of the territory of a kolkhoz or sovkhoz. The public farm supplies the young animals, part of the feed, and some veterinary services, and receives produce of the quantity and quality it contracted for. Above-contract produce may be sold to the farm or elsewhere. It is easy to imagine corresponding arrangements for half-nomadic shepherding in steppe and mountain areas. In livestock production of this kind, the role and autonomy of the family is considerable. Not the output, but certainly most of the production process, may be called individualized, even privatized. A *podryad* family with a private plot and livestock of its own in addition to a contracted land area and livestock practically combines production on behalf of the public farm with that of its plot. Contracting makes its economic activity similar to that of a small *podryad* unit—not wholly private, but certainly individual. This does not apply or applies less so to the frequent cases of a group of kolkhoz- or sovkhoz-owned animals within a large herd and located in a big stable, being tended by a family link with all the feed supplied by the public farm.

The year 1986, and in particular the Twenty-seventh Party Congress, signalled the new stage. With the family being recognized as a legitimate partner, the combination of a *podryad* with contractual production on a family plot and with privately owned livestock became officially desirable. The socialist and the private aspect merged in practice and even in theory. With "tenancy" (*arenda*) added by mid-1987 and fully legalized by the *ukaz* of April 7, 1989, the family was potentially becoming a supplier of labor on leased land and at the same time of produce; the public farm as the landowner was becoming an employer, input supplier, and buyer of produce in a relationship of interdependence.

It is important to remember that two-thirds of the total (gross) value of private plot production consists of livestock and livestock products and that it is these products, especially meat, that are in the greatest demand by the public sector and Soviet consumers at large. Therefore, most attention in dealing with the plot and *podryad* relationship falls to the animal sector. This is reflected in the coverage given this sector in the Soviet press and also in Soviet statistics. Obviously, there are similar flows of produce in crop production, but they seem to be of minor significance. At any rate, they are not shown in the statistics, in which family *podryad* output is part of "social" production.

There is an element of privatization in these arrangements but also one of socialization of production activities, and there is increasing dependence on the public farm, which largely determines the economic activity of the family. Above all, it becomes more difficult, if not impossible under the terms of the contract, to market a stepped-up output other than through the public farm. To put it in somewhat pointed terms, what results might be called a quantitative privatization coupled with a qualitative socialization of individual production.

THE LARGER-THAN-FAMILY INTRA-FARM *PODRYAD*

The great majority of the agricultural labor and production potential under *podryad* is organized in rather large units (see the average sizes quoted above) within the existing kolkhozes and sovkhozes. Most of them are headed by "brigadiers," who, even if elected, are likely to be part of the existing hierarchical command structure and therefore dependent on the management of the big farm. Together with the sheer size of the units, this works towards a continuing "free-rider" mentality among part of the workers.

In view of the still obligatory character of "state orders" for kolkhoz or sovkhoz output, the production tasks for subunits, as stipulated by the *podryad*, cannot be other than assignments of planned output rather than negotiated quantities. Moreover, the determination of necessary labor inputs is based on existing norms and tariffs, and the material inputs largely depend on availability. Thus, the unit or its brigadier has little choice in determining the assortment of inputs and little influence on the quality and timeliness of their supply. Yet the system of remuneration per unit of output, in particular if under the jurisdictional form of tenancy (*arenda*), makes the worker bear a greater income risk in cases of input failure and below-plan output.

Thus, the *podryad* of the brigade and the larger-than-family link (*zveno* or *otryad*), perhaps soon to be renamed "cooperative," is essentially a form of labor organization and only secondarily a form of intra-family contracted production or tenancy. This, together with the circumstances causing its character to be so, may change for the better when plans (state orders) will be less tight and inputs more amply and selectively available. Yet by all indications this is not a prospect for the near future. And if and when such a prospect were to come true, would there still be an urge for Soviet leaders to change the agrarian system, which would have remained essentially collective? What is now in place is a part-transfer of production and labor organization to units that, although large-scale farming by Western standards, are smaller than the giant kolkhozes and sovkhozes. This may lead to a limited improvement of productivity but has nothing to do with privatization.

"PEASANT FARM" OR PRIVATE PLOT?

The term "peasant farm," as distinct from *podryad* or private plot production, adds a new dimension to the discussion. This becomes particularly clear from the decree of April 5, 1989, which spells out what should be done with the fields of a public farm that cannot be saved from continued loss-making and therefore has to be "reorganized or liquidated": they shall be given to other kolkhozes and sovkhozes, to industrial enterprises, to organizations of tenants, to cooperative tenant collectives, to "peasant farms." With the state being the sole legal proprietor of land, such peasants can only be tenants, and the obvious lessor would, though not explicitly identified in the decree, be the local state administration. Where the land is handed over to some other kolkhoz or sovkhoz and through it to tenants, it would make little sense to name "the peasant farm" as a possible other receiver of land.

A special case is that of a tenant from outside—that is, a tenant who is not member or employee of the kolkhoz or sovkhoz that owns the land. Juridically, such a tenant is in a less dependent position, although it remains to be seen whether materially, which is to say in acquiring inputs and marketing outputs, his dependence will be less in real terms. An individual tenant peasant outside the public farm, having contracts not with and not within such a farm, is a significant new legal possibility, but it seems to be a rare phenomenon as yet. Where could such farms be located? The liquidation of kolkhozes or sovkhozes is not a prospect for the immediate future. Their continuing existence is "the main road" for Soviet agriculture, as repeatedly declared by Gorbachev and laid down in policy statements. Because the state organs are required first of all to take steps to bring economically nonviable public farms out of losses within one to two years, even the disappearing of a small number of public farms after that will not happen at once. Moreover, it is also being said that peasant farms or comparable autonomous family *podryad* units should primarily be located in outlying places, where soils are poor or conditions otherwise unfavorable for profitable large-scale farming. Thus, it will take hard-working, risk-taking, and enterprising families with at least two able-bodied members to start a farm of this kind. It should not be denied that such people exist even after two generations of executing work upon order, but the type of families and workers required may be most difficult to find in just those regions with poor conditions and outlying homesteads (central and northeastern Russia, Belorussia). There the outmigration and aging of the rural population has led to profound imbalances in the demographic structure.

The recent Party and government documents did not specifically explain what "a peasant farm" is to be in the Soviet Union, but from the context in which it was mentioned in these documents and from other, nonofficial publications, some of which also use the term "farmer's farm" (*fermerskoe khozyaistvo*), it evidently is, or should be, an autonomous and private agricultural enterprise on rented land with rented or purchased means of production. The mentions of it also make clear that it is different from "personal subsidiary" plot and livestock farming.

At an important regional "seminar-conference" held in Omsk from March 31 to April 1, 1989, with Union-republican and provincial Party secretaries and chairmen of Councils of Ministers or provincial administrations (*ispolkomy*) attending, Ligachev made it clear that what he has in mind is no more than an enlarged plot. He used the term "family farm"(*semeinoe khozyaistvo*) instead of "peasant farm" in his speech, or at least in the published version of it.[27] (It should be pointed out that in both cases the Russian word *khozyaistvo* was used. *Khozyaistvo* is a broad term and is applied to many kinds of economic units, while the traditional Russian peasant had a *dvor*, although it was often called *khozyaistvo* by statisticians, scholars, etc.). Ligachev's words are particularly worth quoting because in other regional conferences that took place later the term "peasant farm" was rarely, if at all, used, while much attention was paid to "personal" plot and garden production. This is what Ligachev said, or wanted to have published:

> An important role is played in supplying the population with food by the personal farms of citizens in villages and workers' settlements, by fruit and berry gardening and vegetable gardening. Actually, what we are talking about is family farms. They produce almost 24 percent of the total volume of agricultural output.
>
> By its very nature, a family farm is a kind of tenancy (*arenda*). The only difference is that not all the output of a family farm is for the market (*nosit tovarnyi kharakter*). As for the principles of operating the farm, they may with good reason be called lease-type (*arendnymi*). The holder (*vladelets*) of a family or—as it is often said, personal—farm receives land, pays the agricultural tax, sells the output produced at his own discretion. This kind of farm is clearly associated with kolkhoz and sovkhoz production.
>
> All of this is a proven, already established form of farming. If its development is given an added impulse, if economic and organizational ties with social production, with consumers' cooperatives, are deepened on a mutually beneficial basis, then it would indeed be possible to obtain a significant increase in foodstuffs. What is more, with minimal expenditures. . . .

---

[27] *Sel'skaya zhizn'*, April 2, 1989, p. 2.

The March plenum of the Central Committee of the CPSU recognized as necessary the restoration of full rights to the personal farms of citizens as one of the forms of agricultural production.... They ... permit drawing into socially useful labor activity a considerable number of students, pensioners, and other categories of people.

This is a program for mobilizing the traditional, if liberalized, Stalinist private sector of Soviet agriculture and those of its labor resources that are not legally obliged to increase its output and market a greater share beyond what they need for their own consumption. Ligachev did not contradict the *ukaz* of April 7 and the relevant parts of the decrees of April 5, 1989; he merely made them look superfluous insofar as individual food production is concerned. In fact, the traditional plot holder has always paid land rent—without the term being applied—by being obliged to work for the kolkhoz or sovkhoz in exchange for the right to farm a plot, to own livestock numbers beyond the upper limits set for nonfarm people, to use some of the public pasture and haying lands, and to receive part of his or her labor remuneration in kind. The upper limits of plot sizes and animal holdings were already lifted before the March plenum on condition of sales or deliveries to the kolkhoz or sovkhoz. Instead of the relative autonomy and negotiating power of individual tenants (*arendatory*) or producers under a labor supply contract (*podryad*), as more or less implicit in the legislation of early April, 1989, Ligachev stressed their being closely connected with kolkhoz and sovkhoz production. As to "collective gardeners," whom Ligachev seems to favor, their conditions were not changed by the recent legislation.

CONCLUSION: POSSIBLE CHANGE, BUT NOT PRIVATIZATION

In the preceding discussion, the fact was neglected that the land in any case remains the exclusive property of the state. A private type of farming could also develop on leased land if other conditions such as free access to free markets and genuine trade of material inputs instead of factual assignment of short supplies were given and, most important, if the farmer himself could choose what to produce and how to produce it, perhaps on the basis of contracts if these were freely negotiated without a chain of command above him.

It may be that at least part of these conditions will be met for family farmers outside the kolkhozes and sovkhozes, as the recent legislation seems to imply. At present, however, such "peasant farms" form an economically neglible minority among the more than twenty-five million farm workers. They are located mainly in the Baltic and Kazkhstan and account for only a tiny fraction of Soviet agricultural production, even if some "family *podryad*" farming on intra-kolkhoz or intra-sovkhoz "tenancy" (*arenda*) in socioeconomic reality achieves a similar kind of production activity. Most of these two kinds of farming will be in livestock production.

Things look somewhat different if one takes a broader view of the private character of small-scale farming. Then the traditional kind of Soviet plot and animal farming may be included, and the individualization will apply also to those kinds of family *podryad* that are combined with plot farming. This tendency is, however, accompanied by an intentional policy of "integrating" private plot farming into socialized production. Its socioeconomic character will thus hardly become more private. Soviet politicians and authors have always maintained that plot farming is "personal" rather than "private". Without engaging in a semantic discussion, it seems to the present writer that the term "individual" (production) is appropriate, as work both on the plot and under family *podryad* is private indeed, but output, except for its share for consumption by the producers and the small percentage going to free markets, is not, nor is the choice of the product mix.

As to the larger-than-family *podryad* and *arenda* units, work may be considered more individualized than it was before. This surely is not privatization, but may be called partial individualization of socialized work. Where it really comes about, it will imply a significant change in the functions of kolkhozes and sovkhozes towards a reduced role of merely overhead activities of supply and marketing. The words "cooperative" and "democratiziation" alone, however, do not suffice to bring about such a change.

The plot-plus-*podryad* sector is likely to expand somewhat in quantitative absolute terms, but in terms of its contribution as a percentage of total Soviet food output it will at best increase and stabilize at 25 percent after its slow but steady decline in recent years. For the foreseeable future, an optimistic but not out-of-the-question assumption would be that new "peasant farms" will total one percentage point to this share, perhaps a little more in livestock production. In certain regions, the percentage might be higher. Yet all this taken together does not permit speaking of a privatization of Soviet agriculture as a whole, at least as long as no measures more far-reaching than the ones now being tried are enacted.

A draft law on property and related rights, which was being discussed by the Supreme Soviet of the USSR in late 1989, does not mainly aim at agriculture, although it is likely to create a somewhat firmer legal basis for already existing "tenancy" and related practices. Depending on the final text of the law, its main importance for genuine private family farming may consist in granting some leeway for specific Union-republican forms on a private ownership basis as they seem to develop in the Baltic republics. Yet such regional phenomena will hardly characterize "the main road" of Soviet agriculture in the foreseeable future.

APPENDIX

The subsequent table attempts to categorize the contract and small-scale forms of agriculture production according to their private and socialist elements. This can be done only in approximate terms, as in real Soviet life the elements may vary, depending on the concrete terms of contracts and of plot farming conditions. The combination of private plot and contract production (see p. 155, above) is not represented as a category of its own, as it forms a mix of elements, which may take different forms but where the common denominator is the family labor input. When, and insofar as, in such a combination privately tended animals remain the property of the public farm, the *podryad* and labor remuneration elements clearly predominates.

In all cases, land as an input remains socialist (i.e., state) property, and therefore is not taken into account. Yet a long-term usage right (plot or tenant farm) also represents a private elements. Except for the Baltic republics, outright private property of land so far is a thing only of discussion and of some reformers' ideas about future developments of Soviet "peasant" farming.

AGRICULTURAL ARRANGEMENTS: SOCIALIST OR PRIVATE?

Category of Farming	Socialist			Private		
	Work	Material Inputs	Output	Work	Material Inputs	Output
Large *Podryad* or its subunits						
Formally	+[1]	+	+[3]	-	-	+[4]
Actually	+[1]	+	+	-	-	-[8]
Autonomous *Podryad* (small group or family)	-	+	+[3]	+	-	+[4]
Private plot						
Formally	-	-[9]	-	+	+[9]	+
Actually	-	+[2]	-	+	+[2]	+[5]
Tenancy (*arenda*), internal	-	+[2]	-[3]	+	+[2]	+[6]
External and Peasant farm	-	-	-	+	+	+[7]

NOTES: (1) Work in the subunits (incorporated small groups or families), although individualized, is essentially assigned under the contract of the big group. (2) Although material inputs in plot and tenancy farming—e.g., supply of feed and young animals, of chemicals, machinery, transport, veterinary, services, etc.,—may originate from the public sector, and therefore in Soviet parlance be called socialist, the graph categorizes them as private if they are paid for by the plot owner or tenant, whether in money or labor, as part of a leasing contract, or in exchange for (instead of legal) sales obligations. (3) Contracted quantities only. (4) Above-plan and part of the contracted outputs. (5) Some sales to public sector often obligatory. (6) Above contract output. (7) Deliveries/sales to public sector state obligatory in actual fact, though not on principle. (8) That part of output, however, which is used for remuneration in kind, may be considered appropriated privately. (9) Formally, most of the material inputs originate in the private, but also in the socialist sector.

8

Perestroika and Innovation in Soviet Industry

Hans Heymann, Jr.

Wнат is probably the most daunting task that Soviet leader Mikhail Gorbachev faces in his gargantuan struggle to revitalize the stagnant Soviet economy is to impart to Soviet industry a propensity to innovate. This is by no means a new issue. When Joseph Berliner wrote his pioneering study of Soviet innovation more than a dozen years ago,[1] he succeeded in directing attention away from the traditional questions that had troubled economists for decades—whether a socialist economy could work at all, whether it could work efficiently, and whether it could sustain a high rate of growth—and in attracting attention instead to the question that has now become so important—whether the Soviet economy can be endowed with the attributes that will grant it the capacity to innovate, to generate rapid technological change.

The Soviet economy's lackluster performance with respect to innovation and its widening technological lag behind the advanced industrial countries has long troubled leaders in the USSR. What is new is that the issue has escalated to the point where it has become, in the eyes of Gorbachev, the key criterion for the ultimate success of his reforms. Indeed, it may prove to be what determines whether the Soviet Union can preserve its vaunted status as a superpower or, for that matter, can even remain a serious contender among the major powers.

Fortunately, so much has been written about the innovation-retarding characteristics of the Soviet command economy by now that a general familiarity with the fundamentals may be assumed, making it possible to proceed directly to the central question to be explored

---

[1] Joseph S. Berliner, *The Innovation Decision in Soviet Industry*, Cambridge, Massachusetts, The MIT Press, 1976.

here—namely, whether the reforms evolving in the Soviet Union today can be expected to have a significant impact on the dynamics of the innovation process in Soviet industry.

In this instance, the word "significant" is taken to mean something more than a mere acceleration in the rate of technological advance. The presumption is that Gorbachev views the problem not simply as one of preventing a further widening of the technological gap between the Soviet economy and the advanced Western economies; that what he is after is a decisive narrowing of this gap and an eventual emergence of the Soviet economy as a credible competitor in the world economy; and that nothing short of this could satisfy his desire to secure for his country the status of a great power in more than just military terms.

This presumption could be mistaken. Perhaps to expect global competitiveness is to set too high a goal for Gorbachev. Assuredly, his political survival would not be jeopardized if he failed to attain that lofty goal. Minimally, he might be satisfied if he managed merely to raise the performance of the economy to modestly respectable levels. It might be argued, though, that achieving the more ambitious goal of global competitiveness must be his optimal objective. If that is a correct assessment, it imposes very tough requirements on the Soviet economy's innovation process: it would have to match the performance of the world's most successful innovators, and its ability to compete with them would have to be judged by the same standards and criteria, by the same success indicators.

Assessing the Efficacy of the Gorbachev Reforms

What, if anything, can be said at this juncture about the prospects for Gorbachev's reforms? As Robert Campbell puts it in his contribution to this volume,[2] *perestroika* looms as a long-term sociopolitical process, the outcome of which can only be dimly perceived at this early stage. The kind of "creeping marketization" that Campbell sees can only develop as a result of a protracted series of sequential policies and programs, arrived at through trial and error and by methods of successive approximation.

Such a fluid process renders the task of assessing the viability of the reforms quite intractable. The task is made even more difficult considering that the most relevant part of the reform package was initiated only a short time ago, at the beginning of 1988; that key elements of the package are yet to be elaborated (e.g., the new tasks that self-financing implies for the banking system); that others have been formally

---

[2]   See "How to Think about *Perestroika*," Chapter 1.

introduced only to be quickly blocked or undercut (e.g., direct contracting and decentralized wholesale trade—the essence of "enterprise autonomy"); and that the program is, at this particular moment, in deep crisis (as evidenced by the unprecedented step of appointing Leonid Abalkin, the most outspokenly critical academic economist among Gorbachev's advisors, to the combined posts of deputy premier of the USSR and head of the new State Commission for Economic Reform.) In sum, reform is not only in its earliest stages but is also in a high state of flux, in which a good deal of confusion and uncertainty are to be expected.

Because of these factors—the fluidity of the program and its dependence on fundamental sociopolitical change—judgments about *perestroika* at this point are hazardous at best. But perhaps enough of its constituent elements and of Gorbachev's style have by now surfaced to permit some insight into the question of whether the reforms hold out some prospect of eventually having a significant impact on the dynamics of the innovation process in Soviet industry.

WHAT MAKES FOR SUCCESSFUL INNOVATION?

What qualities should be looked for that will indicate whether an economy is competitively innovative? By "competitively innovative," is meant an economy that is capable of introducing—rapidly and at "affordable" cost—new products, processes, and services that will be judged in the marketplace to be of superior quality and lasting usefulness.

Berliner has proposed a set of prerequisites for the innovative performance of an economy.[3] To be considered competitively innovative, he suggests, an economy must possess several rudimentary qualities—qualities that have emerged as common characteristics among all leading innovators in the modern industrial world, whether in Western Europe, Japan, or among the newly industrializing "Asian tigers." Specifically, the economies of all of these countries exhibit systems that give their entrepreneurs:

- Production autonomy—i.e., full command of all the resources they need to carry out their innovation tasks;

---

[3] I am indebted to Joseph Berliner for helpful ideas on the measurement of innovation performance. Some of his thoughts on qualities essential to innovative behavior are developed in J. S. Berliner, "Soviet Economic Reform and Technological Progress," Occasional Paper, No. 191, Waltham, Massachusetts, Brandeis University, 1987.

- Sales autonomy—i.e., the freedom to sell to any buyer and invade any market so as to assure the rapid diffusion of innovations;

- Market-based prices—i.e., a mechanism that provides accurate signals for rational entrepreneurial decisions;

- Global linkages—i.e., an environment of pervasive interaction with the world economy and its disciplining effects and competitive benefits; and

- Powerful incentives—i.e., high, tangible rewards that more than offset the risks and uncertainties that innovation typically entails.

Taken together, these qualities provide a convenient standard of measurement for the innovation profile of an economy, particularly if they are accepted as crucial. Thus, it may be useful to examine the Soviet situation with respect to each one of them, to consider the extent to which Gorbachev's reforms take them into account, and to conjecture whether the reforms are likely to instill them in the Soviet economy, perhaps making it possible for the USSR eventually to join the ranks of world-class competitive innovators.

PRODUCTION AUTONOMY

The chief considerations here are: Will an enterprise in fact enjoy the large measure of freedom that it would need to make its own operational decisions? How complete will be its command over resources; how reliable its access to supplies; how open its ability to launch new ventures and close down old ones; how clear and relevant its market signals? All of these considerations are essential to the exercise of production autonomy, but the reforms have so far barely touched them.

What happened, at least initially, was an almost exclusive reliance on the tried and failed remedies of earlier reform cycles: changing the organizational structure and functioning of the bureaucracies and hierarchies. It took Gorbachev and his reformers at least three years before they awakened to the fact that the traditional top-down approach does not work. Two examples illustrate that awakening and the gradual shift towards creating conditions and incentives for innovation and technical change at the enterprise level:

In the Realm of R&D. Here Gorbachev's initial thrust was explicitly directed at better central planning. In his words: "The acceleration of progress in science and technology urgently requires a profound restructuring . . . to increase the efficiency of centralism in planning and management."[4] There followed a spate of measures aimed at improving long-term technological forecasting, at more goal-oriented management of science and technology (a kind of "management by objectives"), and at targeting potential breakthrough inventions that could serve as catalysts for progress. Other measures were aimed at shaking up the commanding heights of the administrative hierarchy—changing the leadership and role of Gosplan (State Planning Committee), re-energizing the GKNT (State Committee for Science and Technology), a top-level coordinating entity, and breaking ministerial barriers by creating superministries and maxibureaus.

One new organizational mechanism, the Interbranch Scientific and Technical Complex (MNTK) has been much touted. It was first mandated in December, 1985, as a vehicle for integrating into a kind of "strike force" under the authority of a lead scientific institute all the forces and facilities (regardless of their ministerial subordination) that could contribute to the accomplishment of an important innovation. Some twenty MNTKs were formed, each focused on a different technology, with lead institutes in most cases being drawn from the USSR Academy of Sciences.

While the resources mobilized by the MNTK network were quite formidable, it appears that successes have been few. Much criticism has been aimed at the leadership of the Academy of Sciences on the grounds that it is deficient in industrial applications know-how and lacks the bureaucratic clout to cope with the powerful ministries. Indeed, the few successful MNTKs were, in every instance, led by prestigious scientist-entrepreneurs with outstanding reputations and high-level Party contacts and patrons. Success may thus be largely a function of the personality and influence of the MNTK's general director.

It has become increasingly evident in the past two years that faith in the efficacy of traditional top-down approaches to accelerating the R&D-to-production cycle has been badly shaken. There is growing recognition now that the real impediment is the dearth of initiative, creativity, and independence at the bottom. The center of gravity has thus begun to shift away from the technology-push to the technology-pull side of the equation.

In the Realm of Production. A second example of the shift is Gorbachev's massive attempt to restructure the machine-building sector, his initial reform priority. Here once more an early preoccupation with centrally energized organizational fixes is evident. As is made clear in an excellent analysis by Andrew and Bonnie

---

[4]   Mikhail S. Gorbachev, *Mikhail Gorbachev: Selected Speeches and Articles,* Moscow, Progress Publishers, 1985, p. 149.

Matosich,[5] Soviet reformers went all out. With the help of large
infusions of new investments into the sector, they introduced a wide
range of top-down administrative measures aimed at boosting
machinery production and improving its quality—two objectives
that were soon found to be incompatible. An improvised system of
quality control (Gospriemka), inserted at the end of the production line
as a kind of *deus ex machina*, proved both infelicitous and pointlessly
demoralizing to the nine hundred machine-building enterprises that
were subjected to it. In addition, the reformers piled on a variety of
measures intended to speed up assimilation of new technology into
production and modernize the antiquated production base.

In this case, however, when these centrally managed efforts proved
ineffectual, the reformers did turn their attention to a more promising,
decentralized, systemic set of measures aimed at changing the motivations and modalities by which machine-builders do their jobs. These
include the kinds of "enterprise autonomy" measures that are clearly
consonant with the innovation-inducing criteria listed above: self-
financing, profit retention, wholesale-trade contracting, foreign joint
enterprise and coproduction arrangements, and at least the prospect of
some type of price reform. There were also some eliminations of intermediate bureaucratic layers, reductions in ministries, and efforts at
improved top-level coordination.

Most of these measures clearly were closer to the mark, but the initial consequences of such an avalanche of reforms were, to say the least,
dismaying. Although considerable momentum for change had been
created in the sector, machine-builders quickly found themselves in an
unaccustomed and highly unstable environment: long-established "rules
of the game," quantitative performance targets, established success
indicators, and carefully cultivated management relationships had
suddenly been invalidated and new arrangements that were often
contradictory put in their place or, worse, superimposed on them.

In trying to fathom the workings of the command economy, Western observers often seem to focus too much on the formal structure of
the system and thus to underrate the importance of the network of
informal relationships—the ad hoc compromises, the collusive
arrangements, the special deals—that have evolved as a matter of
necessity among enterprises, between enterprises and their ministries,
and between ministries and the central planning and supply authorities. These relationships are in fact a kind of lubricant that keeps the
system from grinding to a halt. By dumping too many new demands,
new rules, and new procedures upon the sector, helter-skelter, without
a coherent policy design and in the glare of publicity, the planners

    5   Andrew J. & Bonnie K. Matosich, "Machine Building: *Perestroika's*
Sputtering Engine," *Soviet Economy*, No. 2, 1988, pp. 144-176.

inadvertently disrupted this carefully nurtured web of relationships, throwing machine-building into a state of anxiety and confusion. When performance dropped sharply in 1987, the leadership added fuel to the fire by a campaign of high-level criticism leveled against the machine-builders, adding to their sense of futility and despair.

What is rather more encouraging about the experience in the machine-building sector is that Gorbachev quickly eased back from his high-pressure campaign, recognizing that he may have overloaded the circuits and that this key sector needed some breathing space if it was to assimilate the new ways. At the same time, his attention was diverted by a new political challenge: rising public anger over a visibly deteriorating situation with respect to food, housing, and consumer goods forced him to carry out a drastic reordering of his resource allocation priorities. A major shift in investment and budgetary outlays towards the consumer sectors would be required during the last two years (1989-90) of the Twelfth Five-Year Plan.

It is not likely that Gorbachev will soon resume his campaign to restructure the machine-building sectors with anything like "the storming tactics" so prominent in the earlier reform period, even though he probably still views machine-building as the flagship of his larger drive towards industrial modernization. Other concerns are too pressing—the stark imbalance between the flow of wages paid out and the flow of consumer goods to the shops; an escalating budget deficit that fuels an unprecedented rate of inflation; and food shortages of politically perilous dimensions—matters that Gorbachev must now attend to with utmost urgency.

Given this state of affairs, what can be concluded about the prospects of the "enterprise autonomy" reforms? For the present, the reforms seem stalled at a point where little has been implemented and much effectively blocked. Even if obligatory targets are massively reduced and the scope for decentralized contracting broadly expanded, there remains the worrisome question of how resolutely the reformers will seek to bring the ministries to heel; how obediently the ministries will refrain from microintervention; how patiently they will permit their enterprises to rely on economic instruments to guide economic activity—patterns of behavior that run so deeply against the grain. But if "new thinking" does take hold in these areas, there are still more radical measures that a propensity to innovate would require—the granting of freedom of entry into industries and markets and the introduction of conditions of genuine competitive challenge to pervasively monopolistic economic institutions. The reforms proposed to date show little prospect of significant movement in these directions.

There is, admittedly, one hopeful exception to this somewhat pessimistic assessment—namely, the establishment of cooperative enterprise, which is a potential means of stimulating innovation. The cooperative offered a way of providing some scope for quasi-private competitive economic activity while avoiding the ideological stigma of explicit private ownership. The initiative proved instantly popular, leading to a proliferation of cooperative retail shops, restaurants, and other small-scale service-sector activities. At first, the new private-profit modality was pursued almost exclusively by individual citizens, partnerships, and modest-sized groups, mostly in the urban service sector. Cooperatives quickly gained high visibility and evoked much public resentment for "price gouging." They soon found themselves subjected to heavy taxation and restrictive legislation by the state on the one hand and victimized by extortion from Mafia-like groups on the other. Whether these urban retail cooperatives are destined for a bright future is still uncertain.

What is of much more interest is the recent spread (perhaps it should be termed "migration") of cooperative enterprise to the state sector. A growing number of prestigious Soviet R&D institutes, industrial enterprises, and even their ministries are sponsoring (and sheltering) specialized cooperatives to provide a variety of sophisticated business services for them in such areas as computer maintenance, software programming, information management, and a range of analytic tasks that can be more expeditiously and efficiently undertaken by cooperatives than by the state bureaucracy. The parallels with US governmental contractor-consulting relationships are obvious, and this kind of innovative, flexible, and perhaps in time competitive application of cooperatives appears quite promising as a vehicle for stimulating more innovative responses within the state sector. Such arrangements, however, also provide excellent opportunities for illegal activities such as diversion of state resources.

Where all this may lead is hard to say, but until enterprise-related reforms, including those that have brought the reemergence of cooperatives, evolve more fully and the restructuring process moves to higher levels, attainment of production autonomy will remain at best a hope for the distant future.

SALES AUTONOMY

In the West, vigorous and imaginative pursuit of market opportunities largely determines innovation performance. Innovation occurs not because it is an enjoyable activity but because it is necessary for a firm's survival and prosperity in a highly competitive environment, an environment that is demand-driven, quality-conscious and totally unforgiving. In this environment, great attention is given to merchandising factors such as responsiveness to consumer tastes, market-testing, product-packaging and promotion, advertising, and special financing arrangements; and much effort is devoted to long-term customer confidence-building measures such as comprehensive warranties and reliable after-sales servicing. Indeed, in the Western business community there is now an almost pathological preoccupation with the twin quests for product quality and customer satisfaction.[6]

Among the lessons that Western businessmen have learned about product quality is that it cannot be imposed from above by a system of quality control that operates ex post facto. It must be designed into a product from the outset. Similarly, responsiveness to customer wants cannot be decreed but must be integral to an enterprise's reward structure—i.e., there must be tangible recognition of the link between an enterprise's acuity in satisfying its customers and its bottom-line financial condition.

There is nothing in the Soviet reforms to date that places the pursuit of product quality and customer satisfaction high on the list of entrepreneurial priorities. The reforms focus primarily on easing the petty tutelage that central organs have long exercised over the internal operations of enterprises. The real problem, though, does not lie in the internal operations of enterprises but in their external relations or transactions—with the suppliers of their goods and services and with the customers for their output. There is little, if any, discussion of the degrees of freedom that enterprises are to enjoy in their external transactions and the extent to which a competitive environment is to be encouraged there. Yet the test of the significance of any autonomy that the reform may confer is precisely whether it creates and promotes genuine competition among enterprises, whether it permits an innovating manager to drop an unreliable supplier in the confident expectation that he can place his order with a more reliable one, and whether he feels free to enter the market with a new product or service and be allowed to compete on even terms. The Soviet reforms largely ignore these qualities, and the environment remains one in which "nobody cares." So far at least the reforms fall far short of transforming Soviet enterprises in the matter of sales autonomy to the point of making the economy seriously quality-conscientious and customer-oriented.

MARKET-BASED PRICES

A price system that provides accurate and fair measures of relative scarcities and relative economic contributions is a *sine qua non* for an innovative economy. At this point, there is little reason to expect that such a price system will emerge soon in the USSR. In this realm, the

---

[6] In a recent Carnegie-Mellon University survey of business-school alumni, for example, executives polled cited these two factors as the most important issues US managers will face in the 1990s (see *The Wall Street Journal*, October 11, 1988).

Soviet leaders face their most serious dilemma. Past price reforms—and those now contemplated—have been little more than price revisions, intended to make prices account fully for costs, not to make prices act as an efficiency-signaling and disciplining device. The aim, at least in principle, has been that prices are to be set so that all enterprises can operate profitably. Prices have not been designed to ensure rational production and investment choices—i.e., to reward efficient firms and to force inefficient firms into bankruptcy.

The problem for Gorbachev now is that any price reform that seeks to impose true criteria of economic efficiency on the decision-making process must repudiate the vastly inefficient decisions of the past. It must turn its back on the unproductive legacy of an earlier era. It must suffer the unworthy enterprises and their work forces to go under, while allowing windfall gains to be made by those enterprises (and their work forces) that can meet the new criteria for efficiency—even though in neither case were the human participants necessarily responsible for the decisions of the past for which, under reformed prices, they would be penalized or rewarded. No previous Soviet leadership has been willing to take this step, and neither Gorbachev nor his economists have given much indication that they even fully understand the issue.

Recently, however, economic literacy in the USSR has shown signs of spreading steadily, and the level of sophistication with which complex reform issues are being discussed among Soviet economists seems to be making real headway. There are effective ways in which the painful consequences of a radical price reform can be mitigated, and there is no reason to assume that Soviet economists will not discover them.

GLOBAL INTEGRATION

Even in the West, the extent to which national economies have become involved with and dependent on one another in an ever more encompassing international system is only just beginning to be grasped. For a country to be a competitive innovator in the twenty-first century will require a high degree of global interaction on a very sophisticated level. Increasingly, high-tech enterprise must be multinational in scope, not only because the marketplace for technological innovation is both intensely interactive and truly global but also because today's technologies obsolesce so much more rapidly and their more advanced replacements entail mammoth development costs that few purely national entities can afford. As a result, would-be competitive innovators are both pushed and pulled into multinational relationships. They must find ways to sell globally if they wish to gain the market share necessary to recover costs.

From the perspective of the world economy, what is striking is the virtual absence of the USSR from the international technology exchange market, its lack of productive links with the worldwide R&D community, and its general isolation from the rewards (and penalties) of the international economic system. While some linkage does exist, it is so circumscribed as to exert almost no stimulating or disciplining force. The Soviet economy's unorthodox involvement in technology-"borrowing" from abroad, its ability—within certain limits—to obtain subsidized foreign loans, its as yet half-hearted engagement in "joint ventures," and its (at best symbolic) potential membership in GATT (General Agreement on Tariffs and Trade) mirror the limitations imposed on the system by more than six decades of self-inflicted economic isolation. It will take measures of a much more heroic kind—most notably, domestic monetary and price reform and an internationally convertible ruble—to bring about a fully committed involvement on the part of the USSR in the global economy.

This is not to denigrate the serious interest of a growing number of prominent Soviet economists and political figures in having the USSR, as a major world power, adopt a more consequential attitude towards participation in the international system. Gorbachev's recent reform of foreign-trade institutions and his more hospitable approach towards Western enterprise testify to this interest. The early stages of a break with the past are apparent, but the process will have to go much farther if it is to open the way for a broader, more competitively stimulating exposure of the Soviet economy to the hurly-burly of the world market.

POWERFUL INCENTIVES

The final and perhaps most important prerequisite for fostering innovation in an economy is the structure of material incentives, the set of monetary rewards and less tangible recognitions (personal gratification, prestige) that are held out to the successful, risk-taking, innovating manager and that separate him from his more conservative, risk-averse, noninnovating colleagues.

Soviet leaders have long been troubled by the repeated failure of their "tinkering" with the incentive structure to overcome industrial managers' resistance to innovation. Gorbachev's reforms make another attempt to resolve this stubborn problem. The approach is a familiar one—rewarding successful innovation with more generous special bonus supplements to salaries by drawing even larger shares from enterprises' retained profits. In a restructured economy, it can therefore probably be expected that monetary incentives will be visibly strengthened. But will it be enough to make a real difference?

The mere fact that a highly successful innovation will generate larger incomes than in the past does not mean that the increment will be sufficient to overcome the present, exceedingly adverse ratio of risk to reward facing the Soviet manager. In choosing to innovate, he risks not merely a failure to achieve the promised benefits of the innovation but, more important, a severe disruption of his enterprise's established production process and the loss of the entire enterprise bonus that this could entail. In terms of the balance of risk to reward, he would thus be inclined to view even a sizeable increment in potential bonus income as inconsequential and the overall incentive structure as still quite discouraging whatever the strength of his personal propensity to innovate.

There are two ways of attaining a dramatically more favorable balance of risk to reward: one is by reducing the level of risk facing the enterprise manager, through structural reforms of the kind discussed in the section on sales autonomy above—i.e., increasing the degree of enterprise autonomy over its external transactions; the other is by drastically increasing the level of tangible reward held out to the manager for innovative behavior.

Neither of these two measures is in prospect for plant managers under the Gorbachev reforms thus far proclaimed. Enterprise autonomy remains only a remote possibility, and monetary rewards fall far short of what would be needed to overcome managers' perceptions of risk. Indeed, the potential monetary gains are minuscule when compared with the powerful rewards held out to innovative entrepreneurs in Western countries, where it is not higher current income but large increments in wealth that provide the real incentive. It is the ability to capitalize the stream of future income generated by innovation that constitutes the decisive inducement. Gorbachev's reforms make no provision for wealth incentives, and it is not likely that a socialist economy so intolerant of private ownership and accumulation of wealth will make its peace easily with such a counteregalitarian measure.

CONCLUSION

In sum, in the Soviet case all five of the stated prerequisites for a competitively innovative economy point in the same direction: the industrial reforms that have been enunciated, though hardly implemented to date, may well achieve some respectable improvements in the economy's abysmally poor innovative performance, but short of much more radical departures from hallowed socialist ways, they will not gain for the USSR the position of a world-class innovator to which Gorbachev so fervently aspires.

9

Prospects for Commodity and Financial Exchanges

Perry Patterson

GLASNOST' in the Soviet Union has played a crucial role not just in exposing but also in bringing official acknowledgment of serious institutional defects in the Soviet economy. The continued existence of a whole variety of manifestations of the command-type economic mechanism has been called into question. Among the institutions that are undergoing fundamental rethinking are the state foreign-trade monopoly, the collective-farm system, and the practice of centralized price-setting—to mention but a few.

It is one thing to admit various deficiencies, however, and quite another to evolve and implement concrete, realistic proposals for change. Here, too, *glasnost'* has been a beneficial phenomenon, generating an outpouring of ideas (of varying quality) to remedy the situation. This essay considers a possible reform of current wholesale-supply and capital-allocation mechanisms. The proposed fix, one that has recently surfaced in the Soviet economics literature, is the establishment of *birzhi*, or commodity and financial exchanges. In the essay, some of the theoretical benefits of such a reform are discussed, and a look is taken at Soviet (and Western) attempts to find a justification for commodity and financial exchanges in the experience of other nations and in the Soviet past. Little has been written about the Soviet experience with *birzhi* during the period of the New Economic Policy (NEP) in the 1920s, so the history is reviewed by way of providing a basis for drawing some lessons for today's *perestroika*.

THE REQUIREMENT FOR MARKETIZATION

The centrally planned distribution of goods among Soviet state enterprises at the wholesale level has long been recognized by both Soviet and Western observers as an extremely cantankerous mechanism that is subject to frequent breakdown and that leads to generalized waste of resources and corruption among managerial personnel.[1] Dissatisfaction with the performance of the wholesale distribution system has recently found reflection in a number of specific reform proposals. These include abolishing planning in favor of *goszakazy* (voluntary contracts with the state), requiring managers to contract directly with one another at the wholesale level, reducing bureaucratic interference from the center in horizontal relations, and providing financial incentives based on the profitability of enterprises.

Some of the problems that may arise with current reform efforts in this area are not difficult to foresee. Because prices are still set administratively, managers' efforts to maximize profits, while possibly "rational" in the Soviet context, may in reality lead to uneconomic behavior and a tendency to waste resources. Moreover, managers who have not been trained to look for trading partners are likely to fall back on any *goszakazy* proffered, especially if they are accompanied by guarantees of credit or vital raw-materials inputs. Finally, if the Soviet economy is experiencing repressed inflation or *tovarnyi golod*, then financial incentives may themselves be weak.

Perhaps because of the difficulties of reform in the state industrial structure, another vector has been added to the overall reform picture by the Soviet leadership. This entails a significant increase in the scope of private and quasi-private economic activity and may be viewed as a supplement to the above measures or, perhaps, as supplanting them, getting around much of the institutionalized chaos of the state industrial sector by creating an entirely new non-state-controlled structure. In any case, the expansion of the private sector raises a number of interesting and delicate questions regarding the interaction of state- and private-owned enterprises. How is the state to supply the private sector with raw materials? Can the private sector be a reliable supplier of the state, and vice versa? Are the two sectors to be placed on an equal footing with respect to regulation and taxation?

One obvious institutional need, in the absence of the discredited system of all-encompassing planning, is some form of wholesale market linking all enterprises' supplies and demands of various commodities. Such a market was briefly part of the Soviet economic system during the period of the NEP—in the form of commodity exchanges or *birzhi*.[2]

---

[1]   For Soviet commentaries on this, see V. Romanyuk, "Raspredelyat'? Net, prodavat'!" *Izvestia*, January 3, 1989; and P. Bunich, "Sotsialistichesky rynok sredstv proizvodstva ili razverstka?" *Voprosy ekonomiki*, No. 11, 1988, pp. 55-57.

[2]   Mikhail Svishchev, "Opyt NEPa i razvitie melkogo proizvodstva na sovremennom etape," *Istoriya SSSR*, No. 1, 1989, p. 23.

As Philip Hanson points out in the chapter in this volume on "Ownership Issues in *Perestroika*," a second institutional gap that becomes more obvious as *perestroika* proceeds is the lack of well-developed financial and capital markets. The lack of a market in government bonds makes it more difficult to attract individual savings and perhaps also to contain inflationary pressures, since cash is more likely to contribute to aggregate demand for goods than are less liquid forms of wealth.[3] The lack of markets in enterprise-issued bonds and stocks means that enterprise savings are often misallocated. The lack of a market in foreign currencies makes direct foreign investment a quite complicated affair. Here too these were the sort of markets that were being brought together (at least to some extent) by Soviet *fondovye birzhi*, or financial exchanges, under the NEP.

EXPERIENCE ABROAD AND IN THE SOVIET PAST

The search for viable, politically acceptable market mechanisms for wholesale goods and capital has naturally led Soviet economics writers to evaluate the experience of other (primarily) socialist countries with such mechanisms. While analyses of foreign wholesale-goods markets has been published,[4] little has appeared addressing the issue of commodity exchanges directly. Numerous articles have, however, been devoted to capital markets, financial exchanges, and exchange-rate policies in China, Hungary, Yugoslavia, the United States, and other countries.[5] A number of articles and a conference report have also taken up the question of instituting stock exchanges in the Soviet Union,[6]

---

[3] Martin Feldstein, "Why Perestroika Isn't Happening," *The Wall Street Journal*, April 21, 1989, p. A14.

[4] See, for example, A. Sukhoruchenko, "Organizatsiya optovoi torgovli sredstvami proizvodstva v stranakh-chlenakh SEV," *Planovoe khozyaistvo*, No. 7, July, 1987, pp. 101-105.

[5] See, for example, E. F. Avdokushin, "Teoriya i praktika ekonomiki," *Problemy Dal'nego Vostoka*, No. 5, 1988, pp. 58-64; P. I. Kuligin, "Denezhnye vklady naseleniya v narodnoe khozyaistvo: iz opyta NRB, VNR, PNR i KNR," *Izvestiya AN SSSR, Seriya ekonomicheskaya*, No. 6, 1988; Li Sinshan, "O nekotorykh voprosakh vnedreniya aktsionernoi sistemy v Kitae," *Voprosy ekonomiki*, January, 1989, pp. 78-83; Yu. Malinov, "Valyutnyi rynok v Yugoslavii," *Ekonomicheskaya gazeta*, No. 4, 1989, p. 21; and S. B. Zelenev, "Rynok aktsionernogo kapitala SShA v 80-e gody," *SShA. Ekonomika, politika, ideologiya*, No. 10, 1988, pp. 42-50.

[6] E.g., S. Assikritov, "Tsennye bumagi," *Izvestia*, October 21, 1988; and I. P. Kitaigorodsky, "Aktsii i dividendy," *Ekonomicheskaya gazeta*, No. 45, 1988, p. 23. The conference report is "Nauchno-prakticheskoe soveshchanie v Institute ekonomiki AN SSSR," *Voprosy ekonomiki*, January, 1989, pp. 58-77.

having been prompted by the recent issues of stock- and bond-like instruments by a limited number of Soviet enterprises. Given the limited scope and still experimental nature of such instruments, it is somewhat surprising that such attention has been devoted to the formation of secondary markets. The degree of the current fascination with stock markets in the Soviet Union may even be somewhat unrealistic for a society that still has only rather primitive banking arrangements. Nonetheless, it is clear that Soviet economists have now seriously broached the topic of instituting some form of *birzha*. As they search for workable proposals, it is likely that foreign experience with various forms of exchanges will continue to attract their attention and influence their thinking. It is likely too that the nearly forgotten experience with *birzhi* during the period of the NEP will be reexamined.

There is no question that the NEP has become an important source of inspiration to current reformers.[7] Many of the battles over the role of the private sector, the need for a clearly defined legal system for enterprises, and the nature of interaction between market and plan have already been fought (at least once) under Soviet power,[8] and Soviet scholars have recently been turning to the legacy of the NEP with great frequency.[9] Here too it is likely that the fascination with more or less forgotten mechanisms has gone too far, but the NEP serves the useful function of a symbol of a positive, successful period in Soviet economic history.

Despite the considerable attention paid to the institution of the NEP in general, however, very little attention has been given to *birzhi* in any Soviet writings since 1930. The explanation for this may lie in the circumstance that during the NEP not market mechanisms per se but private versus state participation in them was the central issue. Much of the literature of the late 1920s was more concerned with the elimina-

---

[7]   See the essay by Mark von Hagen in this volume.

[8]   See Alan M. Ball, *Russia's Last Capitalists: The Nepmen, 1921-1929*, Berkeley, University of California Press, 1987, pp. 38-39. See also V. A. Arkhipov and L. F. Morozov, *Bor'ba protiv kapitalisticheskikh elementov v promyshlennosti i torgovle, 1920-nachalo 30-kh godov*, Moscow, 1978; A. Kaktyn', *O podkhode k chastnomu torgovomu kapitalu*, Moscow, 1924; and *Ot kapitalizma k sotsializmu. Osnovnye problemy istorii perekhodnogo perioda v SSSR, 1917-1937 gg.*, Vol. I, *Pobeda sotialisticheskoi revolyutsii. Nachalo perekhodnogo perioda, 1917-1927 gg.*, and Vol. II, *Razvernutoe stroitel'stvo sotsializma v SSSR, 1928-1937 gg.*, Moscow, 1981.

[9]   Arkhipov and Morozov, *op. cit.*; V. P. Dmitrenko, *Torgovaya politika sovetskogo gosudarstva posle perekhoda k NEPu 1921-1924 gg.*, Moscow, 1971; V. E. Manevich, "Likvidatsiya NEPa i dal'neishaya evolyutsiya kreditno-finansovoi sistemy," *Ekonomika i organizatsiya promyshlennogo proizvodstva*, No. 10, 1988, pp. 142-56; and Svishchev, *op. cit.*

tion of private trade than with the institutions that fostered such trade.[10] Literature specifically dealing with the exchanges thus remains quite weak. *Istoriya sotsialisticheskoi ekonomiki SSSR* (Moscow, 1976) devotes approximately a page (Vol. II, pp. 154-155) of vague description to *tovarnye birzhi*. *Entsiklopediya gosudarstva i prava* (Moscow, 1925-1927) has a similar entry (pp. 249-250). Brief notes on related legal issues are to be found in the two-volume *Ekonomicheskaya zhizn' SSSR. Khronika sobytii i faktov, 1917-1965* (Moscow, 1967). Probably the most thoughtful, if brief, recent treatment of related issues is that of Mikhail Svishchev.[11] All modern writings, interestingly, seem ignorant of a very useful summary by Konstantin Shmidt ("Birzha") that appeared in the 1927 edition of *Bol'shaya sovetskaya entsiklopediya.*

The literature on Soviet *birzhi* written in the West is similarly quite limited. Oliver Hayward's article on *birzhi* (pp. 184-188 in *The Modern Encyclopedia of Russian and Soviet History*) contains only three paragraphs on the Soviet period and provides no references. E. H. Carr and R. W. Davies refer to the *birzhi* in passing, and Alan N. Ball provides a few scattered paragraphs, but little else exists in English.[12]

A SHORT HISTORY

THE RISE OF THE SOVIET COMMODITY AND FINANCIAL EXCHANGES

Given the almost total lack of secondary literature on the Soviet *birzhi*, it is surprising to find that they were originally considered to be of great importance, especially in the period 1924-1925. At least 109 *tovarnye birzhi* existed at one time or another on Soviet territory;[13] during the NEP approximately thirteen of these had *fondovye otdely* (see Table 1).

---

[10] I. A. Bialyi, *Chastnyi kapital v g. Irkutske*, Irkutsk, 1929; S. M. Dvolaitsky, (ed.), *Chastnyi kapital v torgovle SSSR*, Moscow, 1928; Andrei Fabrichnyi, *Chastnyi kapital na poroge pyatiletki*, Moscow, 1930; S. L. Fridman, *Chastnyi kapital na denezhnom rynke*, Moscow, 1925; A. M. Ginsburg, (ed.), *Chastnyi kapital v narodnom khozyaistve SSSR. Materialy kommissii VSNKh SSSR*, Moscow-Leningrad, 1927; V. V. Ivanovsky, *Chastnyi torgovyi kapital na rynke Saratovskoi gubernii*, Saratov, 1927; Yu. Larin, *Chastnyi kapital v SSSR*, Moscow-Leningrad, 1927; G. P. Paduchev, *Chastnyi torgovets pri novoi ekonomicheskoi politike (po dannym byudzhetnogo obsledovaniya)*, Voronezh, 1926; and N. N. Ryauzov, *Vytesnenie chastnogo posrednika iz tovarooborota*, Moscow, 1930.

[11] See Note 2.

[12] E. H. Carr and R. W. Davies, *Foundations of a Planned Economy, 1926-1929*, London, Macmillan, 1969; and Ball, *op. cit.*

[13] Most of the secondary literature puts the figure at roughly one hundred.

Table 1
THE SOVIET *BIRZHI*: A PRELIMINARY REGISTER

Aktyubinsk
Alma-Ata
Arkhangelsk
Armavir
Astrakhan
Baku*
Balashov
Barnaul
Bashkir (at Ufa)
Batum*
Biisk
Blagoveshchensk
Borisoglebsk
Bryansk
Bugulma
Bukhara*
Cheboksary
Chelyabinsk
Chistopol
Chita
Dagestan (at Makhachkala)
Ekaterinburg (Sverdlovsk)
Ekaterinoslav (Dnepropetrovsk)
Elets
Elizavetgrad (Kirovograd)
Erevan*
Feodosiya
Gomel
Grozny
Irkutsk
Ivanovo-Voznesensk
Izhevsk
Kaluga
Kazan
Khabarovsk
Kharkov*
Kherson
Kiev*
Kirsanov
Kokand
Kostroma
Kozlov

Krasnodar
Krasnoyarsk
Kremenchug
Kurgan
Kursk
Kustanai
Kzyl-Orda
Leningrad*
Maikop
Minsk
Moscow*
Nikolaevsk
Nizhni Novgorod
Novyi Oskol
Novonikolaevsk (Novosibirsk)
Novorossiisk
Odessa
Omsk
Orel
Orenburg*
Penza
Perm
Petropavlovsk
Petrozavodsk
Poltava
Proskurov (Khmelnitsky)
Pskov
Romny
Rostov-on-Don*
Ryazan
Rybinsk
Samara
Samarkand
Sarapul
Saratov
Semipalatinsk
Severo-dvinsk (Velikii Ustyug)
Simbirsk (Ulyanovsk)
Simferopol
Smolensk
Stavropol
Sukhumi

Table 1 (Continued)
THE SOVIET *BIRZHI*: A PRELIMINARY REGISTER

Syzran	Ust Sysol'sk (Syktyvkar)
Tambov	Verkhneudinsk
Tashkent*	Vinnitsa
Terskaya (Pyatigorsk)	Vitebsk
Tiflis*	Vladikavkaz
Tomsk	Vladimir
Troitsk	Vladivostok*
Tsaritsyn (Stalingrad/Volgograd)	Vologda
Tula	Voronezh
Turkmenskaya (at Ashkhabad)	Vyatka
Tver	Yaroslavl
Tyumen	Zhitomir
Ural'sk	Zaporozhe

* Denotes existence of *fondovyi otdel*

Authorized in 1921, the first *tovarnaya birzha* seems to have been founded at Saratov in July or August, 1921[14] "on the initiative of organs of consumer cooperation."[15]

Indirect evidence of the importance of the *birzhi* can be seen in the great amount of material generated by these institutions. *Torgovo-promyshlennaya gazeta* reported on the *birzhi* on an almost daily basis from 1924 to 1926, in addition to providing daily quotations from the Moscow (and other) financial exchanges and listing major commodity transactions. Furthermore, almost every exchange was producing a *Byulleten'* during these years, some of them on a daily basis, as well as annual reports.

As can easily be imagined, Soviet *birzhi* had a quite complicated existence from the very start. Part of this was owing to political and ideological considerations; part of it had to do with the duties imposed on them. The Soviet *birzha* was to regulate the market; provide a cheap wholesale-trade mechanism for state, cooperative, and private trade in a great variety of goods;[16] assist the new Soviet manager in dealings in

---

[14] In his article in *The Modern Encyclopedia of Russian and Soviet History*, Hayward (seemingly mistakenly) claims that the Moscow *birzha* was first.

[15] *Ekonomicheskaya zhizn' SSSR. Khronika sobytii i faktov, 1917-1965*, Vol. I, p. 82; *Bol'shaya sovetskaya entsiklopediya*, Vol. III, 1927, p. 376; and *Birzhi i rynki: sbornik*, Moscow, 1924.

[16] State enterprises were originally required to conduct or at least register all wholesale trade operations at the local *birzha*.

unfamiliar markets; and give the government complete statistics on volume of trade and the class nature of traders involved not just on the trading floor but in the rest of district wholesale trade as well.

As a result of the many demands placed on the institution, the Soviet *birzha* could never function quite like its Western counterparts. Few of the markets that utilized the *birzha* could have ever tended towards efficient distribution: price controls, low trade volume, and the great variety of nonhomogeneous commodities being traded ensured this. Private interest in conducting trade at the *birzha*, though strong, was surely weakened by the fact that the state was using the *birzha* as a means of acquiring the statistics for correctly waging class war. Only the Moscow exchange was large enough to have a few hundred traders a day. Grain trade may also have been relatively smooth at the larger provincial *birzhi*. The scene on the trading floor must, however, have often been quite dull. Many contemporary writers worried about enlivening trade; the Moscow *fondovyi otdel*, or financial exchange, often reported three traders and no trade on a given day.[17]

THE FUNCTIONING OF THE EXCHANGES

To properly assess the role played by *birzhi* in the Soviet past, some consideration must be given to the differences among *birzhi* in various locations. While coverage of all 109 *birzhi* would be impossible for reasons of space, it will be useful to look at the operating history of the Moscow *tovarnaya birzha*, of the small provincial commodity exchanges, and of the Moscow *fondovyi otdel* in some detail.

The Moscow Commodity Exchange. Founded on January 12, 1922, the Moscow *tovarnaya birzha* quickly rose to a dominant position among all Soviet exchanges (much like the prerevolutionary exchange in St. Petersburg). In terms of transactions conducted directly at *birzhi*, the Moscow exchange had a higher volume of trade than the seventy next biggest exchanges combined for each year between 1922-23 and 1925-26.[18] Rapid growth of trade also made the Moscow *birzha* most like modern Western commodity exchanges, in the sense that it soon became necessary to establish separate trading areas (often in separate buildings) for specific, highly traded items such as grains, textiles, timber, etc. The grain section would seem to have been particularly successful, bringing together in excess of one hundred traders a day.

---

[17]   *Torgovo-promyshlennaya gazeta*, various issues, 1924 to 1926.

[18]   According to Shmidt's article in *Bol'shaya sovetskaya entsiklopediya* (1927), Moscow commodity exchange volumes were 431,500 rubles in 1922-23; 791,700 in 1923-24; 2,056,300 in 1924-25; and 2,855,900 in 1925-26 (see Vol. III, p. 377).

As was generally true elsewhere, the Moscow commodity exchange was a meeting place for all types of traders. While it was certainly the case that state enterprises, syndicates, and trusts conducted the bulk of the volume of trade (88 percent in 1925-26), cooperatives, mixed stock companies with foreign participation, and private traders were also represented.

The dominance of Moscow as a center of wholesale commodity trade, and trade at the Moscow *birzha* in particular, along with its convenient location near the seat of government, also made the Soviet capital the focal point for interaction between *birzhi* and the state. The Moscow exchange was a prolific publisher of daily, monthly, and yearly information and opinions regarding trade at the exchanges and wholesale trade in general.[19] Furthermore, Moscow was the meeting place for congresses of soviets of *birzhevoi torgovli*, which united all the *birzhi* in the Soviet Union, largely for the purpose of lobbying the state to improve operating conditions. Government officials often attended these conferences, at which calls were not infrequently heard for relaxed restrictions on the private sector at all levels. Thus, like the prerevolutionary institutions of the same name, the Moscow congresses provided a form of direct policy feedback to the government that no longer existed following the abolition of both *birzhi* and *s"ezdy* in 1930.

Provincial Commodity Exchanges. Most of the provincial exchanges were quite small compared with that in Moscow in terms of volume of trade, but they nonetheless took on a significant life of their own at the local level.[20] Items traded varied greatly, with individual exchanges specializing in such commodities as grain, textiles, fish, leather, fuels, tobacco, furs, etc. Like the Moscow exchange, the duties of the local exchanges were at first to establish markets and later, increasingly, to monitor the operations of private traders. Similarly too, since all trade (in principle) was to pass through the local *birzha*, a high degree of profitability was associated with many of the exchanges (over 30 percent of revenues in some cases). This circumstance contributed to

---

[19]   See, for example, *Birzhevoe obozrenie, Torgovo-promyshlennaya gazeta*, and *Otchet moskovskoi tovarnoi birzhi*, various years during this period.

[20]   Although the one hundred or more provincial exchanges produced thousands of pages of reports and newpapers, very few of these have found their way to the West or into Soviet scholarship. This section is based on *otchety* for the year 1924-25 provided by exchanges in Vladimir, Armavir; Astrakhan; Vladikavkaz; and, most important, Ekaterinburg, which provided an especially revealing volume. See also, however, *Birzhevoi byulleten'* of Saratov and *Byulleten' Vladivostokskoi tovarnoi birzhi*. It is worth noting that most of the cities that opened *birzhi* in the 1920s probably had them before the revolution as well. Schmidt (p. 376) reports the existence of eighty-six *birzhi* as of 1916.

various kinds of financial pressures exerted on the *birzhi* by local officials. Thus, the Ekaterinburg exchange found itself contributing monies to schools, scholarship funds, prizes for the "two best grain workers" in the region, and an airplane called "Learn to Trade with Good Manners!" In Astrakhan, 5 percent of the budget was going for education subsidies, and in both that city and Leningrad funds were allocated for hurricane and flood victims.

More significant, of course, were the activities of the *birzhi* in encouraging successful trade in and between regions. In this regard, the *birzhi* served as comunications centers—through purchases of radios, installation of telephone lines, and distribution of publications that were sometimes the only source of local and outside economic information. They also performed a consultative function, advising private traders on tax and business matters, and acted as lobbies representing local (including private) interests with respect to credit, material supplies, and rent on state properties. Thus the *birzhi* assumed many of the functions of local governments or chambers of commerce.[21]

The Moscow Financial Exchange. Like the Moscow commodity exchange, the associated *fondovyi otdel* was clearly the dominant exchange for the Soviet Union.[22] The volume of exchange for 1924-25 in Moscow was some 123 million rubles, compared with 58 million rubles in Leningrad, 10 million in Kharkov, and 3 million in all the rest combined.[23] The major traders on the financial exchange were government and cooperative credit institutions, state enterprises and ministries, and mixed stock companies (with foreign participation). Some private concerns were legally allowed to trade as well, but the Moscow exchange seemed not to promote this; private traders made up much larger shares of the volume on the official exchanges in Leningrad and Kharkov.[24] On the other hand, the

---

[21]   It would seem that even more *birzhi* might have been created had the localities had their way. Vladimir, already a very small city, reported that one of its satellite towns had also applied (unsuccessfully) for permission to set up its own *birzha*. This, together with the long existence of similar institutions in the Russian past, suggests that, even though the small exchanges could never provide truly smooth trade flows, they performed a number of useful functions.

[22]   There are very few sources available in the West on *fondovye otdely*. As far as known, the most complete documentation is for the Moscow exchange, as provided by the series of articles published in *Birzhevoe obozrenie* by V. S. Rozenberg during the period from 1924 to 1926. The discussion here is based on those articles.

[23]   See *Bol'shaya sovetskaya entsiklopediya*, Vol. III, 1927, p. 382.

[24]   *Ibid.*

Moscow *fondovyi otdel* tolerated a spontaneous evening financial exchange (the "Amerikanka") that was quoted, where private traders dominated, and where regulations seem to have been much less strict.[25] Furthermore, trade in financial issues and foreign commodities often by-passed the exchange altogether, so that V. S. Rozenberg reported in *Birzhevoe obozrenie* in 1924 that "exchange floor volumes somewhat fail to correspond to the true volume of the foreign-currency market."[26]

It would be hard to choose a "typical" period in the life of the Moscow financial exchange. The statistics for the month of November, 1924, may give a general idea of activities conducted there, however:

Table 2

TRANSACTIONS OF THE MOSCOW FINANCIAL EXCHANGE, NOVEMBER, 1924

CONTRACT	NUMBER OF TRANSACTIONS	RUBLE VALUE OF TRADING*
Pounds Sterling	33	4,168,114
Dollars	5	692,661
Obligations of the Commissariat of Finance	98	4,171,665
Peasant Lottery Loan	11	1,537,861
First State 6% Lottery Loan	4	97,820

SOURCE: V. S. Rozenberg, "Valyutnyi rynok," *Birzhevoe obozrenie*, October-November, 1924, p. 109.

* The ruble traded for approximately $0.51 at this time.

It is also worth noting that the values on the official exchange were very close to those of the evening exchange. Furthermore, a number of foreign exchanges had begun quoting the ruble as well by September, 1925.[27]

---

[25] For example, it was not necessary to register trades, as was the case at the regular exchanges.

[26] See the issue for October-November, 1924, p. 112.

[27] See V. E. Manevich, "O valyutnikh paritetakh i konvertiruemosti chervontsa v 20-kh godakh," *Finansy SSSR*, No. 11, 1988, pp. 50-54.

The Moscow financial exchange served as a sensitive barometer of public expectations regarding government economic policies. Thus, during the summer and fall of 1925, Rozenberg reported in *Birzhevoe obozrenie* that there was a high degree of liquidity in the market for the obligations of the Finance Commissariat and that private citizens were gladly dumping gold in favor of government bonds. Just as noticeably, however, when goods shortages worsened in early 1926, there ensued a "nearly catastrophic" run on savings institutions, and an "unending" demand for foreign currency.[28] Unfortunately, even though the financial exchange continued to exist (and, at least generally, publish some quotations) through early 1930, little is known of its operations, as most related publications ceased by the end of 1926.

THE FALL OF THE *BIRZHI*

Economic Reasons. A number of influences contributed to the short lives of the *birzhi* under the NEP. Continued pressures on the private sector probably limited volumes of trade. Certainly, the attempt to include all wholesale trade in the operations of *birzhi* was mistaken: only certain relatively homogeneous commodities and financial contracts have ever successfully traded on Western exchanges. Forcing all trade to be conducted or registered at the *birzhi* was not the cheapest way to conduct wholesale operations for many producers and goods. This fact became particularly noticeable as the government sought all possible avenues to force down retail prices through cost containment beginning in 1926. Thus, it seems likely that the existence of over one hundred exchanges truly could not be justified on economic grounds, as was asserted in 1927, when fifty-eight exchanges were closed.[29]

Institutional Reasons. Also working against the continued existence of the *birzhi* were a number of institutional factors. As early as 1924, representatives of *birzha* trade who were meeting in Moscow complained that state enterprises were not fulfilling their obligations to conduct trade or at least register trade on time through the exchanges.[30] Thus, the direct use of the exchanges by enterprises remained low, as did the informational value of statistics produced regarding trade. Furthermore, as time went on, the Soviet state, in the interests of planning, began merging enterprises into fewer and fewer big units. It began combining trade operations in large *sindikaty* as well. The effect

[28]   See the issues of *Birzhevoe obozrenie* for March and June, 1926.

[29]   *Torgovo-promyshlennaya gazeta*, February 11, 1927.

[30]   Andrei Lezhava, *Gosudarstvennoe regulirovanie torgovli i birzhi*, Moscow, 1924. See also *Trudy vtorogo vsesoyuznogo s"ezda predstavitelei birzhevoi torgovli, 16-24 aprelya 1924 g.*, Stenographic Report, Parts I and II, Moscow, 1924.

of such measures was to make markets less competitive and to take trading functions directly out of the hands of the exchanges. Eventually (in January, 1927),[31] even the requirement to register state-enterprise trades at the *birzha* was lifted. Soon after, it was judged too expensive to maintain *birzha* operations in most towns.

Political and Ideological Reasons. Even if the above hindrances had not finished off the *birzha*, it is likely that reasons of pure politics and ideology would have done so. The arguments over the role of the *birzhi* that were played out during 1926 in the pages of *Torgovo-promyshlennaya gazeta* were filled with invective and accusations that their main function was to provide a safe haven for "speculation" and political opposition. The editorial staff of *Torgovo-promyshlennaya gazeta* [32] even gloated when the state took action to curtail *birzha* operations, cutting allowable transactions fees, and raising taxes.

Chronology of the Fall. In early 1926, the USSR had 109 *birzhi*. This was not to last long. In June of that year the elimination of eighteen exchanges was announced,[33] followed in February, 1927 by a further list of fifty-eight cuts in the RSFSR alone.[34] The lists were not mutually exclusive, nor do they cover all the exchanges that seem to have been shut down at approximately the same time. By March, 1927, there remained only fourteen exchanges, however.[35] The survivors had always been the largest of the *birzhi*, conducting some 74 percent of the total volume of trade.[36] Furthermore, most of them had some capital market functions[37] up until the liquidation of *fondovye otdely* at all except Moscow and Vladivostok on October 13, 1929.[38] The final legal blow came on February 6, 1930, with the complete liquidation of all *tovarnye birzhi* and their *fondovye otdely*. At this time Gosbank took over all operations in foreign currencies.

---

[31]   *Ekonomicheskaya zhizn' SSSR*, p. 165.

[32]   On this, see "Sovokupnost' momentov i birzhevoi sbor," *Torgovo-promyshlennaya gazeta*, March 16, 1927.

[33]   "Sokrashchenie birzhevoi seti," *Torgovo-promyshlennaya gazeta*, June 29, 1926, p. 4.

[34]   For the announcement of these cuts, see "Sokrashchenie i reorganizat-siya tovarnykh birzh," *Torgovo-promyshlennaya gazeta*, January 6, 1927.

[35]   Those in Moscow, Leningrad, Kharkov, Rostov-on-Don, Kiev, Baku, Sverdlovsk, Nizhni Novgorod, Novosibrisk, Odessa, Saratov, Tiflis, Tashkent, and Vladivostok, (*ibid*.).

[36]   "Perspektivy birzhevoi torgovli," *Torgovo-promyshlennaya gazeta*, March 15, 1927.

[37]   It is not clear what functions were involved here. Market prices being reported as early as 1927 were much too stable to imagine that true free trade of any kind was being conducted.

[38]   *Ekonomicheskaya zhizn' SSSR* , p. 201.

LESSONS FOR THE PRESENT

WHAT A NEW *BIRZHA* COULD CONTRIBUTE

Commodity and financial exchanges in the West, as well as Soviet *birzhi* during the period of the New Economic Policy in the 1920s, are examples of ways in which markets may be organized, but they are certainly not the only ways. Trading does not have to pass through an exchange floor to be efficient. Indeed, for many sorts of operations, markets may today be more efficiently formed by electronic means, through banks, as auctions, etc. *Birzha*-like institutions have, however, proven to be the mechanism of choice for a wide variety of homogeneous, heavily traded commodities and contracts. In the Soviet case, this might mean, once again, markets for government securities; for foreign exchange; and—with respect to commodities—for grains, oil, and cottton, among others.

WHAT IT WOULD TAKE TO MAKE A *BIRZHA* FUNCTION

As noted above, a successful *birzha* requires large trade volumes by a large number of traders. This means, in turn, that any contracts to be traded would have to be accessible to broad numbers of potential traders. At a minimum, this would seem to imply a breakup of existing monopolies or near-monopolies among state enterprises, together with full rights of access by all small enterprises to the markets. In addition, legal issues and taxation levels would have to be made more clear than has been done for at least the past seventy years—that is, limitations on "excessive" or "speculative" profits would have to be carefully and reasonably defined. The state would have to permit enterprises to compete against one another, with some winning and some losing. In light of worker-management reforms, agreements would have to be formulated defining the fiscal responsibilities of managers entrusted with trading enterprise funds. As with other reforms in the USSR, it seems that for the reinstitution of *birzhi* to work well would entail a lot of equally complicated changes.

WHAT ROLE COULD THE STATE PLAY?

The Soviet state would find itself walking a shaky tightrope should it attempt to reinstitute centralized commodity and financial markets. To make the markets function adequately, so that there would be sufficient volume for a true *birzha*, the state would have to interfere and tax at moderate rates. Simultaneously, however, the state would face severe pressures to limit high "speculative" gains, especially those made by foreigners and especially those that might come about through insider information. Such a tightrope is one the West often finds difficult to negotiate, and the Soviet Union seems particularly unprepared (at least at present) for all the tricky legal issues it would encounter. Nonetheless, if *perestroika* continues to move forward, it will do so largely through making progress on many of the above-mentioned obstacles. If so, there may be a place for commodity and capital markets in the Soviet future.

10

Retail Price Reform and the Soviet Consumer

Michael Alexeev

THE KEY importance of a rational system of pricing for the success of the economic reforms currently under way in the USSR has been widely recognized by both Soviet and Western specialists. In one way or another, the point is repeatedly made that without a durable, dynamic base for market-guided decision-making, the vitality of the reforms will eventually be eroded. The introduction of scarcity prices and the creation of a considerably enlarged area of decentralization in the economy are seen as essential to forming such a base and ensuring the efficacy of the reforms. The Soviet leadership itself seems to have come to realize the need to rely on prices for effective signaling of information about scarcities in the economy and for effective decision-making with regard to allocation of resources. For prices to perform their role in the economy well, however, it is not enough for the leadership to permit some or even all economic agents such as enterprises and cooperatives to set prices in a decentralized fashion. The existence of appropriate market institutions, including private ownership of the means of production, capital markets, etc. is crucial for the proper functioning of the price mechanism.

All of this of course implies overlaying elements of a market economy on the traditional Soviet centrally planned economy, whose grave deficiencies have been openly acknowledged and have prompted the current reforms but whose responsiveness and adaptability to extensive marketization are largely unknown. Even if the Soviet leadership were totally committed to the introduction of an essentially market economy, it would be extremely difficult to implement the necessary reforms in the face of resistance on the part of powerful interest groups and because of the unpredictable nature of developments in the transition period that would be required to revamp the entire economic system. A rigorous analysis of the possible consequences of such a comprehensive change taking place all at once is infeasible. It makes sense, therefore, to analyze the elements of comprehensive price reform separately.

A reform of retail prices in the state sector is considered here. To limit the scope of the analysis, changes in the mechanism of price-setting that would be necessary to assure that prices are indeed set at market-clearing levels and are flexible enough to avoid market imbalances in the post-reform economy will be ignored. Possible supply effects generated by such a reform are also disregarded. As will be shown, however, a retail price reform could, in most cases, result in higher prices in the state sector and thus narrow the price differential between it and the nonstate parallel economy. This would in turn influence the choices open to consumers and have certain implications for their welfare as a whole.

DESCRIPTION OF THE MARKET FOR CONSUMER GOODS

It might be helpful in understanding the possible consequences of a retail price reform to review briefly some of the salient features of the Soviet market for consumer goods. While known to many, these features are often overlooked in discussing retail price reform.

Consumers can purchase goods and services either in the state-run retail trade network or in the parallel market, the so-called second economy.[1] Prices in the state network, or first market, are rather rigid and often set below market-clearing levels, which results in constant shortages of many (if not most) consumer goods and services in the USSR. It is important to emphasize that shortages do not necessarily imply anything about the standard of living of the population. A shortage of a particular consumer good means only that its price is below the market-clearing level. Given that wholesale prices of intermediate inputs do not reflect the relative scarcities of these inputs, retail prices based on these wholesale prices do not necessarily reflect relative scarcities of consumer goods either. This means that shortages of consumer goods are only partly attributable to government subsidies on those goods. There is no reason why a subsidized consumer good cannot be in excess supply, just as there is no reason why excess demand cannot exist for a heavily taxed consumer good.[2]

---

[1]   The parallel market is made up of many elements, including some illegal economic activities. For a comprehensive discussion of the Soviet nonstate sector, see Gregory Grossman, "The 'Second Economy' of the USSR," *Problems of Communism*, No. 5, 1977.

[2]   Until recently at least, some types of bread could serve as an example of the first phenomenon. Alcoholic beverages provide an example of the second

Shortages are not costless, however. In particular, they lead to significant nonmonetary expenditures associated with shopping in the first economy. For the most part, these are expenditures of time and take the form of waiting in queues. Other such expenditures may include time spent in searching for a desired good or in getting to the particular outlet where it is available at state-controlled prices. In what follows, these nonmonetary expenditures are, for the sake of convenience, referred to simply as queuing costs.

Because of queuing costs, the price of a consumer good in short supply purchased in the first market represents only part of the cost to the consumer. The full cost is the sum of the price in the first market and the monetary equivalent of the time spent queuing.[3] It is this full cost, and not the price alone, that is the most relevant parameter of consumer choice with respect to purchases in the first market and that makes it possible to talk about the consumer market as a whole being in equilibrium, or what will subsequently be called queue-rationed equilibrium.

It is also important to note that while queuing imposes costs on the buyer it does not constitute income to the seller of goods in short supply. Queues thus represent a waste of real resources. The same allocation of goods achieved without queues (say, through rationing coupons if they could be administered without cost) would obviously be preferable to the kind of rationing by queues that exists at present.[4]

Pervasive shortages are, of course, closely related to the existence of the second economy.[5] Prices in the parallel market are free to adjust to the conditions of supply and demand in that market, and it may be assumed that the nonmonetary expenditures that are associated with shopping in the parallel market are negligible compared with those in the first market.[6] By this assumption, the parallel market price of a good

---

phenomenon. This point is not particularly new (see, for example, A. Deryabin, "Sovershenstvovanie sistemy tsen," *Planovoe khozyaistvo*, No. 1, 1987, pp. 81-87).

[3] Such a monetary equivalent may not exist if income (wealth) constraint is not binding. For most people in the USSR, however, income constraint is binding. It will be argued below that the presence of the second economy makes it binding for virtually everyone.

[4] This statement disregards the possibility that some consumers may actually enjoy spending time in queues or consider searching for goods in short supply to be fun.

[5] Because supply effects are ignored, the focus here is on the distributional aspects of the parallel markets, taking the available supply of all goods as given.

[6] The risk entailed by the illegal nature of part of the second economy may occasionally be significant, but in the overwhelming number of situations in the USSR today it is not.

must be approximately equal to its first market price plus the monetary equivalent of the time spent in a queue or the "full cost" referred to earlier.[7] If the price in the parallel market is "too high" (i.e., greater than the full first market cost of procuring the good), then too many consumers would queue up, purchase the rationed good at the first market price and resell it in the parallel market, creating excess supply there. It is worth emphasizing that these comparisons depend on the transaction costs in the parallel market being negligible.[8] That assumption may not appear to be reasonable to the reader.

What is necessary to know for the discussion below is that the parallel market prices represent the true costs of rationed goods to many consumers and that given first market prices there is a high positive correlation between the parallel market prices and the length of queues in the first market. This will be so as long as the transaction costs of reselling the goods purchased in the first market are reasonably low. These transaction costs might be thought of as a wedge imposed between the full cost of shopping in the first market and the parallel market price. If the transaction costs are prohibitively high, then no one would be willing to perform arbitrage between the markets and the only suppliers to the parallel market would be the second economy producers. The parallel market prices would still have to be greater than, or equal to, the full cost in the first market, but in fact they might be much higher than that.[9]

As part of a description of the market, it is important to call attention to the issue of savings. It is often said that Soviet consumers accumulate significant "undesired" savings, that they are "forced" to save.[10] First, the statement that consumers save involuntarily implies that the mar-

---

[7]   In the absence of transaction costs in the parallel market and privileged access to goods in short supply, this monetary equivalent would be the same for all consumers. It might therefore be more appropriate to talk about the monetary equivalent of queuing time for "a representative consumer."

[8]   For additional simplifying assumptions, see D. O. Stahl and Michael Alexeev, "The Influence of Black Markets on a Queue-Rationed Centrally Planned Economy," *Journal of Economic Theory*, No. 2, 1985, pp. 234-250.

[9]   With no resale of goods from the first market taking place, producers in the second economy might end up selling their goods only to the wealthiest consumers, leaving the poorer consumers far from indifferent on the margin between shopping in the first market and in the parallel market.

[10]   See, for example, M. Bornstein, "Soviet Price Policies," *Soviet Economy*, No. 3, 1987, pp. 96-134, and V. Rutgaizer, I. Glinkin, P. Filenkov, and A. Shmarov, "On the Question of Reforming Consumer Prices and the Monetary Incomes of the Population," *Problems of Economics*, No. 2, 1988, pp. 75-90. See also Michael Alexeev, "Are Soviet Consumers Forced to Save?" *Comparative Economic Studies*, No. 4, 1988, pp. 17-23.

ginal value of money for these consumers is equal to zero.[11] This
implication is obviously false for most Soviet consumers, even with
respect to goods in the first market. The existence of the second
economy belies it for virtually all consumers. Second, the total amount
of savings in the USSR is largely determined by the difference between
aggregate consumer income obtained from the state and the value of
consumer goods sold in the first market at controlled prices. Sales in the
second economy redistribute income, but in one way or another all
rubles that are not spent in the first market must end up as (broadly
defined) savings.[12]

ANALYSIS OF RETAIL PRICE REFORM

For purposes of discussion it will be assumed here that a retail price
reform would result in an increase in the level of retail prices. While it
is true that some prices might be reduced, it is not reasonable to expect
that a meaningful reform could effectively balance price increases for
some goods with price decreases for others, as has been suggested by
Valerii Rutgaizer and his colleagues.[13] Rutgaizer et al. essentially advocate shifting the most severe market imbalances from food to durables
through an elimination of subsidies and a reduction in turnover taxes.
It is, however, difficult to perceive any inherent advantage in eliminating subsidies and reducing taxes as long as shortages remain. If shortages are to be eliminated without reductions in nominal incomes, prices
of both food and durables in the first market would have to go up.[14]
Even Rutgaizer and his colleagues acknowledge that the general price
level would have to rise.

The most important consequence of a price reform is its impact on
the welfare of the Soviet consumer. At present, direct manipulation of
prices by the Soviet government only takes place with respect to the

---

   [11]   If a consumer has a chance to spend his last ruble on consumption in
such a way that his level of welfare goes up but she chooses instead to save it,
then there is nothing "involuntary" about this decision. Consumers in all
economic systems make these sorts of tradeoffs. The authors who talk about
"forced" savings probably mean to say that consumers would have liked to
spend their money buying goods at state-controlled prices but that they often
are not able to do that easily and so they save it instead.
   [12]   It may be more appropriate to call this category savings and currency
in circulation.
   [13]   V. Rutgaizer, A. Shmarov, and N. Kirichenko, "Reforma roznichnykh
tsen, mekhanizm kompensatsii i razvitie potrebitel'skogo rynka," *EKO*, No. 3,
1989, pp. 58-70.
   [14]   See A. Deryabin, "Snachala ispravim tsenoobrazovanie," *EKO*, No. 3,
1989, pp. 41-56, where it is pointed out that shortages in the USSR are universal.

first market. If, as mentioned above, the true indicator of the marginal full cost of purchasing a consumer good in the first market is its price in the parallel market, then what needs to be examined is how an increase in prices in the first market affects the parallel market.

In this connection, S. S. Shatalin has suggested that the elimination of subsidies on consumer goods and services, presumably accompanied by monetary compensation of some kind, would not only raise the price level in the state retail trade network but would also cause runaway inflation in the second economy.[15] Shatalin does not offer any justification for this claim, and it is unlikely that his conjecture is correct, for it can be shown in a simple model of a queue-rationed economy that an increase in the prices of rationed goods in the first market leads to a smaller increase in prices in the parallel market.[16]

The thinking behind this is as follows. Suppose that the price increases are accompanied by a revenue-neutral monetary compensation—i.e., the state pays back to consumers all the money it acquires from price increases on rationed goods. Under such a scheme aggregate savings in the economy remain the same because the difference between the value of all goods in the first market and aggregate income does not change. With the total supply of goods fixed, aggregate consumption of goods does not change either.[17] At the optimal consumption point, the marginal value of a ruble to a consumer must be the same whether this ruble is spent in the parallel market or saved. Assume for the moment that every consumer consumes the same bundle of goods and saves the same amount as before the reform. Then, given that the nominal price of savings remains unchanged (saving 1 ruble always costs 1 ruble), prices in the parallel market have to stay constant as well. Of course, constant aggregate demand for savings and consumption does not imply constant individual demands. For this reason, prices in the market may either increase or decrease somewhat. For consumers with more or less similar Cobb-Douglas

---

[15] *Sotsialisticheskaya industriya*, October 30, 1988, p. 2. Incidentally, Shatalin announced in this article that he had changed his mind and decided that reform of retail prices in the near future was not advisable.

[16] See Michael Alexeev, "Retail Price Reform in a Queue-Rationed Centrally Planned Economy with Black Markets," a paper presented at the Fifth SSRC Summer Workshop on Soviet and East European Economics, Berkeley, California, July, 1989. The model also assumes it is possible to resell goods purchased in the first market at flexible prices in the parallel market with zero transaction costs.

[17] The supply effects of price reform are ignored in this presentation.

utility functions, though, changes in distribution of consumption and savings among consumers do not produce large effects on prices in the parallel market.[18]

What the foregoing suggests is that even a price reform that does not eliminate queues completely would lead to a decrease in the difference between prices in the first market and those in the parallel market. The implication of this is lower nonmonetary expenditures associated with shopping in the first market, shorter queues, and greater aggregate demand for leisure. Increased aggregate consumption of leisure and unchanged aggregate consumption of other goods implies that an appropriate distribution of monetary compensation would make everyone better off as a result of a price reform.[19]

Ideally, a price reform should result in the complete elimination of queues.[20] If this were to be achieved, it would obviously be possible, given the same supply of goods, to make everyone better off than they were before the reform. This would be so regardless of whether the price reform were accompanied by monetary compensation. It does not mean, however, that any equilibrium allocation without queues would make every consumer better off than when there was equilibrium with queues. Suppose that at first no changes in nominal income were to take place during a price reform. It can be shown that queues can be eliminated by raising prices in the first market to levels lower than prices in the parallel market before the reform.[21] Therefore, the consumers who, prior to the reform, procured goods mainly in the parallel market would benefit from lower market prices. The consumers who used to shop mainly in the first economy would gain from the elimina-

---

[18]   A Cobb-Douglas utility function is $U = x_1^{a_1} x_2^{a_2} \ldots x_n^{a_n}$ where x_i denotes the consumption of the i-th good or service. A property of the Cobb-Douglas function that is most important for the current discussion is that all goods are assumed to be substitutes in consumption.

[19]   A monetary compensation giving each consumer an amount of the money equal to the increase in the value of the consumer's pre-reform optimal bundle of goods in the first market would usually qualify as appropriate in this sense.

[20]   Instances are disregarded in which queues may actually be efficient because of the costs of administering market-clearing prices. On this issue, see R. Barro and P. Romer, "Ski-Lift Pricing, with Applications to Labor and Other Markets," *American Economic Review*, No. 5, December 1987, pp. 875-90.

[21]   In the absence of monetary compensation, higher prices in the first market result in lower nominal savings and in a higher value of the last ruble saved. To keep the marginal value of a ruble saved and a ruble spent the same without creating an excess supply of goods, market prices in an economy without queues would have to be lower than prices in the parallel market before the reform. For a formal argument of this, see Alexeev, "Retail Price Reform."

tion of queues (via increased leisure) but would be hurt by higher monetary prices and, on balance, might lose out as a result of price reform.[22] Redistribution of income among consumers may be necessary to make everyone better off. Because such a redistribution would necessarily involve reductions in nominal incomes of some consumers, though, it might be politically infeasible.

If reductions in nominal incomes are to be avoided, a form of monetary compensation for some consumers may be necessary. Contrary to the assertions of almost all Soviet economists writing on the subject of retail price reform,[23] eliminating shortages in the first market while fully compensating consumers for price increases seems to be a real possibility. As argued above, a revenue-neutral compensation would leave aggregate nominal savings unchanged, ensuring that prices in the parallel market remained largely the same despite price increases in the first market. As soon as prices in the first market reached the level of prices in the parallel market, queues would be eliminated.[24]

The question of how to compensate Soviet consumers for price increases in the first market is often discussed by Soviet economists.[25] It is relatively easy to construct a formal model for a compensation scheme that would make everyone better off,[26] but in the real world a compensation scheme must be developed that will be practical to implement. From this point of view, the method of compenstion should probably be based on consumer income.[27] Should the more affluent

---

[22]   At the margin the full costs of shopping prior to the reform would be greater than the post-reform prices for everyone. For those who obtained most of their goods in the first market, though, the average value of time spent in queues prior to the reform would have been a lot lower than its marginal value. This assumes increasing marginal value of time spent in queues.

[23]   Deryabin, "Sovershenstvovanie sistemy tsen" and "Snachala ispravim tsenoobrazovanie"; V. D. Belkin, "Uroki proshlogo," *EKO*, No. 3, 1989, pp. 70-77; and V. Slepov, M. Kokorev, and V. Naumov, "Problemy perestroiki sistemy roznichnykh tsen v SSSR," *Voprosy ekonomiki*, No. 2, 1989, pp. 104-112.

[24]   It is possible to present a numerical example of such an outcome in the framework of the model in Alexeev, "Retail Price Reform."

[25]   Rutgaizer et al., "Reforma roznichnykh tsen." See also I. A. Karimov, "O probleme denezhnoi kompensatsii naseleniyu posledstvii reformy roznichnykh tsen," *Izvestiya Akademii nauk SSSR, Seriya ekonomicheskaya*, No. 1, 1989, pp. 91-96.

[26]   Alexeev, "Retail Price Reform."

[27]   Strictly speaking, compensation should be based on per capita income. As Slepov et al. (*op. cit.*) point out, however, per capita compensation may contradict some goals of regional demographic policies in the USSR.

consumers receive greater compensation than the less affluent ones, as suggested by I. A. Karimov and Rutgaizer et al.?[28] Or should it be the other way around? Or should, perhaps, everyone be compensated equally?

The answer depends mostly on determining what categories of consumers shop in what markets. In the framework of the formal model mentioned above, the more affluent consumers would tend to spend less time in queues and purchase more goods in the parallel markets. The less affluent consumers, on the other hand, would tend to purchase more goods at lower prices in the first market, compensating for their lack of income by spending time in queues. What the model shows is in this respect at variance with the assertion by Rutgaizer et al. that the better-off households benefit from a greater share of price subsidies than the poorer households. They write: "It has been calculated that families with a per capita monthly income of two hundred rubles 'eat up' seven to eight times as much in subsidies as families with per capita income of fifty rubles."[29] Based on a survey conducted among readers of *Literaturnaya gazeta*, A. Shokhin and his colleagues report that "well-paid population groups, thanks to their favorable social status, are able to buy meat at reduced prices," forcing consumers with relatively low incomes to shop in parallel markets.[30] In addition, without providing an exact reference, they cite "budget-statistical data" indicating that "high-income population groups 'attract' three times more subsidies than low-income groups." It is difficult to judge the reliability of this information, especially when details on methodology are insufficient. It should be noted, though, that privileged access to goods in short supply by some consumers does not necessarily imply that they should be compensated at a higher rate in the course of a price reform.[31]

---

[28]   Karimov, *op. cit.*; Rutgaizer et al., "Reforma roznichnykh tsen."

[29]   Rutgaizer et al., "Reforma roznichnykh tsen," p. 61.

[30]   A. Shokhin, A. Guzanova, and L. Liberman, "Prices through the Eyes of the Population, *Problems of Economics*, No. 2, 1989, p. 6-13.

[31]   Unless these more affluent households have other privileges, such as residing in better-supplied cities, in addition to their nominal incomes, it is not clear how they are able to procure large amounts of subsidized goods. Prior to a price reform the USSR may want first to eliminate nonmonetary privileges for higher-income groups of consumers, especially since such privileges may in themselves be detrimental to efficient allocation of goods in the economy (see Michael Alexeev, "A Note on Privileges in a Queue-Rationed Centrally Planned Economy with Black Markets," *Journal of Economic Theory*, No. 2, 1989, pp. 422-30).

Data from the Berkeley-Duke family budget survey fail to support the information from Soviet authors cited in the previous paragraph.[32] Unfortunately, the survey included only questions about consumption of goods purchased privately. Consumption of income inelastic goods such as privately purchased food, does, however, provide a basis for making inferences about consumption of the counterparts of these goods in the first market. Positive correlation between consumption of privately bought food and income would imply that consumption of food bought in state-run stores is negatively correlated with income. To eliminate the influence of geographic location on food support, only the subsample of survey respondents who lived in Leningrad before emigrating from the USSR was considered. Respondents with above-median incomes from all sources reported spending about twice as much money on privately purchased food as the respondents with below-median incomes. Point estimates of income elasticity with respect to purchases of food from private sources came out to be positive and rather large. In the regressions, which included both income and squared income as independent variables, the coefficients of squared income were positive, implying that purchases of food from private sources grew at an increasing rate with an increase in income. (Regression results are presented in the Appendix.) In addition, research in residential housing distribution indicates that the more affluent households do not benefit from subsidies as much as Rutgaizer et al. claim.[33]

---

[32]   The survey covered 1,061 households consisting of persons who emigrated to the United States during the 1970s from different urban regions of the USSR, the largest city subsample being from Leningrad (303 households). The survey put special emphasis on the activities of the respondents and their households in the second economy during their "last normal period" of life in the USSR—i.e., the time not affected by the decision to emigrate. While for many reasons the survey sample may not be representative of the parent population (Soviet urban dwellers), the biases have not proven to be extremely large. For a detailed description of the survey, see various issues of the *Berkeley-Duke Occasional Papers on the Second Economy in the USSR*. Paper No. 7, "Purchases of Food from Private Sources in Soviet Urban Areas," by Vladimir Treml, discusses the sample's pattern of consumption of food purchased privately and compares it with the behavior of the parent population.

[33]   It is not only more affluent households that receive a smaller percentage of their income in the form of housing subsidies (see Michael Alexeev, "Distribution of Housing Subsidies in the USSR with Some Soviet-Hungarian Comparisons," *Comparative Economic Studies*, forthcoming, 1990). The validity of attributing the subsidy to its apparent recipient is not always clear, though (see Michael Alexeev, "The Effect of Housing Allocation on Social Equality: A

On the whole, the Soviet authors' emphasis on subsidies seems to be somewhat misguided. The benefit accruing to a person from consuming a subsidized good purchased in the first market without queuing should be measured by the difference between the price of that good in the first market and its price in the parallel market. For example, high consumption of bread results in "attracting a subsidy," but it does not necessarily point to any great benefit from "favorable social status," as bread usually is not even sold in the parallel market, suggesting that shortages of bread, if they exist at all, are not severe.

If the position is taken that privileges are irrelevant to the issue of monetary compensation and only income is looked at, it is reasonable to hold that, other things being equal, consumers who are better off purchase a greater share of their consumer goods in the parallel markets than do consumers who are not so well off. A price reform that would lead to an equilibrium without queues and offer revenue-neutral monetary compensation would raise prices in the first market to the level of those in the parallel market, leaving the latter essentially unchanged. The more affluent consumers who shop mainly in the parallel market would have to pay approximately the same prices as before the reform, and a relatively small compensation would make them better off. The less affluent consumers who shop mainly in the first market would have to pay more, and any compensation should take this into account.[34] The problem of interpersonal utility comparisons aside, this suggests that the less affluent consumers should receive more money in proportion to their nominal income than the more affluent consumers.[35]

Rutgaizer et al. advocate eliminating income tax as a form of monetary compensation for price increases,[36] but such a scheme would compensate most wage earners at the same rate, disregarding the fact that the benefits from a price reform are differentiated among

---

Soviet Perspective," *Journal of Comparative Economics*, No. 2, 1988, pp. 228-34). Housing subsidies can be "purchased" through the second economy, in which case they would just represent return on investments.

[34]   As mentioned before, the full marginal prices for consumers in both the first and the parallel markets may be the same, while the average prices for those who obtain goods in short supply through standing in queues will be considerably lower than the average prices for those who shop in the parallel market. This is so assuming the increasing marginal value of time spent in a queue.

[35]   The problem of interpersonal utility comparison arises when consumers' welfare is increasing because of price reform. As soon as a consumer's welfare moves to a higher indifference curve, it becomes difficult to ascertain whether one consumer gained more than another.

[36]   Rutgaizer et al., "Reforma roznichnykh tsen."

consumers in different income groups. At the same time, a significant advantage of such a scheme is its simplicity and the fact that it would not alter the accounting production costs of enterprises.

Like Rutgaizer et al., Karimov does not take into account either the second economy markets or rationing by queues and searching time.[37] In fact, Karimov uses a textbook two-good consumption model with the optimal consumption bundle being at the point of tangency of the budget line and an indifference curve. This approach makes it unclear why the USSR needs a price reform to begin with.

Finally, there is the question of the influence of price reform on monetary incentives in the economy. It is sometimes asserted that prices that are "too low" weaken the monetary incentives for workers in the economy.[38] The justification for such statements is not always clear, however.[39] Implicit in these assertions is the idea that money alone is not as useful as it would be in a market without nonprice rationing. In the framework of a queue-rationing model, the equivalent issue is what happens to the shadow price of money as the queues disappear from the system. The shadow price of money for consumers with Cobb-Douglas utility functions would be inversely proportional to the prices of goods other than leisure in the parallel market and to the marginal value of time spent in queuing. If the prices in the parallel market decline (as in a price reform without monetary compensation), the shadow price of money would increase for everyone, and the strength of monetary incentives would increase too. Under a price reform with revenue-neutral compensation, however, the change in the shadow price of money would depend on the compensation scheme. It is possible to show an example within the framework of the model for a compensation scheme mentioned earlier,[40] where, depending on the size of the compensation received by a particular consumer, the value of that consumer's money either increases or decreases under a price reform that eliminates queues altogether. It might be conjectured, however, that there are compensation schemes under which price reform (a) makes everyone better off, and (b) increases the value of money for everyone. This is an issue for future research.

---

[37] Karimov, *op. cit.*

[38] Bornstein, *op. cit.* See also Rutgaizer, et al., "On the Question of Reforming Consumer Prices."

[39] It is certainly not true that money under a price system such as that in the USSR is useless, especially given the existence of the second market. In fact, the possibility of buying goods at below-market clearing-prices in the first market may actually increase the purchasing power of money.

[40] Alexeev, "Retail Price Reform."

Conclusion

In sum, a retail price reform in the state sector entailing price increases is not likely to produce a burst of inflation in the parallel market even when the price increases are accompanied by monetary compensation. In fact, it is quite possible that prices in the parallel market would remain largely the same as before price reform or even decline. In addition, price reform with or without monetary compensation can eliminate queues altogether. Nonetheless, the welfare implications of such a reform are somewhat ambiguous.[41] The price increases alone, or with inadequate monetary compensation, do not necessarily make everyone better off.[42] It is perhaps this fear of insufficient monetary compensation that causes widespread opposition to the suggested reform of retail prices. It is even more difficult to avoid the perception of unequal treatment of different groups of consumers with respect to a monetary compensation. A reform under which some groups of the population benefit more than others, especially if the distance between the currently well-off groups and everyone else increases, may be politically unacceptable to the Soviet leaders.

---

[41]   It should be kept in mind that a model of an economy where price changes generate no supply responses has been considered here. Obviously, if these responses are significant, the welfare implications of price reform may be different from the ones described.

[42]   A similar conclusion was reached by R. K. Sah (see "Queues, Rations, and Market: Comparisons of Outcomes for the Poor and the Rich," *American Economic Review*, No. 1, 1987, pp. 69-77). Sah's framework of analysis differed substantially, however, from that used in the present paper.

Appendix

REGRESSION ESTIMATES OF THE RELATIONSHIP BETWEEN PER CAPITA INCOME AND PURCHASES OF FOOD FROM PRIVATE SOURCES

(Y = Purchases of Food from Private Sources, Rubles per Year)

	Y (TOBIT)	Log (Y) (OLS)	Y (TOBIT)	Log (Y) (OLS)
Constant	-147.0 (.302)	-5.40 (.017)	87.5 (.552)	-1.42 (.470)
Income from All Sources (Rubles per year)	020 (.715)	.898 (.001)	—	—
Income from All Sources Squared (1,000s of units)	.144 (.056)	—	—	—
Legal Income (Rubles per year)	—	—	-.05 (.550)	.520 (.027)
Legal Income Squared (1,000s of units)	—	—	.311 (.013)	—
Average Age of Spouses	4.48 (.016)	1.08 (.004)	2.50 (.306)	.908 (.037)
Family Size	-2..04 (.933)	-.476 (.190)	-22.8 (.406)	-.774 (.041)
Number of Observations	103	85	103	84
R-Square (Adjusted)	—	.35	—	.27
Censored Values (Y = 0)	18	0	18	0

NOTE: All independent variables in the Log(Y) regressions are in logarithms. The values in parentheses are the significance levels of the estimates—i.e., the probability that the estimated coefficient is zero or has the opposite sign given the observed results. These levels are determined from the values of the chi-squares for TOBIT and the t-statistics for OLS (ordinary least squares). TOBIT is a technique for estimating linear regressions when a dependent variable has a truncated (censored) distribution. In the present case, eighteen respondents reported no purchases of food from private sources suggesting that the distribution of the dependent variable in the linear regressions was truncated at 0.

11

Perestroika and Social Entitlements

Aaron Trehub

THE MAJOR SHORTCOMING of *perestroika* to date has been its failure to raise Soviet living standards. This failure has already led to widespread strikes among miners in Siberia and the Ukraine—the most serious labor unrest in the Soviet Union since the 1920s. The lack of success in resolving longstanding social problems has also emboldened Gorbachev's political rivals. Putting them in charge of crucial portfolios (Egor Ligachev to agriculture, Boris El'tsin to construction) where they will have to show results or face the consequences is a clever short-term tactic that could backfire. Finally, in order to succeed, Gorbachev's reforms require nothing less than the enthusiastic participation of millions of Soviet citizens. Mere acquiescence will not do. If living standards do not improve, and quickly, public support for *perestroika*, already flagging, will peter out altogether.

There is another, equally serious problem. The Soviet Union has long prided itself on its status as one of the world's leading welfare states. In his televised interview with Tom Brokaw of NBC in November, 1987, Gorbachev recited Soviet achievements in this area:

> We created a planned economy and guaranteed everyone the right to work. We haven't had any unemployed people for, what, more than fifty years now. The state guarantees free education; the state and society guarantee free medical care; and to a large extent the state has taken upon itself the responsibility for providing working people with housing.[1]

"From the point of view of social protection," the Soviet leader went on to say, "our society is more advanced than yours."

---

[1] *Pravda*, December 2, 1987.

Let us ignore for the moment the fact that the unrest in Uzbekistan and elsewhere in 1989 has given the lie to Gorbachev's claim there is no unemployment in the Soviet Union. The larger point is that *perestroika* cannot but undermine social protection in the Soviet Union—and, with it, the post-Stalin "social contract," which, as Peter Hauslohner has written, rests on egalitarianism, stability, and security.[2] This essay will examine the effect of *perestroika* on four major social entitlements: work, health care, housing, and pensions.

WORK

Perhaps the most important social entitlement in the Soviet Union is the right to work, which is guaranteed by the Soviet Constitution (1977) and which has long been a mainstay of Soviet socialism. In the past several years, however, the theoretical and economic under-pinnings of the right to work have come under attack.

LABOR-SHEDDING

In early 1986, Vladimir Kostakov, a labor resources specialist with USSR Gosplan, raised the specter of mass unemployment in the Soviet Union when he said that between thirteen million and nine-teen million jobs in the manufacturing sector would have to be eliminated by the end of the century if growth targets for labor productivity were to be met.[3] In an article that appeared in the CPSU theoretical journal *Kommunist* in September, 1986, the soci-ologist Tat'yana Zaslavskaya suggested that the prospect of getting the sack might have a salutary effect on labor discipline.[4] The economist Nikolai Shmelev made roughly the same point in his celebrated article "Avansy i dolgi" in the June, 1987, issue of the literary journal *Novyi mir*.[5] In an interview with a Japanese economist that appeared in *Izvestia* in January, 1989, Kostakov complained about overmanning in Soviet enterprises, saying "the labor shortage [in the Soviet Union] is a myth that suits many managers . . . According to the most conservative estimates, over-manning in the economy now amounts to at least ten million peo-ple."[6]

---

[2]   Peter Hauslohner, "Gorbachev's Social Contract," *Soviet Economy*, No. 1, January-March 1987, p. 54.

[3]   "Odin, kak semero," *Sovetskaya kul'tura*, January 4, 1986.

[4]   "Chelovechesky faktor razvitiya ekonomiki i sotsial'naya spravedlivost'," *Kommunist*, No. 13, 1986, p. 70.

[5]   "Avansy i dolgi," *Novyi mir*, No. 6, 1987, pp. 148-149.

[6]   "Pogolovnaya zanyatost' i rynok truda," *Izvestia*, January 11, 1989.

Admittedly, these dire-sounding pronouncements have not been translated into action—yet. "Look," economist Ed A. Hewett of the Brookings Institution told a reporter from *The Washington Post* at the end of 1988, "*perestroika* is a very polite phrase for firing a lot of people, moving people around and closing a lot of bad enterprises."[7] At a press conference held soon after the first session of the Congress of People's Deputies, Academician Leonid Abalkin, director of the Institute of Economics of the USSR Academy of Sciences and now a deputy prime minister, said that all loss-making state enterprises in the Soviet Union must be "liquidated" in the next eighteen months.[8] If Abalkin gets his way, and Prime Minister Nikolai Ryzhkov's remarks at the congress suggest that he will, then at least two and a half million industrial workers alone may find themselves out of a job by the end of 1990.[9]

What will happen to these people? If other labor-shedding exercises (e.g., the Shchekino method and the Belorussian railway experiment) are anything to go on, then it is probable that a large number of them will take early retirement. The rest will have to find jobs with other enterprises, in the service sector, or in cooperatives and individual labor activity. In any event, it looks as if the Soviet job placement system will be getting a workout in the next few years.

JOB PLACEMENT OFFICES

In November, 1987, the CPSU Politburo approved a resolution submitted by the USSR Council of Ministers and the All-Union Central Council of Trade Unions (AUCCTU) entitled "On ensuring the effective employment of the population, perfecting the job placement system, and strengthening social guarantees for workers." In January, 1988, a shortened text of the resolution was published in the central press, and its main provisions were discussed by Igor' Prostyakov, a deputy chairman of the Bureau for Social Development of the USSR Council of Ministers, and Viktor Buinovsky, a deputy chairman of the USSR State Committee for Labor and Social Problems (Goskomtrud).[10]

---

7   David Remnick in *The Washington Post*, November 6, 1988.

8   *TASS*, June 16, 1989.

9   This estimate is based on Ryzhkov's statement that there were nine thousand loss-making enterprises in "material production" in the Soviet Union in 1988 (*Izvestia*, June 8, 1989) and on recently disclosed figures on the average number of employees at Soviet industrial enterprises ("Diktat proizvoditelya i rynok," *Ekonomicheskaya gazeta*, No. 22, 1989, p. 16).

10   "Popav pod sokrashchenie . . . ," *Pravda*, January 21, 1988; "Dela vsem khvatit," *Izvestia*, January 21, 1988.

The fact that this resolution was adopted at all testified to official concern about the fate of workers who will be let go as a result of the economic reforms now under way in the Soviet Union—in particular, the shift of Soviet enterprises to full economic accounting (*polnyi khozraschet*) and the possibility of bankruptcy, which is explicitly spelled out in the Law on the State Enterprise.[11] It would appear that the prospect of being let go—or "freed," in Soviet parlance—is a real one for many workers. The editors of *Pravda* said that the newspaper was getting letters expressing fears about the return of unemployment. "It's as if long-ago, forgotten times are repeating themselves," wrote one Moscow resident.

Prostyakov and Buinovsky tried to put these fears to rest. In an obvious swipe at Shmelev, Prostyakov assured readers that there will be no return of unemployment in the USSR, "even if somebody attempted to revive it, let us say, as a 'lever' of some sort, as 'economic medicine,' and so on." Buinovsky said that there are plenty of new job possibilities in the service sector, in new industries, and in cooperatives and individual labor activity. Both officials admitted, however, that between fifteen million and seventeen million Soviet workers stand to lose their jobs by the end of the century. Echoing other statements that have been made in the past few years, Buinovsky said that it is time for workers to wean themselves away from the notion that a particular job or profession is forever.

Perhaps the most important part of the resolution concerns the creation of a nationwide (*obshchegosudarstvennaya*) system of "centers for the placement, retraining, and professional direction of the population"—i.e., a system of job placement offices. In fact, the Soviet Union has had such a system since the late 1960s. By late 1986, there were job placement offices (*byuro po trudoustroistvu*) in almost seven hundred cities and raions throughout the Soviet Union.[12] Moreover, an especially effective job placement office in Novopolotsk in the Belorussian SSR has long been the subject of laudatory articles in the Soviet press.[13] The news that a job placement and retraining system was to be created in 1988 was, therefore, somewhat confusing.

In his interview in *Pravda*, Prostyakov did little to dispel this confusion, saying that the new offices will have nothing in common with the old labor exchanges (*birzhi truda*), the last of which was shut down in the Soviet Union in 1930. This may be true, but it does not say

---

[11] Article 23, "Zakon SSSR o gosudarstvennom predpriyatii (ob"edinenii)," *Pravda*, July 1, 1987.

[12] "Intensifikatsiya i problemy trudoustroistva," *Agitator*, No. 20, October, 1986, p. 24.

[13] "Est' takaya sluzhba," *Sotsialisticheskaya industriya*, December 29, 1987.

how they will differ from the offices that already exist. Indeed, it is not clear that they will differ at all in any important way; admittedly, the new offices will be self-financing, but so are many of the existing ones. The head of a job placement office in Moscow told the trade-union daily *Trud* in December, 1987, that in many parts of the country the new system will simply be grafted onto the old one.[14]

What is clear is that the existing system of job placement offices has not been very effective at finding people new jobs. This is partly the fault of Soviet enterprises, which prefer to do their own hiring and try to circumvent the official placement service whenever they can. In 1980 in the RSFSR, for example, about 78 percent of all hiring was done by enterprises directly; less than 10 percent was done through the job placement system.[15]

Another problem is the shortage of modern data-processing equipment. Like so much else in the Soviet Union, computers and software are deficit items, and job placement offices are not in a favorable position when it comes to getting them. Moreover, even when offices have succeeded in acquiring computers, they have too often turned out to be almost useless. For example, the Novopolotsk office was generously equipped by Goskomtrud with (Soviet-made) personal computers of the "Agat" type, which have turned out to be little more than "expensive toys." The office has had to buy machine time from other organizations—an obvious disadvantage under conditions of *khozraschet*—and much of its day-to-day work is still done by hand.[16]

The Soviet Union has started enlisting foreign expertise to improve its job placement and retraining system. In February, 1988, Academician Abel Aganbegyan visited Sweden to study that country's highly effective network of job placement offices and training programs for the unemployed.[17] Thousands of handicapped Soviet workers will receive job training in West Germany under an agreement concluded during Gorbachev's visit to Bonn in June, 1989.[18]

In the meantime, the expansion of the job placement system in the Soviet Union is proceeding apace. By the end of 1988, there were over two thousand job placement centers and offices in the USSR. In the first

---

14   "Byuro i byurokratiya," *Trud*, December 30, 1987.

15   "Sistema trudoustroistva v SSSR," *Ekonomicheskie nauki*, No. 3, 1984, p. 53.

16   "Est' takaya sluzhba," *Sotsialisticheskaya industriya*, December 29, 1987.

17   *Reuters* (Stockholm), February 3, 1988. The unemployment rate in Sweden in 1988 was 1.5 percent—the lowest in Western Europe ("Beste Jahre," *Der Spiegel*, May 8, 1989, p. 180).

18   "Erstes sozialpolitisches Abkommen mit Moskau," *Frankfurter Allgemeine Zeitung*, June 5, 1989.

nine months of that year, they succeeded in finding jobs for over two million of the three million people who turned to them for help (it is not clear what happened to the other one million).[19] The number of job placement offices in the Soviet Union was supposed to double in 1989.[20]

Gorbachev has repeatedly stated that the Soviet Union will not tolerate unemployment. "That's not for us," he remarked in reference to Shmelev's suggestion that a little unemployment may not be a bad thing.[21] On the other hand, Gorbachev has attacked the endemic Soviet practice of overmanning and supported such labor-shedding exercises as the Belorussian railway experiment. His ambivalence on this question is typical of his refusal to state publicly that *perestroika* is likely to make life harder for many people in the short run. Soviet economists seem to be more honest about this. In an article that appeared in *Kommunist* early in 1987, Kostakov wrote that the USSR "is not prepared, on either the economic or psychological plane, for drastic changes in the use of labor resources."[22] Despite the rapid growth of leasing arrangements and the cooperative sector, which are described elsewhere in this volume, this judgment still appears valid.

HEALTH CARE

Public health is one of two areas in which Gorbachev has presided over modest but real improvements (the other is housing). The Soviet infant mortality rate dropped from 26 deaths per 1,000 live births in 1985 to 25 deaths in 1987. The crude death rate dropped from 10.6 deaths per 1,000 population in 1985 to 9.9 in 1987—an improvement that Soviet observers attribute, on somewhat dubious grounds, to Gorbachev's ill-fated anti-alcohol campaign. Life expectancy at birth in the Soviet Union, after showing an alarming drop during the later Brezhnev years, is returning to the high point it reached in the mid-1960s. Today, it stands at approximately sixty-five years for men and seventy-three years for women.[23]

Despite these encouraging developments, however, and an emergency increase in funding of almost six billion rubles, the Soviet health-care system is in poor shape. Just how poor has been spelled out repeatedly by the plain-talking minister of health, Evgenii Chazov. It was Chazov, for example, who said that the Soviet Union ranks fiftieth in the world in combating infant mortality, "after Barbados and the United Arab Emirates." It was also Chazov who disclosed that almost

19   *Pravda,* January 22, 1989.
20   "Sokratili. A dal'she?," *Trud,* January 20, 1989.
21   "Vstrecha na izbiratel'nom uchastke," *Izvestia,* June 22, 1987.
22   "Zanyatost': defitsit ili izbytok?," *Kommunist,* No. 2, 1987, p. 85.
23   See *Narodnoe khozyaistvo SSSR v 1987 g.,* Moscow, 1988, pp. 352-357.

half of all medical establishments in the USSR do not have running water. And it was Chazov who said that deficiencies in the state health-care system cost the Soviet economy ninety billion rubles a year.[24]

At the Nineteenth Party Conference in June, 1988, Chazov came close to saying outright that the Soviet Union's pursuit of strategic parity with the United States in the 1970s and the diversion of resources to the military sector had a disastrous effect on the health of the Soviet population. According to Chazov, doctors and scientists tried to get the authorities to do something about the deteriorating health situation in the country but were told that there were "other, more important, state priorities" and that they would have to wait. "So we waited," Chazov told the conference, "and the result is that we now have a grave health situation that it will take more than one five-year plan to correct." Among other things, Chazov spoke with bitterness about the lack of medicines and medical supplies in the Soviet Union. Despite substantial imports of pharmaceuticals, the demand for medicines in the Soviet Union is only 75-percent satisfied.[25]

In recent months, the shortcomings of the Soviet health-care system have been highlighted by AIDS. The USSR registered its first AIDS death in September, 1988, when a twenty-nine-year-old woman succumbed to the disease in a Leningrad hospital. Her doctors originally misdiagnosed her symptoms; then they botched the blood tests, combining her blood serum sample with those of several other patients because there were not enough kits to test each sample separately. When they finally got it right, it was too late. The test results showing that the woman was HIV-positive came back from the laboratory three days after her death.[26] An even more serious case of medical incompetence occurred in a children's hospital in the city of Elista, the capital of the Kalmyk ASSR, where at least fifty-eight children and nine adults were infected with the AIDS virus at the end of 1988. It seems fairly certain that the virus was spread by the repeated use of unsterilized hypodermic syringes.[27] Similar outbreaks have been reported in Volgograd and Rostov-on-Don. The USSR Ministry of Health (Minzdrav) has estimated that the USSR needs over three billion disposable syringes a year; its current production capacity is approximately thirty million.[28]

24   "Zabolel rebenok ... ," *Literaturnaya gazeta*, April 15, 1987; "Na chto zhaluetes', doktor?," *Komsomol'skaya pravda*, June 18, 1988; and "Zdravookhra-nenie: pul's perestroiki," *Meditsinskaya gazeta*, October 30, 1987.

25   "Po tabletke tri raza v god," *Izvestia*, April 10, 1989.

26   See Aaron Trehub: "Soviet Media Report First Soviet AIDS Death," *Radio Liberty Research Bulletin*, RL 470/88, October 19, 1988.

27   *TASS*, February 24, 1989.

28   "SPID podozhdet?" *Komsomol'skaya pravda*, March 26, 1989; Steve Goldstein, *Knight-Ridder Newspapers*, March 18, 1989.

Gorbachev himself drew attention to the shortage of syringes in his speech at the April, 1989, plenum of the Central Committee.[29]

Public dissatisfaction with the poor quality of Soviet health care is strong. At the beginning of 1989, the popular weekly newspaper *Argumenty i fakty* published the results of a poll in which 1,136 Muscovites were given a choice of seven social problems and asked to identify one or two that they considered to be the most important. Half (50.2 percent) of the respondents said they thought that improving the quality of medical care was the most pressing social problem.[30]

PAY POLYCLINICS

There are islands of quality in the Soviet health-care system. Dr. Svyatoslav Fedorov's clinics for microsurgery of the eye are one example. Less well-known but more accessible for ordinary Soviet citizens are fee-for-service polyclinics. Fee-for-service polyclinics (also called pay polyclinics) have existed in the Soviet Union since 1926. Originally intended as an affordable alternative to private doctors, they are now being touted as an affordable alternative to traditional "free" polyclinics, where lines are long and the standard of treatment is poor. In 1986, there were twenty fee-for-service polyclinics in Moscow. In the fall of 1987, the first fee-for-service hospital in the USSR opened in the capital; treatment there generally lasts between twelve and fourteen days and costs between nine and twelve rubles a day.[31]

The Party-government resolution on improving the health-care system by the year 2000 (adopted in November, 1987) says that the volume of paid medical services in the Soviet Union is supposed to increase fivefold by the end of the century.[32] This increase is less impressive than it sounds, however. In 1986, paid services accounted for a mere 0.4 percent of all medical services in the USSR.[33]

How affordable are fee-for-service medical establishments? The evidence is mixed. One study of more than eight thousand clients of pay polyclinics in Moscow discovered that 78.5 percent of them were people with incomes of less than 150 rubles a month; the authors of the survey said that this fact alone "proves that these establishments are accessible to diverse categories of the population."[34] Others are not

29   *Izvestia*, April 27, 1989.
30   "Chto stoit za problemami?" *Argumenty i fakty*, No. 1, 1989, p. 4.
31   "Paying for Health," *Moscow News*, August 30, 1987; "Miloserdie na khozraschete," *Sovetskaya Rossiya*, April 15, 1988.
32   *Pravda*, November 27, 1987.
33   "Platnaya poliklinika: za i protiv," *Izvestia*, July 11, 1986.
34   "Khozraschetnye polikliniki v Moskve," *Sotsiologicheskie issledovaniya*, No. 2, 1988, p. 63.

so sanguine. "With the birth of our child my family's income fell to seventy rubles per person, and with the best will in the world I can't earn more," one woman wrote to the newspaper *Sovetskaya kul'tura* in 1987; "can it really be that my child would be refused help because I don't have any money?"[35] Although it is nearly impossible to get decent medical care in the Soviet Union without paying hefty bribes for basic medications and even fresh bed linen, attempts to expand the volume of paid medical services have encountered strong popular resistance. "It is absolutely clear that the idea of 'medicine for pay' is extremely unpopular," demographer Mark Tol'ts told the newspaper; "people see it as incompatible with the principles of social justice."[36]

MEDICAL COOPERATIVES

Despite strong popular antipathy to fee-for-service medical establishments, pay polyclinics have been joined by another new type of medical service: medical cooperatives. The first medical cooperative in the Soviet Union was set up at the end of 1987 in Moscow. Called "LiK" (for *Lechenie i konsul'tatsiya* [Treatment and Consultation]), the cooperative treated some eighteen thousand patients in the first four months of its existence.[37] In the space of a year, "LiK" had turned into "a powerful organization," with a staff of seven hundred highly qualified specialists.[38] By the end of 1988, there were hundreds of medical cooperatives in the Soviet Union.

This burgeoning sector suffered two serious setbacks at the end of 1988. The first was the promulgation in November of a special directive by the USSR Ministry of Health entitled "On the Use of Costly Medical Technology." This directive, which was signed by Chazov himself, prohibits the leasing of medical equipment by state establishments to cooperatives. The second blow came in late December, when the USSR Council of Ministers issued a decree banning cooperatives from engaging in certain types of business. Medical cooperatives were particularly hard hit; at least 40 percent of the cases now seen in cooperative medical establishments require forms of treatment proscribed under the new decree.[39] The effect of the two

---

35   "Problema nomer odin," *Sovetskaya kul'tura*, September 22, 1987.

36   *Ibid.*

37   See "Pervaya kooperativnaya poliklinika," *Izvestia*, February 22, 1988; and "Mnogolikii 'LiK'," *Moskovskaya pravda*, March 31, 1988.

38   "Novyi 'LiK' meditsiny," *Ogonek*, No. 51, 1988, p. 20.

39   *Argumenty i fakty*, No. 2, 1989, p. 4. For a detailed discussion of the two decrees, see Margot Jacobs, "Are the Restrictions on Medical Cooperatives Justified?" *Report on the USSR*, No. 13, 1989, pp. 9-12.

decrees appears to have been swift and dire: according to a reporter for *The New York Times*, "about 65" of the two hundred medical cooperatives in Moscow went out of business between January and March, 1989.[40]

Unlike pay polyclinics, which have developed rather slowly, medical cooperatives spread much too fast, thereby challenging Minzdrav's near-monopoly on health care in the Soviet Union. It is clear that Minzdrav does not intend to give up its dominant position. "Paid medical services will supplement a guaranteed level of free medical care; they will by no means replace it," said Chazov on the eve of the All-Union Congress of Physicians in October, 1988.[41] "It is the state health-care system, not the cooperatives, that is responsible for [maintaining] the health of the population," Deputy Minister of Health Aleksei Moskvichev told *Meditsinskaya gazeta* in January, 1989.[42] Given Minzdrav's indifferent performance in recent years, this is hardly encouraging news for Soviet patients.

HOUSING

For over thirty years, the CPSU and the Soviet government have been trying to solve the country's chronic housing problem. The Third Party Program (1961) said that every Soviet family, "including newlyweds," would have an apartment or house of its own by 1980. This promise was not kept. The new Party Program, adopted at the Twenty-seventh Congress of the CPSU in 1986, pushed the target date for solving the housing problem to the year 2000.

Gorbachev has made some modest progress in this area. In his first two years in power, housing construction in the Soviet Union rose by more than 20 percent, from 1.9 million apartments in 1985 to 2.3 million in 1987. Gorbachev has also supported the construction of young people's residential complexes, or MZhKs, a form of build-it-yourself housing for young couples tired of waiting in the city or enterprise housing queue. In 1985, the number of MZhKs in the USSR could be counted on the fingers of one hand; by the spring of 1989, there were about five hundred in various stages of construction.[43]

The housing problem remains severe, however. Academician Aganbegyan has said that the shortage of housing is the most serious social problem in the USSR today (Gorbachev thinks that this

---

[40]   Esther B. Fein in *The New York Times*, March 5, 1989.

[41]   *Reuters*, October 14, 1988.

[42]   "Meditsinskie kooperativy: povyshat' otvetsvennost'," *Meditsinskaya gazeta*, January 6, 1989.

[43]   "Dom postroen, chto dal'she?," *Komsomol'skaya pravda*, May 14, 1989.

Table 1
HOUSING CONDITIONS IN CAPITALS OF UNION
REPUBLICS AND OTHER LARGE CITIES

	AVERAGE PER CAPITA LIVING SPACE (SQUARE METERS)	NUMBER OF FAMILIES AND SINGLE PEOPLE ON WAITING LIST EARLY 1988	PERCENT OF FAMILIES ON WAITING LIST	"LIST NORM" (SQUARE METERS)
Alma-Ata	8.9	49,700	15	6
Ashkhabad	6.8	23,600	26	6
Baku	7.9	68,700	26	5
Vilnius	9.7	36,300	21	5
Gorky	9.6	123,100	27	6.5
Dnepropetrovsk	9.6	74,200	20	6
Donetsk	9.9	75,300	22	6
Dushanbe	7.5	31,300	22	6
Erevan	7.5	42,000	16	5
Kazan	9.2	112,900	34	7
Kiev	9.6	208,400	26	5
Kishinev	7.9	69,500	32	6
Kuibyshev	9.2	114,300	29	7
Leningrad	10.6	282,900	20	5.5
Minsk	8.9	34,600	28	6
Moscow	10.7	344,800	12	5
Novosibirsk	9.0	111,600	25	8
Odessa	8.5	80,400	23	4
Omsk	9.4	108,400	31	7
Perm	8.6	106,800	32	6
Riga	10.8	75,700	26	5
Rostov-on-Don	10.0	74,100	23	6
Sverdlovsk	9.2	130,600	31	6.5
Tallinn	11.8	25,400	16	6
Tashkent	8.2	60,100	12	7
Tbilisi	9.5	59,000	19	5
Ufa	8.0	118,800	36	8
Frunze	7.9	31,800	17	7
Kharkov	9.7	113,400	23	5.5
Chelyabinsk	9.5	109,500	31	6

SOURCE: *Argumenty i fakty*, No. 31, 1988, p. 5. The "list norm" (*uchetnaya norma*) is the maximum amount of living space a person can have and still be eligible for re-housing.

distinction belongs to "the food question").[44] In any case, it is clear that housing still ranks high on the scale of everyday miseries that must be endured by ordinary Soviet citizens, millions of whom still live in communal apartments, dormitories, rented rooms, and trailers. At the end of 1988, some fourteen million urban families were on the waiting list for better housing—one million more than in 1987.[45] (See Table 1.) In most large cities, the volume of housing construction is too small to make much of a dent in the number of people already on the waiting list; more discouraging is the fact that it lags behind the creation of new households through marriage and divorce. There were 92,618 marriages and 40,562 divorces in Moscow in 1987; the same year, the city built 57,700 new apartments.[46] There were almost 345,000 families and single people on the housing waiting list in the capital at the beginning of 1988.

Furthermore, around five million Soviet citizens live in dilapidated or dangerous housing—in other words, slums.[47] A lot of the run-down housing in the Soviet Union dates from the last century; a recent description of life in nineteenth-century factory housing in Leningrad today invites comparisons with accounts of living conditions in the proletarian slums of St. Petersburg.[48]

Many Soviet slums are of more recent origin, owing to the miserable quality of Soviet construction. Housing estates from the 1950s are called *"khrushchoby,"* a play on "Khrushchev" and *"trushchoba"* (slum). In August, 1987, then Moscow Party chief (and former construction engineer) El'tsin made one of his meet-the-people visits to a *khrushchoba* in the southern part of the city; there he was all but mobbed by outraged tenants, who showed him cracked walls, boarded-up windows, and basements overflowing with sewage from burst pipes.[49] Shoddy construction can have deadly consequences, as the earthquake in Armenia at the end of 1988 showed.

Another problem is the housing allocation system, which is universally acknowledged to be inefficient, unfair, and corrupt. In 1986, a government investigation conducted in various cities discovered approximately one million apartments that were either not occupied at all

---

[44] "Slagaemye perestroiki," *Nauka i zhizn'*, No. 3, 1988, p. 2; "Arendnyi podryad—kratchaishii put' k prodovol'stvennomu dostatku," *Pravda*, May 15, 1988.

[45] "Uskorit' povorot ekonomiki k cheloveku," *Pravda*, January 22, 1989.

[46] "Statisticheskie materialy," *Vestnik statistiki*, No. 12, 1988, pp. 62-64.

[47] *Pravda*, January 22, 1989.

[48] "Za krasnym fasadom," *Sotsialisticheskaya industriya*, April 28, 1988.

[49] "I vyplesnulos' vozmushchenie, ili Pochemu voznik konflikt v mikroraione," *Moskovskaya pravda*, August 21, 1987.

or occupied illegally.[50] Old people live alone in three- and four-room apartments, while young (and not-so-young) families must make do with single rooms in communal apartments. Efforts to trade up or down are blocked by officials, who fear, with good reason, that they may conceal schemes to make "unearned income." Corruption is endemic, and often involves members of the Party and government *apparat*. In April, 1988, the Central Committee of the Latvian Communist Party dismissed several high-ranking officials for allocating apartments to their buddies.[51] More recently, a journalist from Zhitomir was elected to the Congress of People's Deputies largely on the strength of her exposé of corruption in housing allocation among the local *nomenklatura*.[52]

Finally, there is the sensitive question of rents. Rents for urban state housing in the USSR have remained unchanged since 1928; according to official statistics, they now account for only 3 percent of household expenditures. Like the artificially low prices in state food stores, rents in the USSR are kept down by massive state subsidies—10.4 billion rubles in 1987 alone.[53] Some prominent reform economists (e.g., Aganbegyan, Zaslavskaya, and Natal'ya Rimashevskaya) have suggested cutting these subsidies by charging a higher rate for every square meter of living space above an officially guaranteed minimum. This proposal makes good economic sense but will be hard to sell to a population already suffering from inflation and upset by rumors of price decontrol.

In short, the difficulties in this crucial social sector are so formidable that some knowledgeable observers wonder whether the Party's goal is realistic. "We have declared that by the year 2000 every Soviet family will have a flat," El'tsin told an interviewer from the *Sunday Telegraph* on the eve of the elections to the Congress of People's Deputies in March, 1989; "then we did our sums and it turned out that it is almost impossible. If we don't fulfill the promise we will have betrayed the people again."[54] Mindful of this danger, the Party has started exploring new approaches to solving the housing problem.

INDIVIDUAL HOUSING

One new idea—or rather an old idea that is being dusted off—is private housing. In his speech at the Twenty-seventh Party Congress, Gor-

---

[50]   "Vnov' o pustuyushchei kvartire," *Sotsialisticheskaya industriya*, January 10, 1987.

[51]   "'Dom v tikhom raione'," *Izvestia*, April 9, 1988.

[52]   Kathleen Mihalisko, "Alla Yaroshyns'ka: Crusading Journalist from Zhitomir Becomes People's Deputy," *Report on the USSR*, No. 22, 1989, pp. 17-19.

[53]   *Sotsial'noe razvitie i uroven' zhizni naseleniya SSSR*, Moscow, 1989, p. 84.

[54]   "Where Perestroika Went Wrong," *Sunday Telegraph*, March 26, 1989.

bachev urged Party officials to encourage individual housing "in every way."[55] Two years later, his call was heeded. In February, 1988, the CPSU Politburo adopted a resolution aimed at reviving the individual housing sector.[56] The resolution was the subject of an interview in *Pravda* with Yurii Batalin, the then chairman of the USSR State Committee for Construction (Gosstroi).[57]

In theory, Soviet citizens have long had the right to build private homes. In reality, they have been prevented from doing so by a shortage of building materials and an abundance of red tape. The volume of private housing construction in the USSR has been falling for the past three decades (see Table 2). In 1960, private housing construction amounted to almost 54 million square meters and accounted for almost 50 percent of all housing construction in the Soviet Union. By 1987, these figures had dropped to 19.3 million square meters and 15 percent respectively.

The first step towards reversing this trend, said Batalin, is the removal of "unfounded" legal obstacles to private homes. Although the minister did not specify what obstacles he had in mind, it is likely that he was referring primarily to the ban on private construction in cities with populations of one hundred thousand or more. It should be said that this ban, which dates from 1962,[58] and other restrictions on private housing seem to apply only to ordinary Soviet citizens. Members of the Soviet administrative elite, the *nomenklatura*, have been building private mansions for themselves for years, more or less with impunity.[59] Now, with *glasnost'* and the emphasis on social justice, this practice has come under increasingly heavy attack in the press.

Removing legal strictures will not be enough to revive the private housing sector, however. There is still the question of money. Private homes in the USSR, like private homes elsewhere, cost quite a bit— between fifteen and twenty-five thousand rubles, according to Batalin's interviewer. The average worker and employee currently makes around 234 rubles a month (gross), almost 30 percent of which is spent on food; the average savings bank account at the end of 1987 contained 1,424 rubles.[60] Even allowing for the fact that these are averages and conceal wide variations in income and savings, it is clear that the majority of citizens simply do not have the money to build their own homes.

---

[55]   *Kommunist*, No. 4, 1986, p. 41.

[56]   "V Tsentral'nom Komitete KPSS i Sovete Ministrov SSSR," *Pravda*, February 21, 1988.

[57]   "Svoi dom," *Pravda*, February 16, 1988.

[58]   Article 93, *Sobranie postanovlenii pravitel'stva SSSR*, No. 12, 1962.

[59]   See Henry W. Morton, "Who Gets What, When, and How? Housing in the Soviet Union," *Soviet Studies*, No. 2, 1980, pp. 252-253.

[60]   *Pravda*, April 23, 1989; *Sotsial'noe razvitie i uroven' zhizni naseleniya SSSR*, Moscow, 1989, pp. 100-101.

Table 2
VOLUME OF INDIVIDUAL HOUSING CONSTRUCTION IN USSR

YEAR	MILLIONS OF SQUARE METERS	PERCENT OF TOTAL CONSTRUCTION
1960	53.8	49
1965	33.0	34
1970	26.7	25
1975	22.6	21
1980	16.1	15
1985	16.3	14
1986	17.4	15
1987	19.3	15

SOURCE: *Narodnoe khozyaistvo SSSR v 1987 g.*, Moscow, 1988, p. 455.

In this respect, the resolution adopted in February, 1988, contains some good news. It raises the amount of money Soviet citizens can borrow for building or buying a home from three thousand to twenty thousand rubles, with a repayment term of fifty years in rural areas and twenty-five years in the city (formerly, such loans had to be repaid within ten years). It also allows homeowners to borrow money for major repairs.

Two other problems mentioned by Batalin are the shortage of building materials and the reluctance of contractors to take on individual construction jobs. The first problem is a perennial one and has been the subject of numerous decrees, most recently in July, 1987.[61] Decrees are no substitute for bricks, however, and it remains to be seen whether the decree on private housing will succeed in tackling this problem. Among other things, it assigns two state ministries the job of designing small-scale brick factories. According to Batalin, the first of these factories, which are intended "primarily for rural areas," was to be delivered at the end of 1988. A more promising avenue may be the creation of building-materials cooperatives. Batalin mentioned a cooperative that took over a failing brick factory in Sverdlovsk Oblast in October, 1987, and soon succeeded in turning it into a profitable enterprise. Today, there are over fifteen hundred cooperatives in the home-building and building-materials business, employing some sixty-two thousand people.[62]

---

61 "V Tsentral'nom Komitete KPSS," *Pravda*, July 18, 1987.
62 "Stroitel'nye kooperativy," *Ekonomicheskaya gazeta*, No. 25, 1989, p. 18.

It is too early to tell whether the decree will succeed in boosting the volume of private housing construction in the Soviet Union to the hoped-for level of sixty million square meters a year by 1995. One positive sign is that private home loans have risen sharply since the decree was published. According to the year-end report of Goskomstat, the Soviet statistics agency, Soviet citizens took out 2.7 billion rubles in private home loans in 1988,[63] which is more than twice the amount that Soviet banks lent for this purpose in the years 1966-1984.[64]

COOPERATIVE HOUSING

At the end of March, 1988, the CPSU Central Committee and the USSR Council of Ministers approved a resolution on another neglected form of construction: the cooperative housing sector.[65] Housing cooperatives have had a checkered history in the Soviet Union. The first cooperatives were formed in the early 1920s. In 1937, they were broken up and their housing stock distributed to local soviets. The ban on housing cooperatives lasted until 1958, when they were revived as part of Khrushchev's ambitious housing program of the previous year; they became eligible for state loans in 1962. Although the Soviet leadership has often paid lip service to the need for more cooperative housing, the sector has remained small, accounting for a mere 6.8 percent of all housing construction in the USSR in 1987 (see Table 3).

One Western specialist has rightly remarked that "it is difficult to account for the singular lack of success in this sector as a whole, for it is quite clear that [housing] cooperatives have not developed as rapidly as the state has intended."[66] The main obstacles seem to be money, materials, and motivation. First, until the decree of March, 1988, would-be members of housing cooperatives had to make a cash down-payment amounting to at least 30 percent of the total cost of their apartment (20 percent in the Kazakh SSR, parts of Siberia, the Far East, and the Far North). Since a typical two- or three-room cooperative apartment in the USSR costs between ten thousand and fifteen thousand rubles, this meant that people who wanted to buy into this type of housing had to have between three thousand and four and a half thousand rubles in ready cash. Of course, some people did. In 1986, demand exceeded supply by more than ten to one, with 1.6 million applications on file for 142,000 new cooperative

---

[63]   *Pravda*, January 22, 1989.

[64]   See V. S. Zakharov, *Potrebitel'sky kredit v SSSR*, Moscow, 1986, p. 33.

[65]   "V TsK KPSS i Sovete Ministrov SSSR," *Izvestia*, April 15, 1988.

[66]   Gregory D. Andrusz, *Housing & Urban Development in the USSR*, London, Macmillan, 1984, p. 95.

Table 3

VOLUME OF COOPERATIVE HOUSING CONSTRUCTION IN USSR

Year	Millions of Square Meters	Percent of Total Construction
1965	6.5	6.7
1970	7.7	7.3
1975	5.8	5.3
1980	5.1	4.9
1985	7.8	6.9
1986	8.2	6.8
1987	8.9	6.8

Source: *Narodnoe khozyaistvo SSSR v 1987 g.*, Moscow, 1988, p. 455.

flats.[67] The second problem is building materials. Bricks, tiles, and especially plumbing fixtures are in short supply in the Soviet Union, and the state housing sector gets first crack at them.

The most difficult problem is motivation, however. Neither the local soviets nor the building organizations are interested in cooperative housing. The soviets are not interested because cooperative apartments are not theirs to distribute to people in the municipal housing queue. The builders are not interested because: (a) the plan for state housing comes first; (b) they get 10 percent of all the state-financed housing they build but must forgo this perk in the case of cooperative housing; and (c) members of housing cooperatives are fussier about quality than those who must take what the state provides, and this can cause difficulties—with building inspection commissions, for example. In a word, both soviets and builders view cooperative housing as an additional burden.

The resolution adopted in March, 1988, addresses some of these problems. For example, the minimum down-payment on a cooperative apartment has been lowered from 30 to 25 percent of the apartment's total cost. People who want to join housing cooperatives but cannot manage the reduced down-payment can now borrow up to five thousand rubles, with ten years to repay. Bank credit has also been eased for enterprises and local soviets, who can borrow up to 50 percent of the total cost of a cooperative housing project. Most important, the resolu-

---

67   "Zavtrashnii den' gorodov i sel," *Izvestia*, November 12, 1986; *Narkhoz SSSR za 70 let*, Moscow, 1987, p. 511.

tion allows tenants to form cooperatives to buy apartment houses outright, instead of going through the long and difficult process of having them built. This refreshingly sensible idea was put forward several years ago by Evgenii Gontmakher, then a postgraduate student in economics and now a senior researcher at RSFSR Gosplan, in the RSFSR daily *Sovetskaya Rossiya*.[68] Gontmakher said that it was high time to enlist the Soviet population's pent-up purchasing power in the effort to solve the housing problem by selling finished apartment houses to housing cooperatives. Some readers objected to the idea, saying that it would mean a longer wait for people in the state housing queue.[69] Despite these and other objections, mostly having to do with social justice, it appears that Gontmakher's proposal has become official policy.

Again, it is too early to say whether the resolution will succeed in its goal of tripling the cooperative sector's share of all construction by the end of the Thirteenth Five-Year Plan (1990-1995). The trend seems to be upwards, though. In 1987, construction of cooperative housing reached 8.9 million square meters—an all-time high.

SELLING OFF STATE HOUSING

In December, 1988, the USSR Council of Ministers adopted a resolution allowing local soviets, enterprises, and government institutions to sell apartments in state-owned housing complexes to their tenants, as private property.[70] In order to protect the interests of people in the housing queue, the resolution says that only existing housing stock can be put up for sale; moreover, it can only be sold to the people already living in it. Tenants who decide to buy their apartments must pay at least 50 percent of the cost immediately; the balance can be paid off over ten years (poor and/or large families need pay only 30 percent down and have fifteen years to pay the rest). Apartments bought in this fashion are private property—they can be bequeathed to relatives or sold to strangers (albeit at prices set by the local soviets or state organizations from which they were bought in the first place). The money will go to local soviets and enterprises and, it is hoped, be used to finance the construction of additional public housing. It is also hoped that selling off state housing will soak up Soviet citizens' holdings of unspendable rubles—"the monetary overhang" that is fueling inflation and driving even the most basic goods (soap and salt are the latest items on the deficit list) out of the stores.

---

68   "Kvartira po sberknizhke," *Sovetskaya Rossiya*, June 29, 1986.
69   "Khochu kupit' kvartiru," *Sovetskaya Rossiya*, October 12, 1986.
70   Article 4, *Sobranie postanovlenii pravitel'stva SSSR*, Number 1, 1989.

The privatization of public housing in the USSR got under way in January, 1989. It appears to be making modest progress. The city soviet in Ural'sk, a medium-sized city in Kazakhstan, recently sold a nine-story house with 108 apartments at prices ranging from seven thousand rubles for a one-room flat to thirteen thousand for a three-roomer. The Kiev city executive committee also sold a new house of flats, getting up to twenty-three thousand rubles for three-roomers. Despite the stiff prices, there were four hundred applications for only 88 apartments.[71]

It should be said that the privatization of public housing appears to be a growing trend around the world. In the United Kingdom, Prime Minister Margaret Thatcher has been promoting the sale of council housing for well over a decade; to date, around one million council homes have been sold to private owners. The People's Republic of China started selling off state housing in 1986. In the United States, the new secretary of housing and urban development, Jack Kemp, has made "privatizing the nation's decaying stock of public housing" a top priority. According to *Izvestia*, the decision to sell state housing in the Soviet Union was motivated in part by "the positive experience" of other Socialist countries.[72]

PENSIONS AND SOCIAL SECURITY

There are approximately 58 million pensioners in the Soviet Union today, out of a total population of almost 287 million. The Soviet pension system is based on legislation passed more than thirty years ago. This legislation is clearly obsolete and in need of revision. Its main shortcoming is that it does not guarantee the constitutional right to material security in old age, for the simple reason that in many cases the pensions are too low to ensure a decent standard of living, even by Soviet criteria. The result is widespread poverty among pensioners in the Soviet Union.

POVERTY IN THE SOVIET UNION

A few years ago, the study of poverty in the Soviet Union was almost exclusively the province of Western researchers such as Professor Mervyn Matthews of the University of Surrey, whose pioneering work *Poverty in the Soviet Union* (1986) is still the sole scholarly treatment of

---

[71] "Kuplyu kvartiru, v kotoroi zhivu," *Izvestia*, March 9, 1989.

[72] "The Privatization of Urban Housing," *Beijing Review*, November 14-20, 1988, p. 15; "Kemp's Brave New World," *Newsweek*, January 2, 1989, p. 26; "Sobstvennaya kvartira," *Izvestia*, March 28, 1989.

the subject. Since the advent of Gorbachev and *glasnost'*, however, Soviet researchers have shown a greater interest in the problem, and their findings have been appearing with increasing frequency in the Soviet press.[73]

The problem of widespread poverty in the Soviet Union is now being addressed by the leading political figures in the country. In his speech to the Congress of People's Deputies on May 30, Gorbachev expressed concern for the "more than forty million people with low incomes" in the USSR.[74] The following day, Deputy El'tsin urged the congress to take immediate steps to ease the lot of the Soviet poor and handicapped and forwarded a draft decree on the matter to the presidium for review. Prime Minister Ryzhkov took up the challenge on June 7, outlining a series of measures that should go into effect as early as the beginning of 1990.

EL'TSIN PLAYS UP THE POVERTY ISSUE

In his speech to the congress on May 31, El'tsin criticized the slow pace of Gorbachev's economic reforms and called on the assembly "to resolve at least one concrete social issue" before adjourning in order to restore the Soviet public's lagging faith in *perestroika*. El'tsin proposed that the poor and handicapped be exempted from paying for medicines and public transportation; he also urged the assembly "to solve the pension question, or at least a part of it." He then announced that he was forwarding a draft decree on these matters, "compiled by a very large group of deputies," to the Presidium for review, and spoke of the need for "a law on poverty."[75]

El'tsin showed considerable shrewdness in calling for a war on poverty. There are a lot of poor people in the Soviet Union, and they have the potential to constitute a formidable political constituency. At the beginning of 1989, the trade-union newspaper *Trud* revealed that forty-three million Soviet citizens, or 15 percent of the population, live below the quasi-official poverty level, which currently stands at around seventy-five rubles a month.[76] Furthermore, most of the Soviet poor—thirty-five million, according to one estimate—are pensioners.[77] In general, the material situation of the fifty-eight million pensioners in the USSR is unenviable even by ordinary Soviet standards.

---

[73]   See Aaron Trehub, "Poverty in the Soviet Union," *Radio Liberty Research Bulletin*, RL 256/88, June 20, 1988.

[74]   *Izvestia*, May 31, 1989.

[75]   *Izvestia*, June 2, 1989.

[76]   "300 rublei 'chistymi'," *Trud*, January 12, 1989.

[77]   "Za chertoi bednosti," *Nedelya*, No. 7, 1989, p. 2.

Table 4
DISTRIBUTION OF SOVIET PENSIONERS BY SIZE OF PENSION, 1987

	BLUE- AND WHITE-COLLAR WORKERS (LAW OF 1956)	KOLKHOZNIKS (LAW OF 1964)
Total pensioners, of whom receiving:	47,670,000	10,070,000
less than 60 rubles a month	14,968,380	8,529,290
60 to 80 rubles a month	9,057,300	825,740
80 to 100 rubles a month	7,102,830	365,520
100 to 120 rubles a month	5,386,710	181,260
120 rubles or more a month	11,154,780	171,190

SOURCE: Derived from *Sotsial'noe razvitie i uroven' zhizni naseleniya SSSR*, Moscow, 1989, pp. 88-89. The discrepancy in the kolkhozniks column is due to rounding.

Apart from the sheer number of people affected, the poverty issue is attractive because it raises questions of privilege and social justice—two of El'tsin's favorite themes. The contrast between the pampered life-style of the administrative elite and the borderline existence of the Soviet poor is tailor-made for a populist politician, and El'tsin wasted no time in playing it up. "Why," he demanded, "are tens of millions living below the poverty line while others are wallowing in luxury?"

RYZHKOV RESPONDS

El'tsin's challenge was taken up the following week by Ryzhkov. In the course of his long report to the congress on June 7, Ryzhkov outlined a series of emergency measures that should take effect as early as the beginning of 1990.[78]

First, Ryzhkov said that the CPSU Politburo and the USSR Council of Ministers intend to raise minimum old-age pensions for blue- and white-collar employees and kolkhozniks to seventy rubles a month, which is the current minimum wage in the Soviet Union. Ryzhkov said that this measure should take effect in January, 1990. If it does, it will eliminate one of the more glaring inequities in the Soviet social security system: the fact that minimum old-age pensions for kolkhozniks are ten rubles lower than those for blue- and white-collar workers (forty rubles instead of fifty rubles a month). Ryzhkov said that the raise will affect

---

[78] *Izvestia*, June 8, 1989.

twenty million people, including eight million kolkhozniks. It will not, however, change the pattern whereby the great majority of collective-farm workers fall into the lowest pension brackets.

Ryzhkov said that minimum disability pensions for so-called Category 1 invalids (that is, people with the severest injuries or handicaps) will be raised to eighty rubles a month, while minimum pensions for Category 2 invalids will be raised to sixty rubles a month. These measures will affect more than one million people, Ryzhkov said.

The prime minister then turned to war veterans and veterans of labor. He said that some three hundred thousand war invalids will receive a monthly supplement of fifteen rubles, regardless of the amount of their pensions. Furthermore, some seven million veterans of the "Great Patriotic War" against Nazi Germany or their widows will henceforth receive medicines free of charge. This measure should prove especially popular because, although health care in the Soviet Union is nominally free, medicines are not, and one study has shown that some Soviet pensioners currently spend as much as 40 percent of their monthly income on medication.[79] In addition, war veterans and people who received medals or commendations for their work on the home front during the war will be entitled to use public transportation for free—a perk that will benefit nearly six million people, said Ryzhkov.

The prime minister also announced that, starting in 1990, the ceiling on the combined income of pensioners who continue to work after retirement will be removed. (The ceiling rule says that pensioners who continue working in the administrative apparatus may not earn more than 150 rubles a month, while those who continue working as engineers or technical specialists are limited to a combined monthly income of 300 rubles.) Ryzhkov said that the removal of the ceiling will affect seven million working pensioners.

All in all, Ryzhkov said that the measures outlined above will affect around twenty-two million people and cost nearly six billion rubles.

WHEN WILL THE NEW PENSION LAW BE READY?

Ryzhkov also told the congress that "active work" is proceeding on the new law on pensions (the current law dates from 1956 and is clearly obsolete). This is good news, since this important law has been stuck at the drafting stage for almost three years.

In September, 1986, the CPSU Politburo announced that it had given the go-ahead to start drafting a new law on pensions. The task was assigned to the USSR State Committee for Labor and Social Problems (Goskomtrud), the All-Union Central Council of Trade Unions (AUCCTU), the USSR Ministry of Finance, and the USSR Gosplan.

---

[79]   See the letter from V. Rovinsky in *Ogonek*, No. 6, 1989, p. 3.

Originally, the drafting of the new law was to have taken between one and a half and two years.[80] In fact, it has taken considerably longer. On August 1, 1989 the government passed the "Emergency Measures for the Improvement of Pension Security and Social Maintenance of the Population." The measure, based on Ryzhkov's proposals mentioned above, are designed to improve the living standards of the country's pensioners until a final law on pensions can be implemented. Significantly, the measure declares that kolkhozniks will receive the same pensions as those in the state sector. Benefits for old-age pensioners, veterans and their families, and the handicapped also increase under the emergency measures. Still, most pensions will likely be less than 75 rubles per month, the quasi-official poverty line.[81]

In November, the Supreme Soviet issued a draft law on pensions that builds on the "emergency measures" and stands as a significant improvement over the existing legislation.[82] Important innovations in the draft law are the indexing of pensions to account for cost-of-living increases, and the establishment of the minimum pension at the same level as the minimum wage. If passed, the law would cost an additional 29 billion rubles (on top of the extra 6.5 billion estimated for the cost of the "emergency measures"), a more than 60 percent increase over the 1988 level. Even so, the draft law came under quick criticism in the Soviet press, and more debate is likely before final legislation is ratified.[83]

A SUPPLEMENTARY PENSION PLAN

While work on the pension law proceeds, workers can hedge against poverty after retirement by taking advantage of a supplementary pension plan approved by the CPSU Politburo in August, 1987, and introduced in January, 1988.[84]

The plan is administered by Gosstrakh, the state insurance agency, and can be bought into by men between the ages of thirty-five and sixty and women between the ages of thirty and fifty-five. It provides a guaranteed supplement to the ordinary old-age pension after retirement, which begins at sixty years for men and fifty-five years for women. There are five supplements on offer, ranging from ten to fifty rubles a month in increments of ten. The monthly contribution is taken directly out of a worker's paycheck; its amount depends on (a) the age

---

80   *Argumenty i fakty*, No. 39, 1986, p. 8.

81   See D. J. Peterson, "Supreme Soviet Adopts Emergency Pension Measures," *Report on the USSR*, No. 33, 1989, pp. 7-9.

82   *Pravda*, November 4, 1989.

83   *Ekonomicheskaya gazeta*, No. 48, 1989, pp. 12-13.

84   *Pravda*, August 21, 1987.

at which the worker entered the plan, and (b) the size of the supplement. For example, a man who enters the plan at age forty and chooses the maximum supplement of fifty rubles a month after retirement pays a minimum of 15.05 rubles a month for twenty years. Workers can leave the plan at will, without losing the money they have already paid into it. They can also shift to a higher or lower supplement in accordance with changes in their income. Finally, worker contributions cover only six years of supplementary payments after retirement; the balance is paid by the state.[85]

The number of workers who have taken advantage of the supplementary pension plan has not been made public, so it is hard to say how affordable it is. It is clear, however, that it does nothing to help the millions of Soviet citizens who are already living below the poverty line.

CONCLUSION

Professor Seweryn Bialer of Columbia University has written that perhaps the main weakness of the Soviet welfare state is that it "provides many services which should not be its responsibility."[86] The same point has been made by economists in the Soviet Union. "We have gotten ourselves," said Gennadii Lisichkin on the eve of the seventieth anniversary of the October Revolution, "into a situation in which the state is obligated to feed, clothe, and house everybody."[87] Not to mention employ everybody.

This is starting to change. The right to work is being modified in the direction of economic efficiency, and employment in the nonstate sector is rising. Private health care already exists, and its share of all medical services is supposed to increase several times over by the end of the century. Workers may now buy into a supplementary pension plan, and private charity has reappeared in the Soviet Union after a sixty-year absence. The state is selling off public housing as private property.

Two provisos are in order, however. First, the degree of privatization is still extremely modest. Full-time employment in the nonstate sector (i.e., cooperatives and individual labor activity) in the first half of 1989 amounted to only 1.1 percent of the total work force.[88] It appears that private health care still accounts for less than 1 percent of the total volume of medical services performed in the Soviet Union. Private and cooperative housing construction together account for around 20 percent of all housing construction, and sales of public housing have barely

---

85 "Dopolnenie k pensii," *Izvestia*, September 19, 1987.

86 "Inside Glasnost," *The Atlantic*, February, 1988, p. 67.

87 "Ekonomika na pereput'e," *Literaturnaya gazeta*, No. 23, 1987.

88 "Energichnee perestraivat' ekonomiku," *Pravda*, July 29, 1989.

gotten off the ground. The number of workers who have bought into the supplementary pension plan since 1988 has not been made public, but it is clear that state pensions are still the mainstay of the Soviet social security system.

Second, to the extent that Soviet authorities have resorted to privatization, they have done so in order to augment social entitlements, not replace them. Barring an unforeseen expansion in the cooperative and individual labor sectors, the state will continue to be the main employer in the USSR for the next few years at least. Health Minister Chazov has made it clear that the Soviet Union is not about to abandon the principle of free health care and that the state medical system will continue to take precedence over pay polyclinics and medical cooperatives. The supplementary pension plan is precisely that—supplementary.

Privatization has made its most noticeable inroads in the area of housing. Even here, however, private home ownership is still voluntary, and Aganbegyan's call to sell off at least a third of all new housing remains unseconded by the leadership.[89]

Still, even modest tampering with these entitlements is a tricky business. It strikes at the Soviet social contract and contributes to "the stratification of Soviet society" that El'tsin warned of in his address to the first session of the Congress of People's Deputies. Indeed, this stratification is already taking place, and seems to have been at least partially responsible for the recent disturbances in Turkmenia, Uzbekistan, and Kazakhstan. The dilemma is clear. If Gorbachev does not push ahead with *perestroika*, living standards will stagnate or even decline, thereby fueling popular discontent. If he does, then he risks turning the Soviet Union into a society of economic winners and losers, thereby fueling popular discontent. The Soviet leader will need all his formidable political skills to resolve this dilemma.

---

89   "'We Made Some Serious Mistakes'," *Newsweek*, March 13, 1989, p. 12.

Contributors

Robert Campbell is Distinguished Professor of Economics, Indiana University. His publications include general analyses of the Soviet economy, and more specialized studies in the areas of energy policy, research and development, and military affairs in the USSR. His current research deals with Soviet telecommunications as an infrastructure for the information revolution. He is on the editorial board of the journal *Soviet Economy*.

Elizabeth Teague is Senior Research Analyst, Radio Free Europe/Radio Liberty, Inc., where she is a specialist on Soviet domestic politics. Her publications include *Solidarity and the Soviet Worker*, published by Croom Helm in 1988, and "Gorbachev's 'Human Factor' Policies," in the Joint Economic Committee's 1987 compendium, *Gorbachev's Economic Plans*.

Mark von Hagen is Associate Professor of History and Associate Director of the W. Averell Harriman Institute for Advanced Study of the Soviet Union at Columbia University. A specialist on the early Soviet period, he is the author of *Soldiers in the Proletarian Dictatorship: The Red Army and the Soviet Socialist State, 1917-1930,* published by Cornell University Press in 1990.

Philip Hanson is Professor of Soviet Economics and Acting Director, Centre for Russian and East European Studies, Universtity of Birmingham. He is on the editorial board of the journals *Soviet Economy* and *Detente*, and is a frequent contributor to the Radio Liberty publication *Report on the USSR*. Recent publications include *Western Economic Statecraft in East-West Relations. Embargoes, Sanctions, Economic Warfare and Detente,* published by Routledge and Kegan Paul in 1988.

Vladimir Sobell is Chief Economic Analyst, Radio Free Europe/Radio Liberty, Inc. A specialist on East European economics, he is the author of *The Red Market: Industrial Cooperation and Specialization in the CMEA,* published by Gower Press, 1984, and numerous articles and book chapters on various aspects of East European economics and trade.

John Tedstrom is Senior Research Analyst, Radio Free Europe/Radio Liberty, Inc. His publications include chapters and articles on Soviet economic reform and Soviet defense economics. His current research interests include the Soviet cooperative movement, Soviet defense economics, and fiscal federalism in the USSR.

Karl-Eugen Wädekin is a former Professor of Foreign and Socialist Agrarian Policies at Justus-Liebig-Universität, Gießen, a member of the Kommission für Erforschung der Agrar- und Wirtschaftsverhältnisse des europäischen Ostens, and coeditor of the monthly *Osteuropa*. Most of his publications deal with Soviet agrarian affairs, including social and regional aspects, and his current research continues to concentrate on this subject.

Hans Heymann Jr. is Distinguished Professor of Political Economy at the Defense Intelligence College. A long-time student of the Soviet economy, his early work focused on estimating Soviet national income. His more recent research interests include Soviet technological development and economic reform. He serves on the editorial board of the journal *Soviet Economy*.

Perry Patterson is Assistant Professor of Economics, Wake Forest University. He has taught economics and Russian language at Northwestern, Vanderbilt, and Indiana Universities. His recent research includes studies on the impact of Soviet reform on Eastern Europe and comparative economic problems of the US and the USSR.

Michael Alexeev is Assistant Professor of Economics, George Mason University. His research focuses on the microeconomic aspects of planned economies. His publications on the Soviet second economy, the Soviet housing problem, and other topics have appeared in *Comparative Economic Studies* and *The Journal of Comparative Economics*, among other economics publications.

Aaron Trehub of The Johns Hopkins University is formerly an analyst of Soviet social affairs with Radio Free Europe/Radio Liberty, Inc. He is a frequent writer on social problems in the Soviet Union.

Index